The Yachtsman's Pilot
Clyde to Colonsay

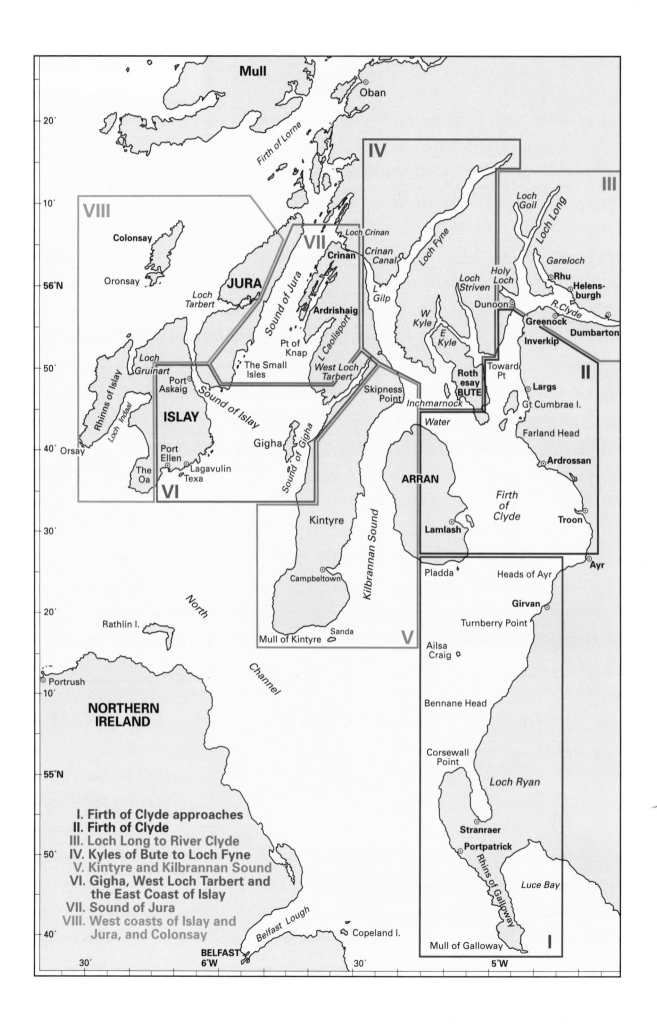

Mull

20′

Firth of Lorne

Oban

IV

10′

VIII

Loch Crinan

Colonsay

VII

Crinan

Crinan Canal

Loch Goil

Loch Long

III

Loch Fyne

Gareloch

56°N

Oronsay

JURA

Sound of Jura

Crinan

L Gilp

Loch Striven

Holy Loch

Rhu

Helens-burgh

Loch Tarbert

Ardrishaig

Dunoon

Greenock

R.Clyde

Inverkip

Dumbarton

Pt of Knap

L Caolisport

W Kyle

E Kyle

50′

Loch Gruinart

The Small Isles

West Loch Tarbert

Roth esay
BUTE

Toward Pt

II

Port Askaig

Sound of Islay

Skipness Point

Inchmarnock

Largs

Gt Cumbrae I.

Rhins of Islay

Loch Indaal

ISLAY

Water

Farland Head

40′

Orsay

Port Ellen

Gigha

Sound of Gigha

ARRAN

Ardrossan

The Oa

Lagavulin
Texa

VI

Firth of Clyde

Troon

30′

Kintyre

Kilbrannan Sound

Lamlash

Pladda

Heads of Ayr

Ayr

North

Campbeltown

Girvan

Turnberry Point

Sanda

V

Ailsa Craig

Mull of Kintyre

20′

Rathlin I.

Channel

Bennane Head

10′

Portrush

NORTHERN IRELAND

Corsewall Point

Loch Ryan

55°N

Stranraer

Portpatrick

Rhins of Galloway

50′

I. Firth of Clyde approaches
II. Firth of Clyde
III. Loch Long to River Clyde
IV. Kyles of Bute to Loch Fyne
V. Kintyre and Kilbrannan Sound
VI. Gigha, West Loch Tarbert and the East Coast of Islay
VII. Sound of Jura
VIII. West coasts of Islay and Jura, and Colonsay

Luce Bay

40′

Belfast Lough

Copeland I.

BELFAST
6°W

Mull of Galloway

I

30′

30′

5°W

The Yachtsman's Pilot
Clyde to Colonsay

MARTIN LAWRENCE

Imray Laurie Norie & Wilson

Published by
Imray, Laurie, Norie & Wilson Ltd
Wych House St Ives Cambridgeshire PE27 5BT England
☎ +44 (0)1480 462114 *Fax* +44 (0)1480 496109
E-mail ilnw@imray.com *Web* www.imray.com
2007

© Martin Lawrence 2001
First edition 1989
Second edition 1993
Third / Fourth edition 2001
Fifth edition 2007

ISBN 978 085288968 8

British Library Cataloguing in Publication Data.
A catalogue record for this title is available from the
British Library.

CAUTION
Whilst every care has been taken to ensure accuracy,
neither the Publishers nor the Author will hold themselves
responsible for errors, omissions or alterations in this
publication. They will at all times be grateful to receive
information which tends to the improvement of the work.

CORRECTIONAL SUPPLEMENTS
This pilot book will be amended at intervals by the issue
of correctional supplements. These are published on the
internet at our web site www.imray.com and may be
downloaded free of charge. Printed copies are also
available on request from the publishers at the above
address.

PLANS
The plans in this guide are not to be used for navigation.
They are designed to support the text and should at all
times be used with navigational charts.

Most of the plans in this book are based on British
Admiralty charts with the permission of the Hydrographer
of the Navy and the sanction of HM Stationery Office.

The last input of technical information was January 2007

Printed and bound in UK by CPI Bath

Contents

Preface

'...the accidents of weather keep in ceaseless change...'.

Along the whole length of this noble sheet of water, lofty hills rise on every side and numerous arms of the sea resembling Norwegian fjords branch off at various points into the deep recesses of mountainous districts, whilst the shores of the Firth are studded with numerous watering places, the summer resort of Glasgow citizens, the whole presenting a panorama of almost unequalled beauty and grandeur.'

Few scenes surpass in grandeur the view from the anchorage in Brodick bay diversified as it is by mountain, glen, and wood, and rendered more resplendent by the marked lights and shades, which the accidents of weather keep in ceaseless change; whilst with a clear atmosphere the soft azure tints of the Ayrshire coast complete a picture from which no element of beauty is wanting. The many natural attractions of this lovely bay cause it to be much frequented during the summer months.'

For many yachtsmen the two previous paragraphs, written by a naval officer in the *Sailing Directions, West Coast of Scotland* in the 19th century, are sufficient attraction. Even the phrase about the 'accidents of weather' merely hints at circumstances which at worst discourage the crowds seeking guaranteed sunshine.

The Firth of Clyde and adjacent waters can be enjoyed simply for their superb scenery and sheltered water, more easily than ever now that several former industrial and commercial harbours have been converted to yacht havens and marinas.

More adventurous yachtsmen can find anchorages providing more or less shelter, where some effort is needed to select a place with neither too much depth nor too little, and free from private moorings and the floating cages of fish farms.

At yet another level of adventurousness are the true rock-dodgers, often in the smallest boats – pocket cruisers, bilge keelers, Silhouettes, Cornish Crabbers, Drascombe Luggers, and even kayaks. These provide probably the most entertainment in proportion to cost, and this book and the others in the series are particularly dedicated to this class of sailor for whom local knowledge has to be gathered at a level of detail more intimate than any Admiralty chart (although these remain essential).

Although I have been exploring inshore in Scotland and elsewhere for more than 30 years, I have no monopoly on the information published here, nor can I guarantee its accuracy. Some of the information comes from others (often in fact from visitors, who see features with a fresh eye), some from published accounts, some from old, large-scale charts which are no longer published, and some even from original surveys carried out 150 years ago.

Rocks don't move, do they?

This remark is frequently used as justification for not using the most up-to-date charts and pilot books. Some rocks, though, aren't shown in their correct positions; some have been discovered since the most recent survey, which may have been 150 years ago.

The datum to which sea level relates on Admiralty charts has changed, and the horizontal datum is in the process of being changed; buoyage has changed, fish farms have been established and many, many moorings have been laid, both for permanent residents and for visitors – and some charted features have been removed again.

Aids to navigation, both floating and fixed, lit and unlit, are subject to change.

Formally designated anchorages are about to be indicated on charts, and these will have a legal significance.

Mistakes are very occasionally made, and corrected when they are brought to light.

No pilot book is a static, fixed, authoritative publication, and supplements are issued for these *Yachtsman's Pilots* from time to time by the publishers, both on paper and on their web site.

Do, please, make sure that you have the latest supplement (for which, see Appendix I) and, if you come across features which differ from the contents of the pilot, please share them with me and other yachtsmen.

Inevitably a book of this kind is flavoured by the author's outlook and experience, and it may be helpful to know that for 14 years we have owned *Thomasina*, a Bowman 36 with a centreboard, which perhaps influences my attitude to shallow water, and helps me to appreciate the needs and qualities of smaller boats.

For the previous ten years I owned a steel ketch of traditional character and perhaps took a slightly more light-hearted view of rock-dodging than the owner of a less robust vessel would do. On the other hand *Erraid* is not so handy as most GRP cruiser-racers, and any place into which she could find her way should present little difficulty to a modern yacht of moderate size.

'...accidents of weather keep in ceaseless change...'

Sources of information In addition to current Admiralty charts, older charts often include additional information about tidal streams, etc.

I have also been able to refer to original Admiralty surveys, many of them made about 1860 and earlier in meticulous detail and drawn at a much larger scale than published charts.

In addition to my own aerial photos, a series of aerial survey photos taken by the RAF in the 1950s reveal a wealth of detail when they were taken under suitable light conditions.

Published accounts of cruises supply occasional clues, and individual yachtsmen provide information including, occasionally, sketch plans. Sometimes, however, there are conflicts between different accounts and a choice has to be made between them.

Even where the information seems adequate it has to be compared with other sources and checked for new developments (and rumours of developments).

In the end these directions can be no more than the sum of my own, and other people's, observations together with a summary of all that I have read, and gleaned from charts and aerial photos, and various published sources. There could well be hazards which I have missed by luck rather than good management and in spite of all the efforts of Imray's editorial team there may be simple errors which have been overlooked; in the days when new editions of Admiralty Pilots were published every 15 years or so the supplements would contain the occasional instruction 'for E read W'.

The directions should be compared with charts and all other information available before an approach is made, to ensure that they are understood and that they correspond. If you find directions which you think are inaccurate, or changes which have occurred since the publication of this volume (and the most recent supplement), I should be very grateful if you would let me know, through the publishers.

Acknowledgements

The production of the book itself owes an enormous amount to the work put in by various people: The final form of the plans is due to the work of Imray's cartographers, to whom I gave only the outlines and rough notes.

Information and advice were provided by too many people to name individually, some of them annonymous, but including harbourmasters, local authority officials, office bearers of yacht clubs, marina operators and staff, distillery operators, local residents and traders.

Everyone who sails to the east coast of Islay owes thanks to Michael Gilkes for pointing me in the direction of original survey information at the Hydrographic Office. We should all be grateful to Jon Hallam for his meticulous survey of the inner reaches of Loch Tarbert last year. David Vass (Secretary of WHAM) John Shepherd, Ian Wallace (Chairman of WHISCA), Kevin Williams (Tayvallich Bay Association), Dennis Pogson and Mark James all contributed specifically to this edition. The publishers are grateful to Elizabeth Cook who compiled the index.

Martin Lawrence
Perth

Introduction

The series of Yachtsman's Pilots of which this is one part sets out to provide useful information for visitors to the west coast of Scotland as clearly as possible. It is not trying to 'sell' the West Coast; anyone reading it is probably already considering sailing there. The upper limit of size for which it caters is a draught of 2 metres, but there is also information specifically for shoal-draught boats – centreboarders, trailer-sailers, twin-keel boats and multihulls, and of course motor-cruisers, who tend to be forgotten by writers of 'sailing directions' who usually seem to own deep-keeled sailing boats.

The Clyde and west coast of Scotland have traditionally been regarded as deep-water areas, but some anchorages or parts of anchorages are only accessible to shoal-draught boats, particularly those which can dry out fairly upright. In most other cruising areas, having a shoal-draught boat is the best way to avoid the crowds, and this is increasingly becoming the case on the west coast of Scotland.

The smallest boats, even dinghies, may be able to cruise in much of the area described in this pilot, but they must be soundly equipped and competently handled by experienced crews. Except within some very sheltered lochs, the Clyde and west coast of Scotland are not suitable for those who are unable to deal with adverse conditions which may arise unexpectedly.

Some harbours and anchorages are only suitable for small shoal-draught boats or, for larger boats, a brief visit above half flood under favourable conditions, but I hope this will be clear from the description.

For trailer-sailers the easiest place on the Clyde to launch a boat trailed from a distance is Barrfield Slip at Largs. However it is moderately exposed, and marinas may have a slip available for a charge.

Much of the area covered by this volume is sheltered by islands or within lochs which penetrate far among some of the highest hills in Britain.

This shelter creates problems of its own, particularly the squalls which are generated in the lee of hills, as well as the higher rainfall.

Anyone who is capable of managing a yacht at a comparable distance from the shore whether in the North Sea, the Baltic, the English Channel, the Atlantic coast of France or the Irish Sea will have little problem on the west coast of Scotland.

Outwith the main channels of the Firth of Clyde there is little traffic, although a good lookout needs to be kept for fishing boats, and naval vessels (especially submarines) on exercises.

Visibility is usually good, except in rain: fog as such is fairly rare. The climate is wetter and cooler than, for example, the south coast of England (although the further west you go, away from the mainland hills, the drier the weather. A compensating factor is the longer daylight in summer, so that it is rarely necessary to sail at night.

One of the main attractions of the West Coast is the sheer variety of anchorages and passages which occur within quite a small area. The directions in this book are divided into eight chapters, each covering waters of quite different character, from the industrial (and post-industrial) surroundings of the upper parts of the Firth of Clyde to the absolute remoteness of the west of Jura.

Charts

It is essential to carry adequate charts to cover both the intended passage and any likely diversion. The most comprehensive range of charts is published by the UK Hydrographic Office but the most convenient are those published by Imrays, which are now approved by the Maritime and Coastguard Agency, for carriage by vessels up to 24m. All charts available are listed in Appendix I. This includes Leisure Folios, printed on A2-size sheets, both from Imrays and UKHO.

Note that older copies of charts, as well as some current charts are referred to a horizontal datum known as OSGB36, on which a position given by geographical co-ordinates may differ by as much as 100 metres from the position on current charts. The datum on current charts is WGS84, or ETRS89 which is indistinguishable from WGS84. It is possible for the difference between OSGB36 and WGS84 / ETRS89 to cause critical inaccuracies in plotting, for example, positions of new aids to navigation, or plotting a position given by a satellite navigation system, and it is essential to know which datum is referred to.

The conversion of current Admiralty charts of the Firth of Clyde, from OSGB36 datum to WGS84 datum, or ETRS89 which is effectively identical, is complete, and the conversion of those outwith the Clyde is in progress. Current editions of Imray charts, as well as Admiralty Leisure Folios, are referred to WGS84.

When attempting precision navigation by electronic means, the navigator needs to be aware of the datum to which the chart refers, and the datum to which his satellite navigation equipment refers. Some satellite navigation equipment offers a choice of datum, but some does not, in which case it refer to WGS84. Older charts will either refer to OSGB36 or an unknown datum, and the difference needs to be taken into account, particularly when working at larger scales.

Corrections for both Imray (www.imray.com) and Admiralty charts (www.ukho.gov.uk/weekly_nms) are published on the internet.

In a few cases, older large-scale charts, some dating from the 19th century, may be useful to supplement current charts.

Maps

Ordnance Survey maps at 1:50,000 are well worth having on board to make up for the lack of topographical detail on current charts. In places where the charts are at a small scale the Ordnance Survey maps actually provide useful navigational detail.

In some cases the OS *Pathfinder* and *Explorer* series of maps at 1:25,000 supply essential detail where there is no Admiralty chart at an adequate scale.

Note that OS maps use a different grid of co-ordinates which do not even align with those of an Admiralty chart. Some GPS receivers can display OS co-ordinates.

Equipment

This should be as robust and reliable as for a yacht going a similar distance offshore anywhere in the English Channel or the North Sea.

Anchors

A boat needs at least two anchors, of the sizes recommended by anchor manufacturers or independent reference books, rather than those supplied as standard by boat manufacturers which are often on the light side.

Chain rather than rope will prevent a yacht roving around in gusts, but if you do use rope it will help to have a weight ('angel', 'chum') which can be let down to the seabed on a traveller.

So many yachts are now kept in marinas and only sail to another marina or harbour that for many yachtsmen anchoring is no longer an everyday operation, but on the West Coast it is essential that the crew is thoroughly familiar with anchor handling.

It is no use relying on visitors' moorings being available; where they do exist they are quite likely to be already occupied.

Chartering and instruction

Plenty of boats are available, both for bareboat and skippered charters, and also instructional cruises. Many of the operators are members of the Association of Scottish Yacht Charterers, for whose brochure see Appendix I.

A good way to gain experience on the West Coast is to take a berth on one of the skippered charter yachts or instructional courses which are available. There are also shore-based instructional courses in dinghies; for any of these courses see the current edition of the publication *On the Water*, available free from Sail Scotland, see Appendix.

Travel

Transport/public transport in the area is fairly comprehensive. Most places on the east side of the Clyde are served by rail, including Helensburgh, Garelochead and Arrochar at the head of Loch Long, but excluding any part of the coast between Ayr and Stranraer.

Details of services throughout Argyll are contained in the Area Transport Guide, distributed widely throughout Mid Argyll. To obtain a copy call the Council's public transport helpline 01546 604360 or email public.transport@argyll-bute.gov.uk

Most other parts of the mainland have a bus service, as do Arran, Bute and Islay.

All inhabited islands (except Inchmarnock, Little Cumbrae and Holy Island) have a regular car ferry service. The ferry to Colonsay runs from Oban.

Campbeltown and Islay have an air service from Glasgow.

For information about travel see Appendix.

Most parts of the mainland are served by good roads, but those on the Cowal peninsula, between the Firth of Clyde and Loch Fyne, are not suitable for trailers.

Trailed boats can be launched at Largs which is convenient for roads from the south. Each of the marinas has a mobile hoist, suitable for launching boats delivered by road.

Passage making

With the exception of a passage round the Mull of Kintyre, and south and west of Islay, most passages covered by this volume are within sounds or lochs or along a shore entailing only short hops across open sea, so that navigation is, in the main, a matter of pilotage by eye and satisfying yourself that what you see corresponds to the chart. It is useful to pick out from the chart transits such as tangents of islands, or beacons in line with headlands to give you position lines from time to time. Check by compass bearings as well, starting from some unmistakable prominent object.

Traditional clearing marks for avoiding unmarked dangers, based on transits of natural features, are often much easier to use than compass bearings particularly where there are strong currents. Bearings are given in the text as a check on identification, and drawings and photographs provided where possible.

At night main channels are very well lit, but lights may be difficult to pick out against shore lights. Most other channels are just adequately lit; for a passage under power or with a fair wind. A few anchorages or passages are very well lit for local commercial users. During June and July there is little need to sail at night unless you are going further afield.

Other Traffic

Except within the upper Clyde estuary, there is not a lot of traffic, but yachts need to be particularly aware of certain vessels. Very large bulk carriers may be encountered and, north of the south end of Bute they may be constrained to narrow channels. These channels include the east side of Cumbrae Islands as well as a separate channel north of Cumbrae, to the east of the main Firth of Clyde Channel; this channel, known as the Skelmorlie Channel, is significantly deeper than the Firth of Clyde Channel.

Other commercial traffic of all sizes may be encountered throughout the Clyde, as well as west of Kintyre, and some of it has increased enormously in recent years, including cruise ships, such as the *Hebridean Princess* and paddle steamer *Waverley* which could, for example, be met with in the Kyles of Bute. Transport of timber by sea has beeen reintroduced and ships carrying timber may be encountered in unexpected places, such as Ardrishaig, Craighouse on Jura, and even Portavadie.

Wherever there are ferry routes it is as well to be aware of expected movements of ferries. For sources of timetables see Appendix 1.

Beware fishing boats, and warships, which may behave unpredictably.

If not participating, you may wish to avoid concentrations of yachts taking part in races, or musters, or cruises in company. RYA Scotland publish a programme of races and regattas, but the social events organised for members of individual clubs maybe harder to anticipate.

More recent information about moorings may be found at:
www.bluemoment.com/scotmoorings.html

Clydeport's *Marine Leisure Guide* should be available at Clyde marinas, otherwise by phoning 01475 726221.

Submarines

Certain areas are designated on charts as 'Submarine Exercise Areas' and a good lookout should be kept for submarines in these areas.

Information, known as 'Subfacts', about areas where British submarines may be active, is broadcast by Clyde Coastguard every four hours as part of Maritime Safety Information.

Submarines on passage, both inbound and outbound, may be towing sonar equipment. Other vessels are recommended to remain 1500 metres clear when crossing astern of a surfaced submarine. It is intended that information on passages by submarines with these towed arrays will be included in Coastguard Marine Safety broadcasts.

Tides

Within the Firth of Clyde and to the west of Islay and Jura the range of tide is up to 4 metres, but in the area covered by Chapters VI and VII it is less than 2 metres. In several passages between the Mull of Kintyre and Colonsay tidal streams run at up to 6 knots. Tidal streams are strong wherever the movement of a large body of water is constricted by narrows, and there are often overfalls at the seaward end of narrow passages, particularly with wind against tide. Overfalls also occur off many headlands, and eddies are formed, usually down-tide of a promontory or islet or even a submerged reef, but sometimes in a bay up-tide of the obstruction. There are also usually overfalls wherever two tidal streams meet. These eddies and overfalls are so common that they are often not mentioned individually.

Tidal streams The flood tide generally runs north and west; but see also the paragraphs on tides in the Notes on Plans and Pilotage Directions below.

Tides between Kintyre and Jura are influenced by a feature known as an Amphidrome. This is defined by the Proudman Oceanographic Laboratory as a point in the sea where the tidal amplitude is zero due to tidal waves cancelling each other out. Co-tidal lines radiate from an amphidromic point and co-range lines encircle it. An amphidrome occurs between Port Ellen, Islay and Machrihanish Bay, Kintyre. As a matter of curiosity, an amphidrome may also be located on the shore, with a similar effect as above on the adjacent waters, In this case it is known as a Degenerate Amphidrome, and defined as a terrestrial point on a tidal chart from which co-tidal lines appear to radiate, and further described as 'an imaginary point where nothing happens'.

Weather forecasting

A new schedule for forecasts, broadcast by the Coastguard on VHF has been introduced at the beginning of 2007, as follows:

• HMCG will broadcast forecasts three hourly, that is eight times a day and will complete most transmissions around the coast within one hour. Four broadcasts will provide new forecasts and four will be repeats.

• Two of the new forecasts will include gale warnings, the shipping forecast and inshore waters forecast and outlook, as well as navigation warnings and the three day fisherman's forecast when applicable.

• The other two new forecasts will include inshore waters forecasts, a repeat of the previous 24 hour outlook and any gale warnings or strong wind warnings. Mariners will thus have new inshore waters forecasts every six hours.

• The repeats are for the benefit of mariners who missed the new forecast made three hours previously and will consist of the inshore waters forecasts and gale warnings and any new strong wind warnings.

• The full broadcasts will be based on 0710 and 1910 start times so as to catch navigators at the beginning of the sailing day or night passage. All broadcasts will be in local time to avoid confusion between UTC and BST.

• Forecasts for UK inshore waters are issued four times a day at 0500, 1100, 1700 and 2300 GMT and cover the next 24 hours. Outlooks for the following 24 hours are only issued at 0500 and 1700.

• Warnings for all forecasts will be transmitted on VHF Ch 16, indicating the forecast on VHF Ch 23, 84 or 86 (perhaps 10), which will remain unchanged. Aerials will be combined for the warnings to avoid apparent repetition.

• Warnings will be brief: 'All stations – this is Stornoway Coastguard – for a weather information broadcast listen channel 83', but made slowly. The forecast broadcasts will be made clearly and at dictation speed.

Information is available at:
www.metoffice.gov.uk/weather/marine/guide/
Frank Singleton's Weather Site:
www.franksingleton.clara.net/
is the most useful overall guide to weather services available.

Anchorages and Moorings

Within the sailing lifetime of many of us the only way to remain in one place – overnight, or to go ashore – used to be to put down an anchor and to go ashore in a dinghy, usually with the exertion of a pair of oars. In very rare cases one might moor alongside a quay in a working harbour, taking ones chance along with fishing boats and working vessels. Only when passing through the Crinan Canal did one have the luxury of mooring to a fixed structure and stepping ashore at deck level. One's boat was kept on a home mooring which the owner had laid himself or, if he could afford it, was laid by a boatyard or contractor.

Now, many of the most sheltered anchorages are fully occupied by permanently moored yachts or inshore fishing boats, if not by commercial fish farms, and it is usual for a yacht to be kept, when not in use (which is probably most of the time), in a commercial yacht harbour, moored between pontoons.

Currently, moorings for visiting yachts are increasingly provided by local traders, hotels and restaurants to attract custom, as well as by local authorities on behalf of the traders, and sometimes by independent interests. These may be free or charged for, or may be free of charge to customers of a particular establishment. Increasingly, pontoons as well as moorings for visitors are being established. In consequence, using an anchor is becoming less common and a yacht's crew may not be really familiar with the techniques involved.

Where visitors' moorings are provided it is the crew's responsibility to find out whether payment is due, and to whom – and to pay it. Some people have avoided paying in the past by claiming that they weren't asked for it, although many providers of moorings cannot afford the expense of employing staff to collect payments.

This Pilot aims to provide details of less familiar anchorages and passages, although it makes no claim to be comprehensive. Some of these anchorages may only be suitable for use by limited classes of boats, such as shoal-draft boats able to take the ground, and it is the skipper's responsibility to assess, using all available information, whether an anchorage is suitable to use in the circumstances prevailing.

As well as published sources, I have drawn on individual observations by many users. More than 25 years ago, an article by Michael Gilkes in *Roving Commissions* led me to the archives of the Hydrographic Office, which made available copies of original surveys of waters around Islay which, although dating from the early nineteenth century, are of enormous value, and are further confirmed by photos by the RAF from the 1950s, and more recently, my own air photos.

Loch Sween

Aerial photos, as well as some from ground and sea level, are used to supplement charts and maps, and this edition has more than 50 new photos. No claims are made to artistic or technical quality due, partly, to the constraints under which they were taken. Apart from the weather and availability of the aircraft and pilot, photographic flights are planned to coincide with the lowest tides, to show as much detail as possible below water. Two flights were made early in 2006, on the first of which the wind rose much more than forecast and at times the aircraft was leaping around like a leprechaun. Some photos were unusable, but I hope the remainder will be found helpful. With cooperation from Prestwick Air Traffic Control we were able to take new photos along the Ayrshire coast within controlled air space – but not encouraged to linger. Even so we crossed the tracks of three incoming airliners, whose wake vortex can affect a light aircraft for up to five minutes after their passing. Apart from those published, examination of the photos provided new information, as in the example of one remote anchorage, where the salient points at the sides of the channel are clearly shown to be marked by perches.

Where appropriate, a date is included in the captions of photographs, so that the reader may assess how recent the information is.

Many places are only suitable for a short daytime visit in settled conditions and the inclusion of an anchorage is no indication that it is suitable for all conditions. It is the skipper's responsibility to decide whether to use an anchorage at all, and for how long in light of conditions (both current and predicted) and all the information available. Even the most apparently sheltered place will sometimes have the crew standing anchor watches throughout the night.

The description 'occasional anchorage' is intended to convey that the place described is only suitable for use under certain conditions; perhaps for a brief visit ashore during daylight, or in winds from certain directions to await a change of wind or tide. I prefer this description to 'temporary anchorage' which might imply that the anchorage is always (or only) suitable for a brief daylight visit. Conversely, the absence of the description 'occasional' should not be taken as a recommendation that an anchorage may be used in any weather.

Some anchorages, and particularly piers and boat harbours, are only suitable for shoal-draught boats, and this should be obvious from the description; the inclusion of an anchorage does not imply that it is suitable for all yachts.

Within some anchorages there are often several suitable places to lie depending on conditions and it is not always practicable to describe them all, or to mark each one on the plans. In any case, an anchorage suitable for a shoal-draught boat 6 metres long may be inaccessible to a 15-metre yacht with a draught of 2 metres, and a berth which would give shelter for the larger yacht might be uncomfortably exposed for the smaller.

Steep high ground to windward is unlikely to provide good shelter; in fresh winds there may be turbulent gusts on its lee side, or the wind may be deflected to blow from a completely different direction.

After a hot windless day there may be a strong katabatic wind down the slope, usually in the early morning; such conditions are by no means unknown in Scotland.

A valley to windward will channel and accelerate any wind through it.

Trees to windward will absorb a lot of wind and provide good shelter.

Rivers, burns and streams generally carry down debris, often leaving a shallow or drying bank of stones, sand or silt, over which the unwary may swing, invariably in the middle of the night.

Within any anchorage the quality of the bottom may vary greatly. Mud is common, (usually where there is little current) but its density may not be consistent and there are likely to be patches of rock, boulders and stones; also clay, which tends to break out suddenly. Sand is also common, but sometimes it is so hard that an anchor, particularly a light one, will not dig in. Weed of all kinds appears to be on the increase, but it does vary from year to year.

Man-made obstructions Fishing floats, often insufficiently conspicuous, may be encountered even in very deep water, and a lookout has to be kept for them at all times but especially when motoring.

Fish farms have been increasing at an alarming rate, usually outwith the most popular places, but attempts are sometimes made to establish them in recognised anchorages as well.

Permission to establish any permanent fixture on the seabed, such as a mooring, has to be obtained from the Crown Estates Commissioners who own the rights to the seabed; they consult the Department of Trade and Industry, who in turn consult RYA (Scotland), who consult whichever group of yachting interests may be appropriate, and they consult either the Clyde Cruising Club or the Royal Highland

Fish cages are a universal hazard

Girvan harbour

Yacht Club, one of whose more senior members will be asked for his comments; the comments are then passed back up the chain. The CEC have become more aware of the needs of small craft.

In the past, moorings were laid within established anchorages for fishing and other workboats as well as for yachts, and some traditional anchorages are now unusable by visiting boats.

The designation of anchorages (to be kept free of permanent moorings and equipment) has been formalised following discussions between various parties.

The limits of designated anchorages will be shown on future editions of charts.

The West Highland Anchorages and Moorings Association, (WHAM), was set up to resolve conflicts between users. For the address and web site see Appendix.

Visitors' moorings generally have large blue rigid plastic buoys marked with the maximum displacement. There is often no pick-up, and a rope has to be fed through a ring on top of the buoy. If your bow is so high that the buoy is out of reach and you cannot pass your rope through the ring, the best way to secure to one of these moorings is to lead a rope from the bow to the lowest point amidships, pick up the buoy there and take the end of the rope back to the bow. It is desirable to take an extra turn round the ring to reduce chafe, and some owners use a length of chain with rope tails, and/or a snap shackle at one end.

The provision of visitors' moorings in many places is under review, and they may cease to be provided or, where formerly free of charge, may be charged for. Additional moorings may be provided, in some cases for the customers of an adjacent hotel (see also Appendix).

For latest details of moorings, and facilities for visiting yachts see the publication *Welcome Ashore*, available free from Sail Scotland (see Appendix).

Several marinas have been established in the Firth of Clyde, and a berth or mooring will usually be found for a visiting yacht. If planning to leave a boat at as particular marina for a time, it should be arranged beforehand.

Commercial harbours

Some harbours, mainly in the Firth of Clyde, are used by commercial and fishing vessels, whose crews either do not understand the needs of, or are out of sympathy with leisure craft.

Piers and jetties

Even in the most remote anchorages, may be privately owned or are treated as such by regular users, and should be considered in the same way as private moorings. Some are used by fishermen or workboats which may not treat an unattended yacht with as much delicacy as the owner would wish. Some piers are derelict and dangerous.

Eating ashore

Hotels, restaurants and pubs, being essential to any crew's wellbeing, are mentioned in the text, although not always by name, and without specific recommendations as management and standards may change rapidly.

Activities ashore

For many yachtsmen (and particularly their families) the places visited are as much part of a cruising holiday as the sailing itself. Indoor entertainments are sometimes welcome, if only as a refuge from bad weather; museums are mentioned where appropriate.

There are castles and antiquities, birds and wildlife, and hills for walking but details would extend each volume to an unmanageable size.

Some general books and other pilot books are referred to in Appendix I.

Access to Land

New access rights and responsibilites relating to open country in Scotland came into effect in February 2005. The Access Code, published by SNH defining the terms and obligations governing access is available from tourist offices, etc. and may be downloaded from the Internet at:

http://www.outdooraccess-scotland.com

Communications

Public phone boxes

These are fairly well distributed and are referred to where known.

Coverage by mobile phone companies is improving rapidly (at the expense of further degradation of the landscape).

VHF radiotelephones

The hilly nature of parts of the coast puts some areas out of range of the coastguard. Marinas and yacht centres have VHF R/T, but they may not be continuously manned.

Place names

Place names need to be communicated verbally, for example between the navigator, helmsman and lookout, so I have used the popular form of a name where there is one, as well as the name which appears on current charts.

Admiralty charts and sailing directions follow the Ordnance Survey convention of printing academic renderings of Gaelic names, with a variety of accents as they would appear in a Gaelic dictionary. Some of these are quite unpronounceable other than by Gaelic speakers (and, I believe, sometimes unrecognisable even to them).

Both authorities sometimes use anglicised versions, or translations, of Gaelic words, apparently quite arbitrarily; for example you may come across 'Old Woman Rock' among a patch of Gaelic names on a chart, or alternatively a Gaelic name alongside its equivalent anglicisation.

The early surveyors often made up their own names, based on natural features, their own translations of the Gaelic, or events or personalities connected with the survey, and these names were used on earlier charts, but have not often survived to the present time. Some names (such as Wreck Bay on Bute) are only used by yachtsmen.

The spelling of names in this pilot should match that on the Admiralty charts. You may find some discrepancies, but I hope they will not be so great as to cause confusion. For translations of some of the more common Gaelic words see Appendix.

Emergencies

Serious and immediate emergencies (including medical ones) are usually best referred to the coastguard. If you don't have VHF R/T but are able to get ashore (for example, if a crew member is ill), phone the coastguard or police. For less serious problems, such as a mechanical breakdown out of range of a boatyard, mechanics experienced at least with tractor or fishing-boat engines, will often be found locally.

Coastguard

The Maritime Rescue Co-ordination Centre for the area is Clyde Coastguard, ☎ 01475 729988.

Auxiliary Coastguards are based in the following locations, but mariners are not normally able to communicate with them direct.

Clyde Sector: Dunoon, Greenock, Helensburgh, Rothesay, Cumbrae, Kames, Kilcreggan, Loch Goil, Largs, Inverary

Kintyre Sector: Campbeltown, Jura, Gigha, Port Charlotte, Tarbert, Ardpatrick, Carradale, Port Ellen, Southend

Galloway Sector: Ardrossan, Arran, Drummore, Girvan, Stranraer, Ayr, Ballantrae, Portpatrick.

In addition to the Coastal Teams described above, a naval rescue helicopter squadron is based at Prestwick.

Lifeboats

All-weather lifeboats are based at: Troon, Girvan, Portpatrick, Campbeltown, Islay, Oban and Tobermory. Inshore lifeboats are based at Helensburgh, Largs, Tighnabruaich, Arran, Stranraer and Campbeltown.

Notes on plans and pilotage directions

Generally the conventions used on Admiralty charts have been followed so that this pilot may be used in conjunction with them. Please refer to the heading *Charts* on page 1.

Passages are described as far as possible for an approach from seaward, but this is not possible in the case of sounds between islands, and the Kyles of Bute are described from east to west, and Kilbrannan Sound from north to south to fit in with a continuous sequence of chapters.

In each chapter information relating to the whole chapter about charts, tides, marks and dangers comes first; then any passage directions, sometimes including certain anchorages where it is necessary to relate these to plans associated with the passages; then any branches from the main passage; and finally individual anchorages, usually in the same sequence as the passages described.

Conspicuous features are listed to help identification in poor visibility.

Lights, and any directions for making a passage or approach by night, are described separately from the Dangers and Marks to which they relate, as most of us sail by day for most of the time, and this reduces the amount of information to be absorbed.

Bearings

Bearings are given from seaward and always refer to true north. A few of the plans are not orientated with north at the top in order to make the best use of the space available, but reference to the north point on the plan will make this clear.

Distances are given in nautical miles and cables (tenths of nautical mile); distances of less than ¼ cable are generally expressed in metres.

Depths and heights

These are given in metres to correspond with the current Admiralty charts. Depths are related to the current chart datum which is generally lower than that on older charts. This datum is the lowest level to which the surface of the sea is expected to fall owing to astronomical causes. If high barometric pressure and/or strong offshore winds coincide with a low spring tide the water may fall below this level, in which case there will be less depth than shown on the chart, or sketch plan.

Tides

Heights of tides are represented by five figures; these are: Mean High Water Springs, Mean High Water Neaps, Mean Tide Level, Mean Low Water Neaps, Mean Low Water Springs. The word *Mean* is important because (for example) Low Water Springs in any particular fortnight may be substantially higher or lower than the mean.

If you have tide tables which give heights of tides at Greenock or Oban (depending on whether you are east or west of Kintyre) you will be able to relate the height of tide on any particular day to the mean figures there (4.0 2.9 2.4 1.8 0.7 for Oban, 3.4 2.9 1.9 1.0 0.4 for Greenock) and judge whether the rise and fall is greater or less than the mean.

The difference between times of tides at Greenock or Oban and at Dover may vary by as much as 40 minutes, so that local tide tables will give more accurate results than those for Dover. In addition to Admiralty tide tables and commercial almanacs, pocket tide tables for Greenock and Oban are supplied by local chandlers, boatyards and marinas.

Plans of anchorages and passages in this pilot are often at a larger scale than those on current charts, and the information in them is compiled from many sources. These include the Admiralty's original surveys; air photographs, observations by other yachtsmen; and my own surveys, both from the air and by sea, as well as from land. Some of them are based directly on British Admiralty charts, with the permission of the Hydrographer of the Navy.

Photographs

Those taken from the air and from hilltops often show more detail than can be included in the plans.

Photos and views from sea level are used to illustrate transits and clearing marks, or to help identify landmarks.

Transits are in some cases more clearly illustrated when the marks used are not actually aligned; where this is done the marks are indicated by pointers.

Aerial photos were taken as far as possible at low spring tides to reveal as many hazards as possible. However it takes many years to visit each place at a specific time of day or month, whether by sea, land or air – with no guarantee that conditions will be suitable for photography when one gets there. Accordingly, some of the coverage isn't as comprehensive, and some of the photos not as clear as I would wish.

With increasing frequency, photos which were once satisfactory become superseded by new developments and some photos may not include features which exist on the ground.

Details change, new passages, and new hazards, are discovered. Amendments are published on Imray's website www.imray.com

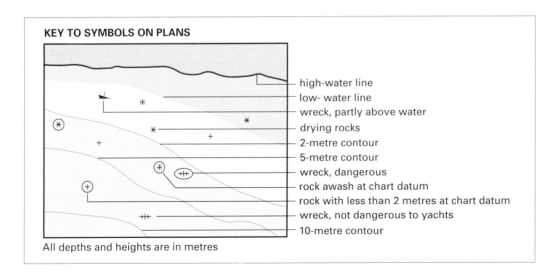

KEY TO SYMBOLS ON PLANS

- high-water line
- low-water line
- wreck, partly above water
- drying rocks
- 2-metre contour
- 5-metre contour
- wreck, dangerous
- rock awash at chart datum
- rock with less than 2 metres at chart datum
- wreck, not dangerous to yachts
- 10-metre contour

All depths and heights are in metres

I. Firth of Clyde approaches

The distance from the Mull of Galloway to Heads of Ayr is about 55 miles. In that distance there is one natural inlet, a couple of harbours neither of which is accessible at low water or in strong onshore winds, and a few smaller harbours accessible only to shoal-draught boats.

Passages round the Mull of Kintyre are described in Chapter V.

Charts

2198 (1:75,000), 2126 (1:75,000)

Tides

In the middle of North Channel tidal streams run at up to 4 knots along the line of the channel.
The southeast-going stream begins about +0440 Greenock (+0600 Dover).
The northwest-going stream begins about –0120 Greenock (HW Dover).
South of the Mull of Galloway for several miles streams run at up to 4 knots in an east–west direction.
The east-going stream begins about +0530 Greenock (–0545 Dover).
The west-going stream begins about –0030 Greenock (+0045 Dover).
Eddies run SSE along the shore of the Rhins south of Portpatrick.

Passage notes

The passage from the Irish Sea to the Firth of Clyde is generally straightforward except near the Mull of Galloway when there are eddies and overfalls.

The passage round the Mull of Kintyre is described in Chapter V.

Lights

At night the approach to the Firth of Clyde is well lit, but Ailsa Craig light is obscured over a wide sector on its west side.

Look out for other traffic, particularly fishing and naval vessels which may not maintain a steady course and speed.

The following are the major lights in the approach to the Clyde (parts of this list are repeated where relevant to individual sections of the coast but are included here for the benefit of a yacht approaching the Clyde at night):

Mull of Galloway lighthouse Fl.20s99m28M
Crammag Head lighthouse Fl.10s35m18M
Killantringan Head lighthouse Fl(2)15s49m25M
Group of four radio masts 5 miles north of Portpatrick with red obstruction lights
Corsewall Point Al.LFl.WR.74s34m18M
Ailsa Craig Fl(6)30s18m17M (028°-obscd-145°)
Turnberry Point Fl.15s29m24M
Pladda (south of Arran) Fl(3)30s40m23M
Pillar Rock Point (Holy Isle, east of Arran) Fl(2)20s38m25M
Lady Isle (southwest of Troon) Fl.2s19m11M (racon)
Sanda Island (south of Kintyre) LFl.WR.24s50m19/16M
Island Davaar (east of Kintyre) Fl(2)10s37m23M

Shelter

East Tarbert Bay on the east side of the Mull of Galloway, provides shelter from the west but strong tides and very heavy seas off the Mull itself may make the approach hazardous when shelter is most needed.

Loch Ryan is easily entered although there may be heavy seas under some conditions off the west side of the entrance.

Lamlash Bay on the east shore of Arran provides shelter around its shores and is easily entered by day or night.

The Rhins of Galloway

The hammerhead-shaped peninsula of the Rhins, 26 miles long, has an inhospitable rocky coast with a few bays and the partly ruined harbour of Portpatrick. Several groups of radio masts stand on the Rhins.

CHART
2198 (1:75,000)

TIDES
Eddies and overfalls occur inshore along the coast of the Rhins.
The south-going stream begins about +0310 Greenock (+0430 Dover).
The north-going stream begins about –0250 Greenock (–0310 Dover), running at up to 5 knots at springs south of Black Head, decreasing further north to 2 knots at Corsewall Point.

DANGERS AND MARKS
No hidden dangers affecting a yacht on passage in good visibility lie outwith a cable from the shore. About 2¼ miles southwest of Corsewall Point the drying rock Craig Laggan, two cables from the shore, is marked by a stone beacon with a blunt pointed top. The main landmarks on the Rhins of Galloway are:

Mull of Galloway lighthouse at the south end of the Mull of Galloway, a white tower 26 metres high on top of a cliff.

Crammag Head lighthouse, 4 miles WNW of Mull of Galloway, a 6 metre white tower 30 metres above sea level.

Portpatrick village 10 miles south of Corsewall Point, with a single radio mast with dish aerials on it behind the village.

Killantringan Head lighthouse, 1½ miles northwest of Portpatrick, a 22-metre white tower at sea level.

Various groups of radio masts in the northern part of the Rhins are easily confused with each other, but the principal group of four masts stands a mile inland, 5 miles north of Portpatrick.

Corsewall Point lighthouse at the north end of the Rhins, a 34-metre white tower.

LIGHTS
Mull of Galloway lighthouse Fl.20s99m28M

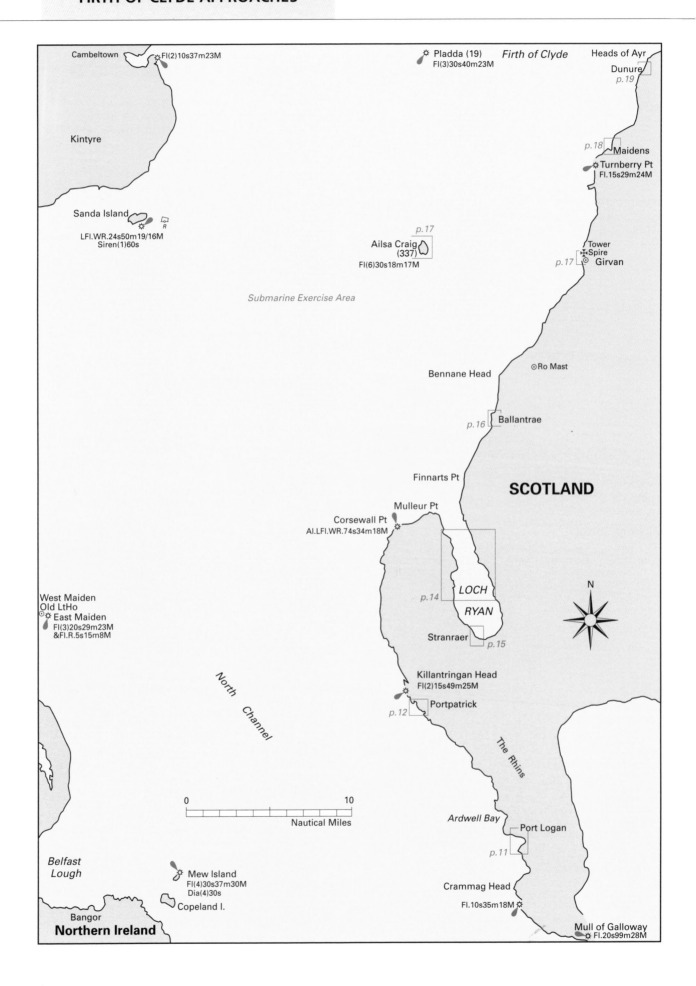

Cambeltown ☼Fl(2)10s37m23M

Pladda (19) ☼ *Firth of Clyde* Heads of Ayr
Fl(3)30s40m23M
Dunure
p.19

Kintyre

p.18 Maidens

☼ Turnberry Pt
Fl.15s29m24M

Sanda Island
LFl.WR.24s50m19/16M
Siren(1)60s

p.17

Ailsa Craig
(337)
Fl(6)30s18m17M

Tower
✠ Spire
p.17 ⊙ Girvan

Submarine Exercise Area

Bennane Head ⊙Ro Mast

p.16 Ballantrae

Finnarts Pt

SCOTLAND

Mulleur Pt

Corsewall Pt
Al.LFl.WR.74s34m18M

p.14 **LOCH**
RYAN

N

West Maiden
Old LtHo
⊙☼ East Maiden
Fl(3)20s29m23M
&Fl.R.5s15m8M

Stranraer *p.15*

Killantringan Head
Fl(2)15s49m25M

North Channel

p.12 Portpatrick

The Rhins

0   10

Nautical Miles

Ardwell Bay Port Logan

p.11

Belfast
Lough

Mew Island
Fl(4)30s37m30M
Dia(4)30s

Crammag Head

Bangor Copeland I.
Northern Ireland

Fl.10s35m18M ☼

Mull of Galloway
☼ Fl.20s99m28M

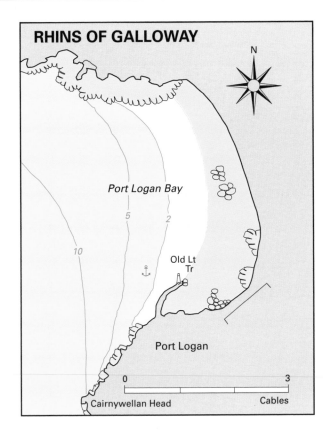

RHINS OF GALLOWAY

N

Port Logan Bay

5   2

10

Old Lt
Tr

Port Logan

0   3

Cairnywellan Head   Cables

Crammag Head lighthouse Fl.10s35m18M
Killantringan Head lighthouse Fl(2)15s49m25M
Group of four radio masts 5 miles north of Portpatrick
with red obstruction lights
Corsewall Point AlLFl.WR.74s34m18M

OCCASIONAL ANCHORAGES

Port Logan Bay 54°43′.5N 4°58′W 3½ miles north of
Crammag Head, has moderate depths for anchoring
offshore. A stone breakwater 180 metres long on the
south east side of the bay provides shelter for small
shoal-draught boats able to take the ground.

Ardwell Bay 54°46′N 5°00′W nearly 3 miles further
north, provides shelter in offshore winds.

Portpatrick

54°50′.5N 5°07′W

Attempts were made in the late 18th and early 19th
centuries to develop a harbour here for Irish traffic,
but the breakwaters were destroyed by the sea, and
the harbour was formally abandoned about 1870
with the coming of steamships able to negotiate the
length of Loch Ryan.

The entrance is 35 metres wide between low water
lines, with ruined breakwaters on both sides, a
broad drying rocky shore on its south side and
several drying rocks on the north side, the most
easterly of which, Half Tide Rock, is marked by an
unlit red buoy. The Inner Harbour is small, but it is
popular with Irish crews, especially at weekends.

From northwest the entrance is not easily
identified until it is abeam. A single radio mast east
of the village has many dish aerials on it, and there
is a single plain mast close north of the village.

From south the hotel on the north side of the
harbour is conspicuous.

Once inside, shelter is good although with strong
southwest winds some sea may work in even to the
inner harbour. In the channel to the inner harbour
the depth is only 0·5 metre.

TIDES

Tides run at over 4 knots northwest and southeast 2
cables off the entrance.
Constant +0022 Liverpool (+0037 Dover)

Height in metres

MHWS	MHWN	MTL	MLWN	MLWS
3·8	3·0	2·0	0·9	0·3

DANGERS AND MARKS

Half Tide Rock is marked by a red unlit buoy, and shoal
ground/submerged rock on the NE side of the channel
may be marked by a green unlit buoy, as shown in the
photo of the leading line.

Port Logan provides temporary shelter for small boats

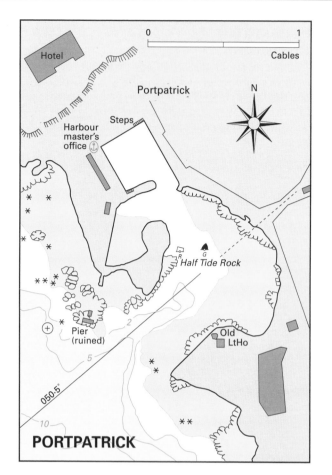

PORTPATRICK

rear mark · front mark · 'Half Tide Rock'

Approach

The harbour should not be approached within 2 hours of LW, more if there is any onshore sea, owing to the shoal depth in the approach to the inner harbour. It is essential to pick up the leading marks: an orange vertical stripe on the harbour wall and another on the left-hand corner of a building in the main street 050·5°, as illustrated.

Portpatrick   *Patrick Roach*

Portpatrick was never ideal as a ferry harbour in the days of sail

As soon as the inner harbour opens up to port bear round to that side to avoid the drying sandy bay to starboard. The only berths are in the inner harbour, the southwest side of which is reserved for the lifeboat. Avoid mooring in front of stone steps; you will be asked to move.

Lights
At night F.G lights are shown on the leading line, but their existence cannot be relied on.

Supplies
Shops, post office, telephones, hotels, showers, refuse disposal, Calor Gas, petrol, diesel at Esso garage in main street, water at inner harbour, EC Thursday. Harbourmaster ☎ 01776 810355.

Loch Ryan
Loch Ryan provides the best and most accessible shelter south of Troon. The approach is straightforward but there may be heavy seas off Milleur Point at the west side of the entrance, especially in northwest winds with an ebb tide.

The inner part of the loch is shallow with The Spit, which dries, extending southeast for over a mile from the west side of the loch, providing some shelter in the bay behind it, known as The Wig.

Car ferries, including high-speed catamarans, run between Larne and both Stranraer and Cairnryan in Loch Ryan.

CHART
1403 (1:10,000)

TIDES
The stream turns northwest about HW Greenock (+0115 Dover) and southeast about 5½ hours later, running at 1½ knots at springs.

Constant −0020 Greenock (+0055 Dover)

Height in metres

MHWS	MHWN	MTL	MLWN	MLWS
3·0	2·5	1·6	0·6	0·2

DANGERS AND MARKS
The principal mark is Cairn Point lighthouse on the east shore.

Milleur Point, the west point of the entrance, has a north cardinal buoy 3 cables NNE of it.

A drying rock lies a cable off the point and another lies a cable offshore ½ mile SSE of the point.

Jamieson's Point is the most prominent feature of the west shore, 1½ miles SSE of Milleur Point. Rocks drying and submerged extend over 4 cables from the west shore south of Jamieson's Point, merging with The Spit.

In mid-channel, between Jamieson's Point and Cairn Point, port- and starboard-hand light buoys mark underwater hazards which were discovered by ferries but of no concern to yachts.

A south cardinal light-buoy lies northwest of Cairn Point.

The Spit extends over a mile southeast from Kirkcolm Point opposite Cairn Point, its outer end marked by Spit G conical light buoy.

South of Spit buoy three green light beacons mark the west edge of the channel to Stranraer Harbour.

Yachts which can sail outwith the channel must give way to ferries or any other large vessels confined to the channel.

Agnew Monument stands on the skyline west of the loch.

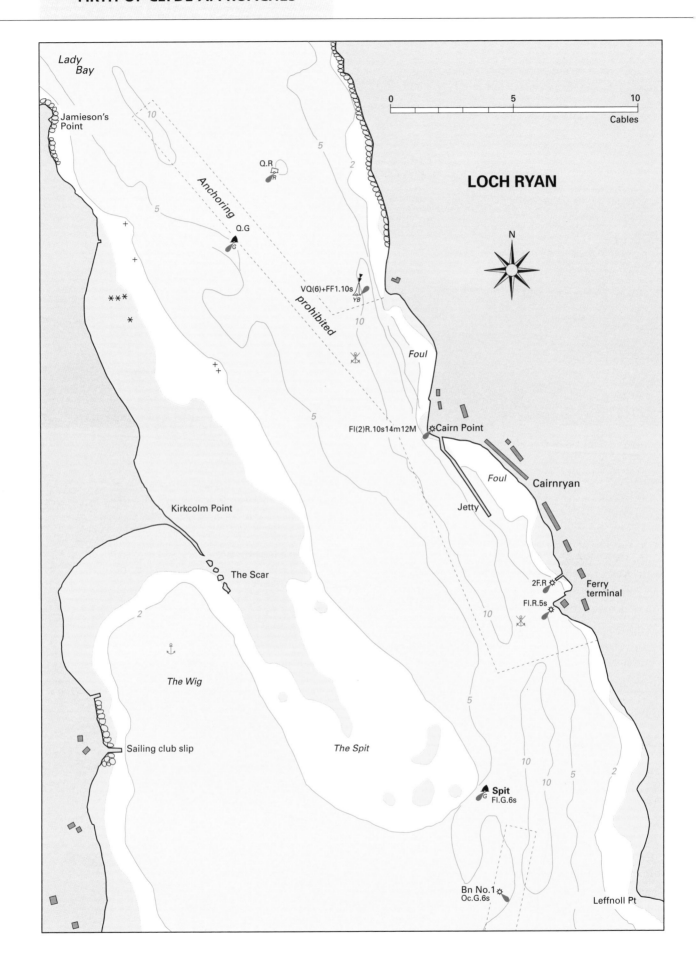

LOCH RYAN

Lady Bay

Jamieson's Point

Anchoring prohibited

Q.R

Q.G

VQ(6)+FF1.10s

Foul

Fl(2)R.10s14m12M

Cairn Point

Foul

Cairnryan

Jetty

Kirkcolm Point

The Scar

2F.R

Fl.R.5s

Ferry terminal

The Wig

Sailing club slip

The Spit

Spit
Fl.G.6s

Bn No.1
Oc.G.6s

Leffnoll Pt

0   5   10

Cables

N

Anchoring is prohibited in the fairway off Cairn Point, and between the fairway and the east shore from ½ mile north of Cairn Point to 2 cables south of the light beacon at Cairnryan Ferry Terminal; also in the channel on the east side of beacons 1 to 5 and in the area northwest of the East Pier at Stranraer where the ferries turn round.

Approach

Keep a lookout for ferry and other traffic and keep well off the west shore as Cairn Point is approached; pass east of Spit buoy. Watch Ch. 14 for announcements of vessel movements

Lights

Milleur Point north cardinal buoy Q
Buoys NNW of Cairn Point Q.R.5s and Q.G.5s
South cardinal lightbuoy VQ(6)+L Fl.
Cairn Point lighthouse Fl(2)R.10s14m12M
Cairnryan Ferry Terminal Fl.R.5s5m5M with 2 F.R(vert) lights inshore.
Spit buoy Fl.G.6s
No.1 beacon Oc.G.6s
No.3 beacon Q.G
No.5 beacon Fl.G.3s

Anchorages

The Wig on the west shore provides some shelter from northeast behind The Spit.

From Spit buoy head southwest with Agnew monument on the skyline 030° on the starboard bow for ½ mile, west for ½ mile, then northwest towards moored yachts.

Anchor off sailing club slip clear of moorings or, in northeast winds, as far up to north shore as depth and swinging room allow. Loch Ryan Sailing Club is at the head of the concrete slip.

The sailing club welcomes visiting yachts and can provide showers when the clubhouse is open; there is usually someone about on Wednesday evenings and Saturday and Sunday afternoons. Keep clear of yachts which may be racing.

In strong winds from south to southeast The Wig is uncomfortable and Stranraer Harbour is better; north to northwest winds send a swell into the harbour and The Wig then provides better shelter.

Supplies

Provisions at Kirkcolm (1 mile). For water and fuel yachts need to go to Stranraer.

Stranraer Harbour

Stranraer Harbour consists of three piers of which the East and Centre piers are reserved for RoRo ferries.

Small craft moor on the east side of the root of West Pier.

High speed ferries no longer operate from Stranraer Harbour and pontoons and an extended breakwater are being installed for small craft.

Make fast at the inner end of West Pier, south of the 'knuckle' and find the harbourmaster at the Seacat office.

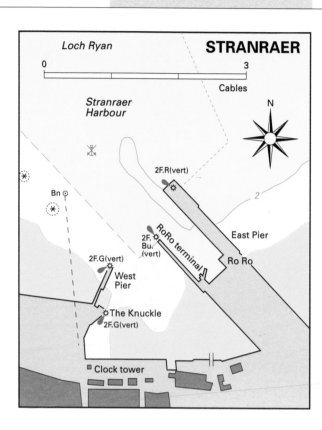

Alternatively anchor outside the harbour northwest of West Pier, clear of the prohibited area and clear of the outfall pipe, and rocks inshore.

Lights

At night the approach beacons are lit (see above) and the harbour has a colourful display of fixed lights competing with the town lights:

East Pier 2F.R(vert)9m
Centre Pier 2F.Bu(vert)
West Pier head 2F.G(vert)10m4M
West Pier knuckle 2F.G(vert)5m4M

Supplies

Shops, post office, bank, phones, hotels, *Calor Gas*, petrol, diesel at garage, water, EC Wednesday. Metered electricity, toilet block with showers, swimming pool.

Communications

Harbourmaster Mike Watson ☎ 07734 073421.

Lady Bay and Finnart Bay in the outer loch are subject to disturbance from ferry traffic.

Stranraer Harbour from west. The ferry terminal at lower right has been removed   *Patrick Roach*

Loch Ryan to Heads of Ayr

CHARTS

2199, 2126 (1:75,000). Of these *2126* is the most useful particularly if a passage to or round Kintyre is envisaged. OS Landranger maps *70, 76*.

TIDES

Tidal streams are not significant except close inshore.

DANGERS AND MARKS

Between Corsewall Point and Arran no hidden dangers in reasonable visibility lie outwith ½ mile from the shore.

Ailsa Craig, 55°15′N 5°07′W, 11 miles south of Arran, 337 metres high, is the principal reference point.

Turnberry Point, 55°20′N 4°50′W, a white lighthouse 24 metres high.

Culzean Castle, 55°21′N 4°47′W, an ornate building on a cliff 3 miles northeast of Turnberry Point.

Occasional anchorages

Ballantrae 55°06′N 5°00′W, about halfway between Corsewall Point and Girvan, is most easily identified by Knockdollan, a conspicuous conical hill 3 miles northeast of the village. A stone pier which dries, at the north end of the village, provides some shelter from south at high water or to boats which can take the ground. Access to the drying basin at the pier is obstructed by mooring lines for lobster and angling boats. Supplies in the village.

Ailsa Craig 55°15′N 5°07′W, 8 miles offshore, is steep-to all round but a timber jetty on its northeast side has a depth of 0·6 metre at its head.

Depths are suitable for anchoring in very quiet weather close inshore northwest of the jetty but

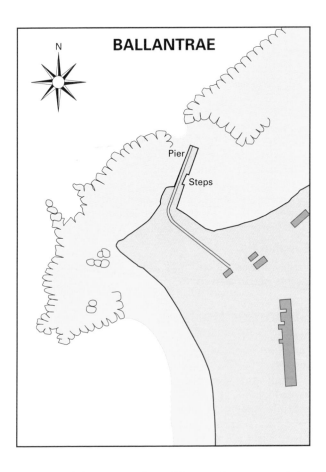

beware of the ruins of an old jetty close west of the existing jetty. Use a tripping line as the steeply shelving bottom consists of granite boulders under which an anchor may be jammed.

Ailsa Craig; jetty in right foreground

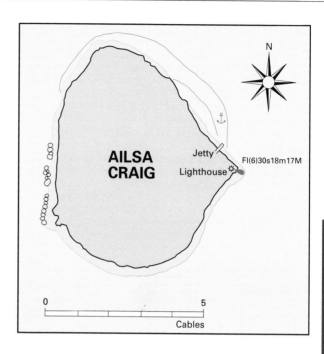

A yacht should not in any case be left unattended, either at anchor or alongside to avoid obstructing supply vessels or helicopters.

Girvan

55°14´.5N 4°51´.5W

Difficult to enter owing to shoaling of the channel, although there are proposals for permanent improvements. Girvan is often crowded with fishing boats, but a pontoon is provided for visiting yachts.

CHART

Plan on *1866* (1:6,250)

TIDES

Constant –0032 Greenock (+0043 Dover)

Height in metres

MHWS	MHWN	MTL	MLWN	MLWS
3·1	2·6	1·8	0·9	0·4

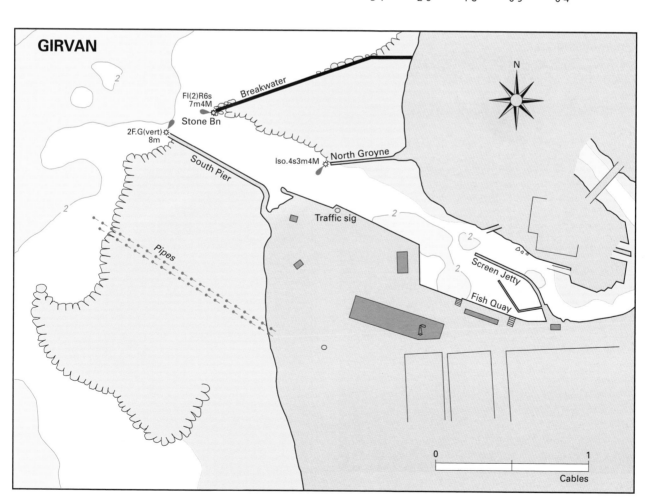

DANGERS AND MARKS

Depths in the entrance vary owing to movement of the bottom. Girvan Patch, with a least depth of 1·7 metres, 4 cables SSW of the entrance and 4 cables offshore, is a hazard if approaching from south, as are drying reefs 1½ cables SSW of the entrance.

Northwest winds cause heavy seas in the entrance, and there is a strong current from the river after heavy rain.

The head of the North Breakwater is marked by a light beacon.

Enter only within 3 hours of high water except in quiet conditions. Keep closer to the South Pier than to the North Breakwater.

A screen jetty keeps debris from the river away from the South Pier, which is used by fishing boats, and a single long pontoon lies between the screen jetty and the pier.

Moor temporarily at the pontoon and find the harbourmaster in order to be allocated a suitable berth.

Traffic signals

Signals are shown at the east end of the South Pier; by day two black discs horizontally disposed, at night two red lights, indicate that the harbour is closed.

Lights

South Pier 2F.G(vert)8m4M
North Breakwater Fl(2)R.6s7m4M
North Groyne Iso.4s3m4M
2F.R(horiz) at South Pier indicate harbour closed.

Supplies and services

Shops, post office, telephone, bank, hotel, *Calor Gas*, petrol, diesel, water, EC Wednesday, indoor swimming pool, showers.

Communications

Harbour office ☎ 01465 713648. VHF Ch 16, 12 (0900–1700, Mon–Fri). Mobile 07970 844057.

Maidens Harbour is being dredged to extend its use for small craft. Note Keown Rock at left

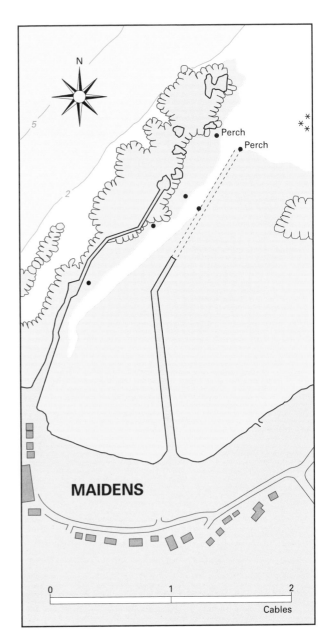

MAIDENS

Girvan   *Patrick Roach*

Maidens Harbour (2006)

Maidens

55°20′N 4°49′W

A drying harbour on the south side of Maidenhead Bay, 1½ miles northeast of Turnberry lighthouse, which can be entered in settled conditions by yachts able to take the ground, but it is fairly fully occupied by local boats and there may not be any space alongside the quay. Extensive dredging and other improvements are being carried out.

The harbour is formed by a stone quay and breakwater connecting a line of rocks on its west side, and an incomplete breakwater on its east side. The channel within the harbour is marked by iron beacons.

Keown Rock in the middle of the bay, ¼ mile north of the harbour entrance, covers at half tide. Temporary anchorage can be found in 2 metres between Keown Rock and the harbour entrance.

Shops, post office, telephone, hotel, Calor Gas at caravan site, diesel at garage.

Harbourmaster (part time) ☎ 01655 331665, water and fuel can be arranged through her.

Culzean Bay provides temporary anchorage in settled weather in 5 metres.

Dunure

55°24′.5N 4°45′.5W

A small artificial drying harbour 2 miles southwest of the Heads of Ayr, foul with small-boat moorings, Dunure is identified by a ruined castle on the shore at the south end of the village, and the harbour has a stone beacon on the head of the breakwater.

It should only be attempted if there is no sea running and at not less than half-flood, and only by a boat able to take the ground, unless for a very brief stay. All berths are allocated to permanent berth-holders and there is no provision for visiting boats.

Dunure Harbour (2006)

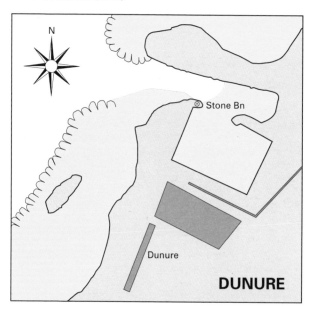

TIDES

Constant −0032 Greenock (+0043 Dover)

Height in metres

MHWS	MHWN	MTL	MLWN	MLWS
3·1	2·6	1·8	0·9	0·4

II. Firth of Clyde

Traffic in the Firth of Clyde has diminished in recent years, but a sharp lookout needs to be kept for naval vessels (especially submarines) and fishing boats, all of which may behave unpredictably, and very large tankers and bulk carriers.

CHARTS

Imray chart folio *2900* (1:50,000)
2126 (1:75,000), *2220* (1:36,000)

SHELTER

Lamlash Bay on the east side of Arran provides shelter around its shores and is easily entered by day or night.

Troon and Ardrossan are the only artificial harbours on the east side of the Clyde south of Cumbrae Islands which are accessible in strong onshore winds. However, in strong southwesterly winds there may be heavy seas on the shoals with nowhere to run for, and in these conditions Lamlash may be a better refuge.

Largs Yacht Haven provides shelter and the approach itself is sheltered and well lit, but there is little space to enter under sail.

MARKS

Heads of Ayr, a dark cliff about 80 metres high on the south side of Ayr Bay; a group of 3 radio masts stands on Bron Carrick Hill about 1½ miles south of Heads of Ayr.

Lady Isle, 55°31′.5N 4°44′W, 2 miles southwest of Troon Point, is 3 metres high and has a white tapering light beacon 16 metres in height with vertical red stripes.

A long light-coloured building (a paper mill) a mile north of Troon is conspicuous, especially in afternoon or evening light.

Horse Island, northwest of Ardrossan, has a single tapering beacon on it but it is stone coloured and the island is close inshore.

DANGERS

Unmarked rocks, submerged and drying, extend over half a mile from the shore between the Heads of Ayr and Irvine, and between Ardrossan and Farland Head.

Saltpan Spit, with a least depth of 1·6 metres 1¾ miles NNW of Ayr harbour entrance.

Black Rocks, drying 6 cables from the shore 2 miles SSE of Troon, are charted as having a beacon near their south end, but it was missing in May 1988.

Lady Isle has drying rocks all round it, up to 2 cables to the northeast.

Lappock Rock 1½ miles north of Troon has a stone tower on it.

Yellow light buoys in Irvine Bay 1–1½ miles offshore are of no significance to yachts but may provide a useful check on position in combination with chart.

By remaining outwith the 15-metre contour a yacht will keep clear of these dangers, but several isolated shoals outwith this depth will puzzle any navigator who is

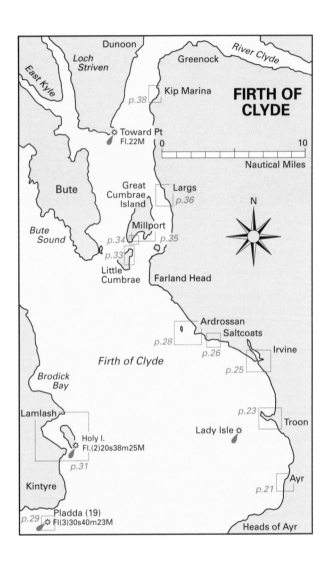

relying on his echo sounder and has not kept his track on the chart. Passing Ardrossan the 15-metre contour is the closest distance at which it is safe to be from the land, and west of Horse Island a 6-metre shoal will be found on this line.

LIGHTS

At night there are no major lights on the east shore and harbour lights are difficult to see against lights ashore.

Lady Isle Fl(4)30s19m8M

Harbour lights are shown under the respective harbours.

Ayr

55°28′N 4°38′W

A commercial harbour, with a visitors' pontoon east of the commercial quays. The entrance is straightforward except in strong onshore winds when it should be avoided.

CHART

Plan on 1866 (1:10,000)

TIDES

Constant –0025 Greenock (+0050 Dover)

Height in metres

MHWS	MHWN	MTL	MLWN	MLWS
3·0	2·6	1·8	1·1	0·5

DANGERS AND MARKS

St Nicholas Rock and submerged rocks extending ¼ mile WSW of the south pier head are marked by a starboard-hand light buoy, Outer St Nicholas, 4 cables west of the south pier head.

Traffic signals are shown from a mast at the outer end of North Quay, two cables within the entrance: two black balls vertically disposed by day; two red lights by night indicating that the harbour is closed.

Entrance

Before entering harbour call the harbourmaster on VHF to check on movements of any large vessels.

Pass north of Outer St Nicholas buoy and between the South Pier and the North Breakwater. Bear slightly to starboard and follow the river to a pontoon on the north bank, not more than ¼ mile from the entrance to the Griffin Dock (otherwise you will run out of water), and put a crew member ashore to ask for a key to the gate at the Ship Inn, opposite the gate. The pontoon on the south side is reserved for permanent berthing for club members only. There is no water or electricity on the pontoon, nor showers nearby, but the town centre provides full shopping facilities within a short walk, details from the Ship Inn. The pontoon is provided by the Ayr Yacht and Cruising Club; pay at the Ship.

Lights

Outer St Nicholas buoy Fl.G.2s

South Pier Q.7m7M, with F.G.5m5M showing southwest over St Nicholas Rock, but part of water over which the F.G light does not show has less than 1·5 metres

North Breakwater Q.R.7m5M

Leading lights 098° *Front* F.R.10m5M. *Rear* Oc.R.10s18m9M

Traffic signals (as above) 2F.R(vert) at North Breakwater indicate that the harbour is closed.

Supplies and services

Shops, post office, bank, telephone, hotel, Calor Gas, petrol, diesel, water, EC Wednesday.

Communications

Harbour office at North Quay ☎ 01292 281687, VHF Ch 14.

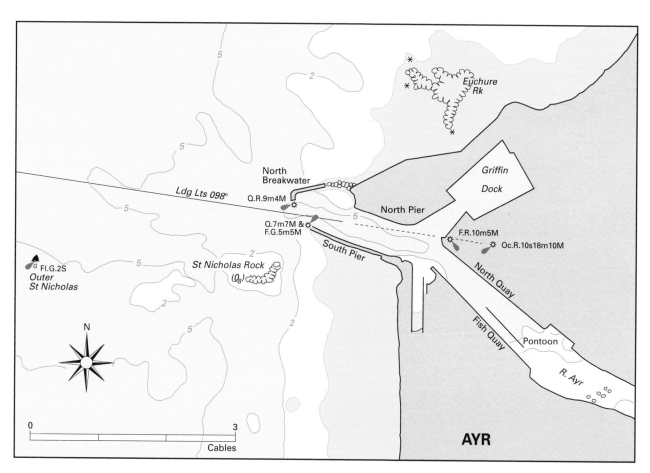

FIRTH OF CLYDE

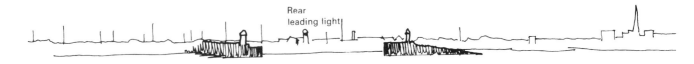

Ayr Harbour approach

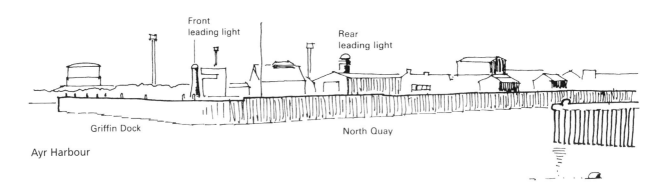

Ayr Harbour

Visitors' pontoon at the Ship Inn on the north side of the river (2006)

Ayr Harbour: visitors' pontoon at left side of river (2006)

Troon

55°33′N 4°41′W

The easiest harbour to approach on this part of the coast. Troon Marina is in the inner harbour. A new ro-ro terminal has been built on the north side of the East Pier.

CHART

Plan on *1866* (1:6,250)

TIDES

Constant –0025 Greenock (+0050 Dover)

Height in metres

MHWS	MHWN	MTL	MLWN	MLWS
3·1	2·6	1·8	0·9	0·4

DANGERS AND MARKS

Strong southwest winds build up very heavy seas in the approach and in these conditions it may be better to make for Lamlash or Largs Marina.

Troon Rock, a mile west of the entrance, breaks in heavy weather.

Heavy seas build up in the entrance in strong northwest winds.

Lady Isle, 3 metres high with a white tapered light beacon with red vertical stripe, lies 2 miles southwest of the entrance, with rocks and shoals all round, up to 2 cables to the northeast.

Crab Rock, more than a cable west of West Pier is marked by a starboard-hand light buoy a cable northwest of the rock.

A new steel beacon 'Approach' stands 1½ cables north of the East Pier head, together with a new dolphin close off the end of the East Pier head.

Mill Rock, which dries 0·4m, 4 cables NNE of the entrance, is marked on its south side by an unlit can buoy.

Lappock Rock, 1½ miles north of the entrance, is marked by a stone tower.

Car ferries, including high speed ferries, operate from a terminal at the West Pier. Watch Ch 14 for announcements of vessel movements.

Approach

From south or west identify Crab Rock buoy and pass north of it.

From north identify Mill Rock can buoy and pass clear west of it.

Watch out for commercial traffic and fishing vessels which may be hidden behind the entrance piers. Call the marina on Ch 37 or 80 for advice, especially if traffic signals (see below) are showing.

Make for the inner harbour (note that the south part of the passage is obstructed by the sloping end

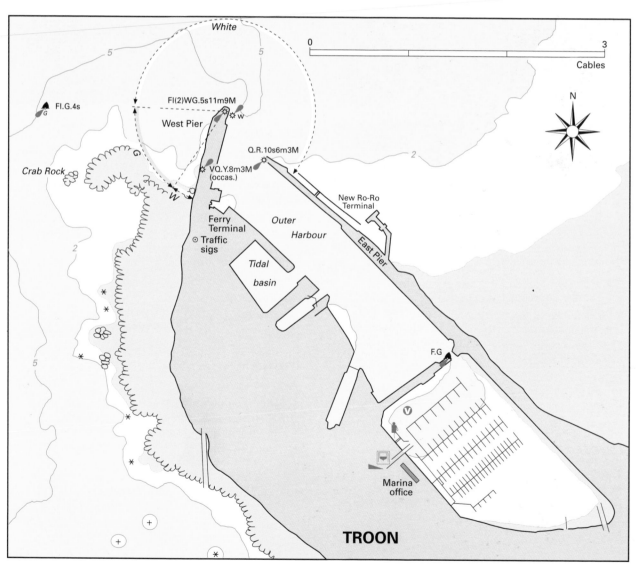

FIRTH OF CLYDE

Troon Harbour: new high-speed ferry terminal in foreground (2006)

of the wall separating the two parts of the harbour, marked by a stbd-hand light buoy), make fast temporarily at the outer end of the second pontoon, and report to the marina office. The tidal basin in the outer harbour is used by fishing boats.

Traffic signals

By day two black balls vertically disposed on a mast a cable south of the north end of West Pier indicate that the harbour is closed. A VQ flashing light on the west breakwater indicates that a ferry is about to leave the harbour.

Lights

Lady Isle Fl.2s19m11M (racon)
Crab Rock light buoy Fl.G.4s
West Pier Fl(2)WG.5s11m9M
Approach Bn Fl.R.2s.4M
East Pier dolphin Q.R.3M
East Pier head Fl.R.10s6m3M
Traffic signals (as above) show 2F.R(vert) at night
At night
From southwest keep outwith the 5-metre contour until in the white sector of the West Pier light.

Services and supplies

At marina telephone, Calor Gas, petrol, diesel, water, slip, hoist. Hull, mechanical and electrical repairs. Laundry, restaurant, bar, showers.

In town (10 min walk) Shops, post office, bank, hotel, EC Wednesday.

Communications

Marina ☎ 01292 315553 VHF Ch 80.
Harbourmaster ☎ 01292 281687

Irvine

55°36′N 4°42′W

A former industrial harbour inside a shallow river mouth with yacht berths on the south side.

The sliding bridge across the river is at present left permanently open. If the situation changes, it will be noted as soon as practicable.

The Scottish Maritime Museum, Seaworld Centre, and Magnum Leisure Centre stand on the south side of the river.

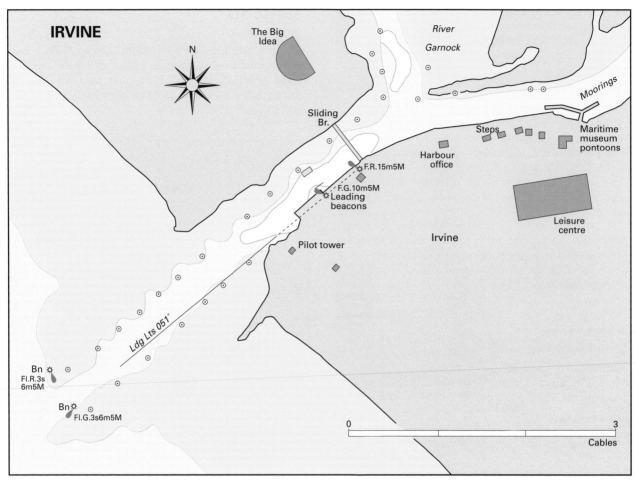

IRVINE

CHART

Plan on *1866* (1:10,000)

TIDES

Constant –0015 Greenock (+0100 Dover)

Height in metres

MHWS	MHWN	MTL	MLWN	MLWS
3·1	2·6	1·8	0·9	0·4

Tidal streams run across the entrance together with currents depending on winds. Seas break on the bar if the wind is blowing against the ebb; during or after heavy rain the current flowing out of the river is increased.

DANGERS AND MARKS

Yellow light buoys in Irvine Bay 1–1½ miles offshore are of no significance to yachts.

A bar, on which the least depth is 0.5 metres, lies between light-beacons at the outer end of the channel. The shallow channel has groynes on either side, marked by perches.

The old pilot tower at the entrance is conspicuous.

Directions

The bar should not be approached within 3 hours of LW, or more if there is any sea.

The leading marks, standing east of the old pilot tower on the south side of the river bearing 051°, are two tall lattice beacons. The leading line leads along the LW line on the southeast side of the channel.

Lights

Lappock Rock beacon is not lit
Entrance beacon northwest side Fl.R.3s6m5M
Entrance beacon southeast side Fl.G.3s6m5M
Leading lights bearing 051° *Front* F.G.10m5M. *Rear* F.R.15m5M

A wharf on two levels for visiting yachts extends 90 metres beyond a line of posts upstream of the inner leading beacon on the south bank, with a least depth of 2.2m, bottom soft mud. The lower level is 0.3m

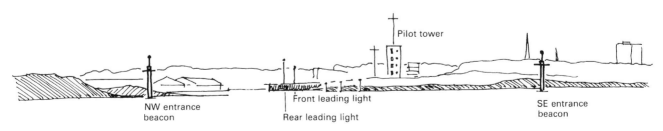

Irvine River entrance

above MHWS and the upper level 1.1m. Moorings further up the river are not available for visiting yachts, and anchoring is not permitted. The harbourmaster's office is the white cottage beside the wharf.

Supplies

Water tap in a locked box at road level by the visitors' wharf; key from Maritime Museum during office hours (including weekends).

In town, ¼ mile, are shops, post office, telephone, hotel, *Calor Gas*, petrol, diesel, water.

Leisure centre near wharf provides most indoor sports, an indoor swimming pool, showers and a sauna.

A concrete slip beyond the Maritime Museum pontoons can be used for launching trailed boats by arrangement with the harbour office. The outer end, at a level of about MLWS, extends 10m beyond a tall marker pole.

Irvine Water Sports Club beside the slipway has showers, and offers assistance and hospitality to visiting yachts.

Communications

Water Sports Club ☎ 01294 274981
Magnum Leisure Centre ☎ 01294 278381
Scottish Maritime Museum ☎ 01294 278283

Saltcoats

55°38′N 4°47′W

A small drying harbour built before 1700 and abandoned for commercial traffic, but now used by local small craft. Usual supplies and services in town: two supermarkets have been built at the east end of the harbour.

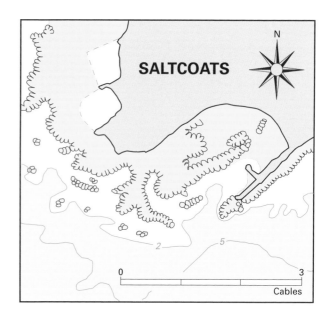

Irvine Harbour: at present the bridge is permanently open (2006)

Saltcoats Harbour (2006)

Ardrossan

55°38'.5N 4°49'W

Clyde Marina is in Eglinton Dock, but access may be restricted owing to traffic movements or heavy weather.

Traffic Signals

All traffic is controlled by light signals displayed on the roof of the control tower at the north side of the marina entrance throughout 24 hours. The signals have the following meanings:

3R(vert)	Harbour closed, but pleasure craft may proceed to and from marina
3G(vert)	Pleasure craft may proceed to and from marina, but commercial vessels requiring permission may not enter, leave, or manoeuvre within harbour
2R(vert) over G	Pleasure craft must clear the outer basins, canting area, and approach channels immediately.

CHART

Plan on *1866* (1:7,500)

Tides

Constant –0010 Greenock (+0105 Dover)

Height in metres

MHWS	MHWN	MTL	MLWN	MLWS
3·2	2·7	1·9	1·1	0·5

DANGERS AND MARKS

Horse Isle, ½ mile WNW of the entrance, has a stone beacon at its south end.

West Crinan Rock, which dries 1.1 metres 1½ cables northwest of the harbour entrance, is marked by a red can light buoy.

Eagle Rock, just above water nearly 3 cables south of the entrance, is marked by a green conical light buoy on its west side.

The channel east of Horse Isle is obstructed by drying rocks, and drying reefs extend 1½ cables SSW of the island.

Approach and entrance

Pass at least 2 cables south of Horse Isle, identify the two buoys and pass between them. Call the harbourmaster on VHF before entering.

Car ferries for Arran berth at Winton Pier, southeast of the entrance.

The marina entrance is 10 metres wide and may be closed by storm gates in very severe weather (normally only mid-winter).

Lights

Horse Isle beacon is not lit
West Crinan light buoy Fl.R.4s
Eagle Rock light buoy Fl.G.5s
Breakwater, south end Fl.WR.2s12m5M
Lighthouse Pier Iso.WG.4s11m9M
A directional 055° DirF.WRG.15m9M light, with a
    F.R.9m9M light leads into the harbour entrance

Supplies

In marina: Water, diesel, Calor Gas. In town: shops, post office, telephone, hotel.

Communications

Harbour office at north side of Eglinton Basin, VHF Ch 12, 14.
Marina VHF Ch 80 (office hours), ☎ 01294 607077.
Ardrossan Harbour Control Tower is manned from 30 minutes prior to the scheduled arrival of ferry services, up to the departure time of the ferry.
Outside of these times, Mariners should contact Clydeport Estuary Control

FIRTH OF CLYDE

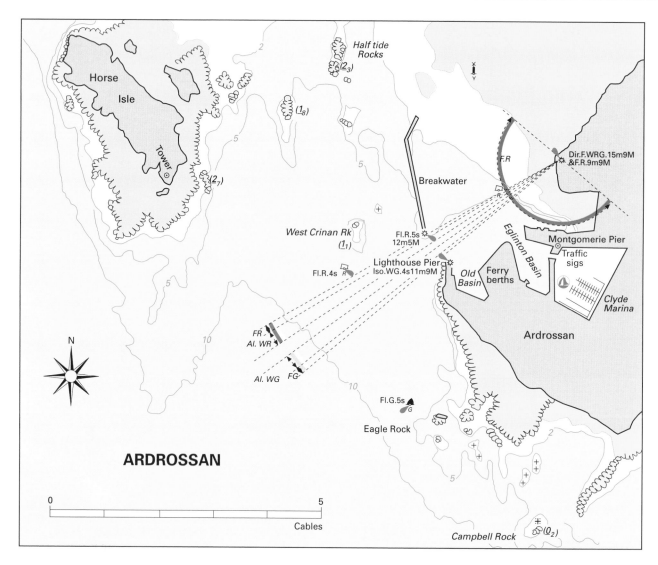

ARDROSSAN

Half tide Rocks

Horse Isle

Tower

Breakwater

F.R

Dir.F.WRG.15m9M &F.R.9m9M

West Crinan Rk

Fl.R.5s 12m5M

Montgomerie Pier

Traffic sigs

Lighthouse Pier Iso.WG.4s11m9M

Fl.R.4s

Old Basin

Ferry berths

Eglinton Basin

Clyde Marina

Ardrossan

FR Al. WR

Al. WG FG

Fl.G.5s G

Eagle Rock

N

0   5
Cables

Campbell Rock

Ardrossan Marina (2006)

East side of Arran

CHARTS
  2126 (1:75,000), 2220, 2221 (1:36,000)

DANGERS AND MARKS

  A race extends for about 2 miles south and southwest of Pladda during out-going tides.

  The east shore of Arran is generally clean beyond a cable from the shore, but for a mile northeast of Kildonan Point at the south end of the island several drying reefs extend 2 cables from the shore.

  Pladda Island south of Arran is 19 metres high with a 29-metre white lighthouse.

  Holy Island, on the east side of Arran, is 311 metres high with a white lighthouse 23 metres in height near the shore on its east side.

LIGHTS

  Pladda lighthouse Fl(3)30s40m23M
  Holy Island Inner light Fl.G.3s14m10M
  Pillar Rock lighthouse Fl(2)20s38m25M

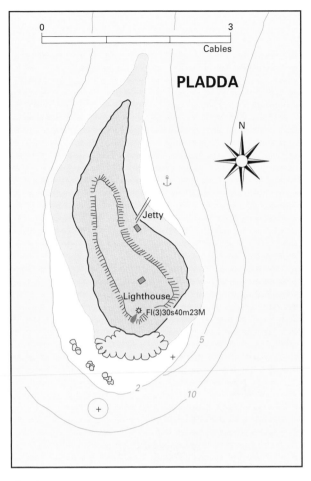

PLADDA

Pladda lighthouse

Pladda from north (2006)

Anchorages

Pladda provides some shelter on its east side, close inshore north of the jetty, on sand and weed.

The channel between Pladda and Arran is obstructed by rocks, and tidal streams there run at over 3 knots.

Whiting Bay stands a mile south of the south entrance to Lamlash Harbour, has a long stone slipway.

FIRTH OF CLYDE

Lamlash Harbour

55°32′N 5°06′W

Sheltered by Holy Island, this is the main anchorage on Arran, although possibly more suitable for a fleet of warships than a yacht. In northwest winds the bay is affected by violent squalls from the mountains. Easterly winds send some sea into the harbour, affecting even the anchorage at Holy Island.

CHART
Plan on *1864* (1:20,000)

TIDES
Constant 0000 Greenock (+0115 Dover)
Height in metres

MHWS	MHWN	MTL	MLWN	MLWS
3·2	2·7	1·9	1·0	0·4

Approach

In the south entrance pass east of Fullarton Rock red can light buoy.

In the north entrance a red can light buoy in mid-channel marks a spit extending from the north shore which has a depth of 5 metres a cable north of the buoy, so the buoy can be passed on its north side by yachts in quiet conditions.

Lights

Holy Island Inner light, at the east side of the south entrance, Fl.G.3s14m10M, obscured from east of 147° and north of 282°
Fullarton Rock buoy Fl(2)R.12s
Hamilton Rock Buoy in north entrance Fl.R.6s
There are no navigation lights within the bay.

Anchorages

For ½ mile northeast and ¼ mile south of Lamlash Pier the shore dries for over ¼ mile. Permanent moorings are laid off Lamlash Pier, as well as visitors' moorings.

Both moorings and fish cages lie north of Kingscross Point on the west side of the south entrance.

Depending on wind direction anchor clear of moorings north of Kingscross Point; or 4 cables west of Clauchlands Point at the north side of the north entrance; or clear of moorings east of Lamlash Pier.

In easterly winds anchor to the south of the house at the northwest end of Holy Island, clear of the mooring and slip.

Lamlash Harbour; Holy Island Inner light on the right (1987)

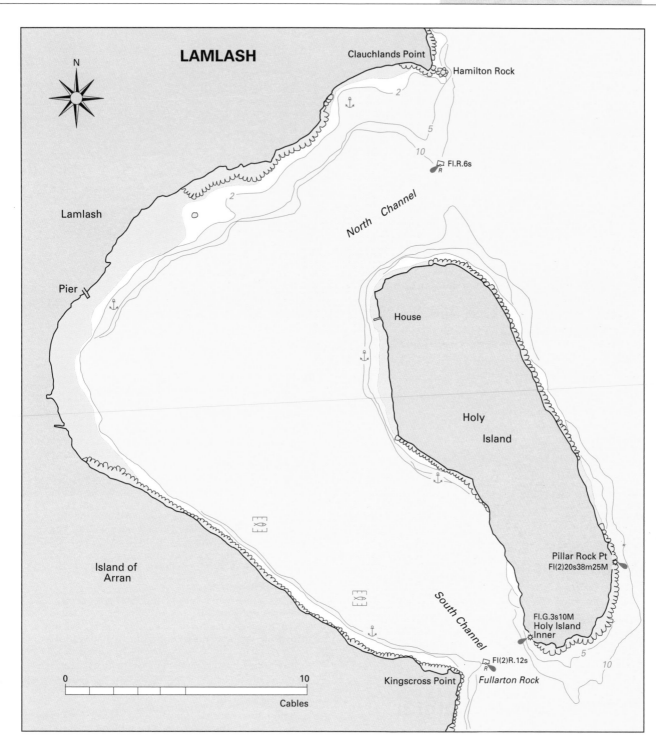

Supplies and services at Lamlash

Shops, post office, bank, telephone, hotel, *Calor Gas*, petrol, diesel, water, EC Wednesday. Chandlery, diver and marine engineer Johnston's Marine Stores ☎ 01770 600333.

Brodick

55°35′N 5°09′W

The village is on the south side of the bay and Brodick Castle is on the northwest side. Fierce squalls are to be expected from the valley at the head of the bay in westerly winds. A rough wharf lies at the mouth of a burn close north of the ferry terminal, and may be convenient for crew of small boats to go ashore briefly towards HW.

Shoal draft boats able to take the ground may be able to use two boat harbours at Corrie (see OS map), and the burn mouth at Sannox.

CHART

Plan on *1864* (1:25,000)

TIDES

Constant 0000 Greenock (+0115 Dover)

Height in metres

MHWS	MHWN	MTL	MLWN	MLWS
3·2	2·7	1·9	1·0	0·4

Map labels: LAMLASH · N · Clauchlands Point · Hamilton Rock · Fl.R.6s · North Channel · Lamlash · Pier · House · Holy Island · Island of Arran · Pillar Rock Pt Fl(2)20s38m25M · Fl.G.3s10M Holy Island Inner · South Channel · Fl(2)R.12s · Kingscross Point · Fullarton Rock · 0 ... 10 Cables · FIRTH OF CLYDE

Corrie Pier and Boat Harbour, Arran (1987)

Anchorage and berths

Depths are suitable for anchoring on the northwest side of the bay below Brodick Castle.

Piermaster ☎ 01770 302166. Visitors' moorings are available.

Supplies

Shops, post office, telephone, hotel, *Calor Gas*. Moped and bicycle hire.

Lights

Pier head 2F.R(vert)9m4M

Minor Harbours

Corrie on the north side of the masonry pier lies a drying boat harbour used by local boats.

Sannox a drying boat harbour lies at the mouth of the river Sannox. A submerged rock lies at a depth of 1.5 metres, 2 cables off shore, in the mouth of the bay.

Firth of Clyde Channel

CHART
1907 (1:25,000)

TIDES
South of Garroch Head, the south point of Bute, overfalls occur on the ebb tide.

Streams in the Firth of Clyde Channel run at 1 knot at springs and more over banks (causing turbulence, particularly with wind against tide), turning about 20 minutes before high and low water.

Constant at Millport, Cumbrae, is −0015 Greenock (+0100 Dover).

Height in metres

MHWS	MHWN	MTL	MLWN	MLWS
3·4	2·8	1·9	1·0	0·5

DANGERS
The passage from Cumbrae to Cloch Point is generally clean outwith 1½ cables from the shore except for the dangers described below.

On the west shore a mile north of Toward Point a reef known as The Bridges extends 4 cables from the shore, marked by a red stone beacon, **Innellan**, inshore of its outer end.

Just over 5 miles NNE of Toward Point and 3 cables SSE of Dunoon Pier lies The Gantocks, a detached drying reef which is marked by a red light beacon at its southeast corner and a north cardinal buoy on its northwest side. The clear passage northwest of The Gantocks is 2 cables wide.

On the east shore, Lunderston Bay, 1¼ miles south of Cloch Point, dries out for nearly ¼ mile.

SHIP CHANNELS
Ship channels which may be used by vessels constrained by their draught, are marked by buoys as follows:

Firth of Clyde Channel, marked by a total of five high focal plane buoys in the centre of the channel, spaced several miles apart.

Skelmorlie Channel, marked by lateral buoys branches eastwards from a point northwest of Great Cumbrae, for vessels of deeper draught than those which can use Firth of Clyde Channel.

Hunterston Channel, east of the Cumbraes, marked by lateral buoys. This is described on subsequent pages.

It is useful to know which channel large vessels are making for and for this purpose they show numeral pennant 1 for the Firth of Clyde Channel and pennant 2 for Skelmorlie Channel.

MARKS
Cumbrae Elbow old lighthouse, a white tower 11 metres in height, stands on the west side of Little Cumbrae, with the new Little Cumbrae light beacon close south of it.

Rubha'n Eun light beacon, a white metal tower 8 metres in height, stands on the southeast point of Bute.

Hunterston Nuclear Power Station, consists of two blocks 63 metres and 70 metres high, on the mainland east of Little Cumbrae.

Ascog Patches pile beacon, stands 7 cables off the Bute shore 1¼ miles southeast of Bogany Point, black with two red bands and a topmark of two balls, is of no significance to yachts, but a useful reference point.

Toward Point lighthouse (pronounced with the accent on the first syllable of 'Toward'), a white tower 19 metres in height, stands at the north side of the entrance to Rothesay Sound with lattice radio masts north of the lighthouse.

Innellan Beacon, red with ball topmark, a mile north of Toward Point.

A large quarry on the west shore, 4 miles north of Toward Point, stands a mile south of The Gantocks.

Inverkip Power Station chimney, 238 metres high, on the east shore, is the principal mark in this passage.

Cloch Point lighthouse, a low white stone tower with a black band, stands 2½ miles north of Inverkip Power Station.

LIGHTS

Many buoys in the Firth of Clyde Channel are lit but these are generally of no significance to yachts except insofar as they mark the deep-water channels. The principal lights are as follows:

Little Cumbrae light beacon Fl.6s28m14M
Rubha'n Eun light beacon Fl.R.6s8m12M
Ascog Patches pile beacon Fl(2)10s5M
Toward Point lighthouse Fl.10s21m22M
The Gantocks Fl.R.6s12m6M
Cloch Point Fl.3s24m8M
Innellan beacon is not lit

Occasional anchorages on the east coast of Bute

Glencallum Bay, immediately southwest of Rubha'n Eun lighthouse; only 1 cable wide, with a rock drying 2.1 metres near the north east side.

Kilchattan Bay, 1½ miles north of Rubha'n Eun. The head of the bay dries for 3 cables and then the bottom drops steeply. There is a narrow shelf off the east end of Kilchattan village on the south side of the bay, and a more extensive area ¼ mile off the north side of the bay.

Visitors' moorings with a capacity of 15 tons have been laid by St Blane's hotel at the south side of the bay.

Hunterston Channel

Overfalls form off the south end of Little Cumbrae which should be given a good berth particularly with an ebb tide against a fresh southerly wind. Fishing floats are laid up to ½ mile south of Little Cumbrae.

On the east side of the channel, Hunterston Sands, part of which was reclaimed for an oil rig building yard to be built, dry out for a mile.

Hunterston Ore and Coal Loading Jetty, with large travelling cranes on its head, extends 4 cables from the shore 1 mile NNE of the oil rig yard.

Brigurd Spit extends up to 4 cables from the shore south of the oil rig yard. South of Brigurd Spit the outfall from Hunterston Power Station, which is marked by a yellow conical light buoy, causes severe turbulence.

Little Cumbrae

55°43′N 4°56′.5W

Anchorage on the east side of the island in the bay between Castle Island, which has a ruined castle at its north end, and Broad Island, 3 cables further north. Drying reefs extend north and south of Trail Isle, ½ cable east of Castle Island. The anchorage is subject to a disturbing tidal swell.

A shoal lies 1 cable offshore ¼ mile southeast of Sheanawally Point, the north end of Little Cumbrae, and a bank dries ½ cable northwest of the point. A light column stands on Sheanawally Point.

Landing on Little Cumbrae is no longer discouraged by the proprietor.

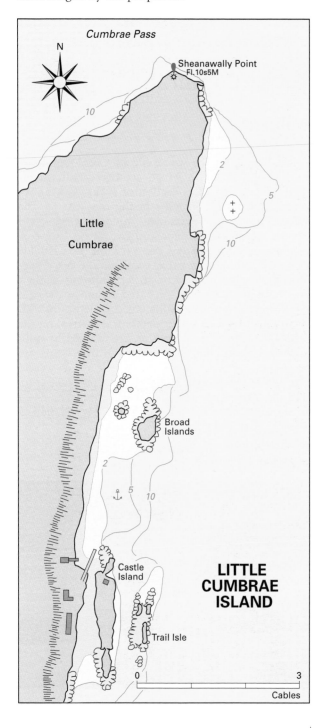

Cumbrae Pass

N

Sheanawally Point
Fl.10s5M

10

Little

Cumbrae

2

5

Broad
Islands

2

5   10

Castle
Island

LITTLE
CUMBRAE
ISLAND

Trail Isle

0   3

Cables

Little Cumbrae anchorage from south west (1987)

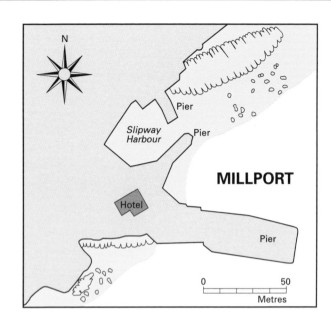

MILLPORT

0 — 50
Metres

Great Cumbrae

Millport

55°45′N 4°55′W

A small town at the south end of Great Cumbrae, built round a bay in which are two small islands (The Eileans) and a collection of rocks both above water and drying. In most of the bay east of The Eileans there are permanent moorings wherever depths are suitable for anchoring.

National Watersports Centre lies on the east side of Great Cumbrae a cable south of the ferry slip. Visiting yachts may moor at the pontoons at their own risk, but must be prepared to move away if conditions deteriorate. Submerged concrete blocks, over which there is a least depth of 2 metres, on the landward side of the pontoons, are marked by unlit spherical plastic buoys. Recreational dive boats are frequently active around the wreck of a second world war flying boat, half way between the Centre and the ferry slip, and a clear berth should be given to stationary boats flying the diver's flag. ☎ 01475 530757. Bar and showers.

CHART

Plan on *1867* (1:12,500)

TIDES

Constant –0015 Greenock (+0100 Dover)
Height in metres

MHWS	MHWN	MTL	MLWN	MLWS
3·4	2·8	1·9	1·0	0·5

Approach and moorings

Approach the pier with its head showing between The Eileans and The Spoig rock bearing 333°. The church tower in line with the pier head is on this bearing.

An extensive drying rock lies ½ cable south of the Eileans.

An alternative approach is along the shore from southwest inshore of The Clach and The Leug rocks, taking care to avoid the drying reef at Nupkur Point.

Visitors' moorings have been laid SSE of the pier and there is also space to anchor southwest of the pier, clear of the moorings and rocks. Berths alongside north side of pier. Do not obstruct access to steps. A shower block has been built but is not at present in commission.

Lights

Ldg Lts 333° F.R.7m5M lead to the pier
Eileans, west point Q.G.2m5M shown between 1/9 and 30/4 only.

Cumbrae, National Watersports Centre (2006)

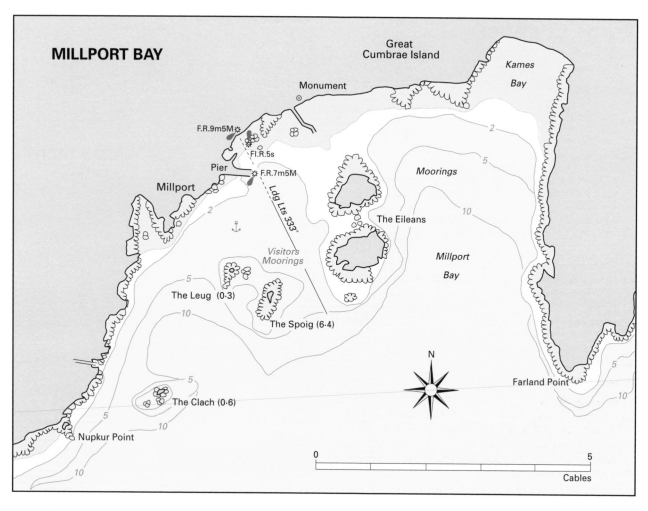

MILLPORT BAY

Great Cumbrae Island

Kames Bay

Monument

F.R.9m5M

Fl.R.5s

Pier

F.R.7m5M

Millport

Moorings

The Eileans

Millport Bay

Visitors Moorings

The Leug (0·3)

The Spoig (6·4)

Farland Point

The Clach (0·6)

Nupkur Point

N

0   5

Cables

Supplies

Shops, post office, telephone, hotel, Calor Gas, petrol, diesel, water at pier, EC Wednesday. Boatyard, Stuart Macintyre ☎ 01475 530566

Communications

Chandlery ☎ 01475 530806.

Millport, Cumbrae (2006)

Largs Channel

CHARTS

Plan on *1867* (1:12,5000), 1907 (1:25,000)

DIRECTIONS

Fairlie Roads, 55°45′.5N 4°52′W, 4·5 cables northeast of Hunterston Jetty head and 3 cables SSW of Fairlie Pier provides occasional anchorage within ¼ mile northwest of the west cardinal perch at Fairlie Yacht Club slip.

An unlit mooring buoy, 3 cables SSW of the Fairlie Pier elbow, is a hazard if approaching by night.

Fairlie Patch, with a depth of 0·3m ¼ mile ENE of Hunterston Jetty head, is marked on its west side by a starboard-hand light buoy

Avoid obstructing access to any of the piers, and keep well clear of vessels manoeuvring.

LIGHTS

There are no major lights but many lateral light buoys.

Hunterston jetty 2F.G(vert) at both ends of its head, and it is lit up like a Christmas tree

Fairlie pier 2F.G(vert) at both ends of its head

Largs Yacht Haven Oc.G.10s4m4M on the south side and Oc.R.10s4m4M on the north side of the entrance

Largs Pier 2F.G(vert)7m5M at its north end

Largs Yacht Haven

55°46′.5N 4°51′.5W

TIDES

Constant–0005 Greenock (+0110 Dover)

Height in metres

MHWS	MHWN	MTL	MLWN	MLWS
3·4	2·8	1·9	1·0	0·5

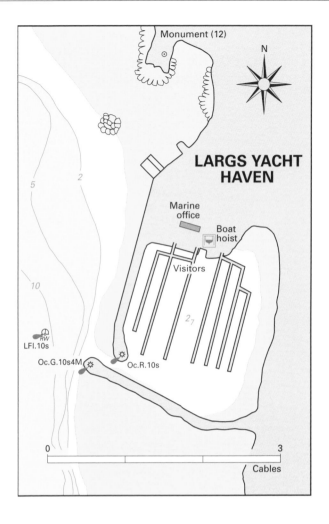

Largs Yacht Haven (2006)

Directions

Close north of the NATO Pier, the marina is accessible at all states of tide. The shore dries off south of the entrance to the end of the south breakwater, for about 50 metres on the outer side of the north breakwater, and the entrance channel is very narrow. Make for the RW entrance buoy before entering.

In easterlies strong winds are funnelled down Kelburn Glen, inland from the entrance.

Lights

At night the RW light buoy off the entrance is lit LFl.10s, and there is a light on the head of each breakwater, Oc.G.10s on the south side, Oc.R.10s on the north side, but they may be difficult to pick out at night against shore lights.

Supplies

At marina: *Calor Gas*, diesel, water, chandlery.

At Largs, 1½ miles: post office, telephone, hotel, petrol, EC Wednesday.

Communications

Marina office VHF Ch 80 ☎ 01475 675333. Slip, 45-ton hoist, repairs to hull, machinery and electrics.

Train/bus to Glasgow.

Largs Pier

55°47′.7N 4°52′.3W

Temporary anchorage north or south of the pier, approximately east of the north end of Great Cumbrae, or at the pier itself, which has 2 metres alongside, but take care to avoid obstructing approach to the car ferry ramp inshore of the pier.

Lights

At night lights, 2F.G(vert), are shown at the north end of the pier

Supplies

Shops in town. Train/bus to Glasgow.

BARRFIELDS SLIP

3 cables north of Largs Pier, the slip is 12 metres wide and is suitable for launching trailer-sailers. The slip is also used by an RNLI inshore lifeboat for which space must be left at all times. No charge is made for the use of the slip, but launching a boat there would be an appropriate occasion to put a contribution in the RNLI collecting box.

Beacons about ¼ mile north west of the slip mark a drying reef and a sewer outfall.

Wemyss Bay Pier

55°52′.5N 4°53′.5W

Temporary anchorage north or south of the pier, leaving space for the Bute car ferry to manoeuvre at the pier. A yellow pile structure with a cross topmark 4 cables NNW of the pier in a depth of 15 metres (lit Oc(2)Y.10s) is a convenient marker for the anchorage.

Kip Marina

55°54′.5N 4°53′W

A marina formed from a gravel pit at the mouth of Kip Water, ½ mile north of Inverkip Power Station is entered from Kip G conical light buoy through a dredged channel marked by pairs of buoys. The depth in the channel is more than 3 metres.

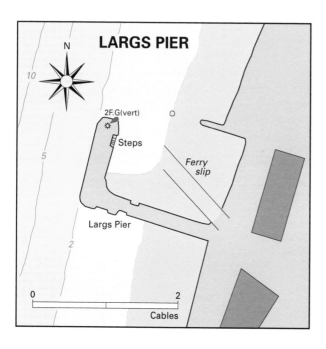

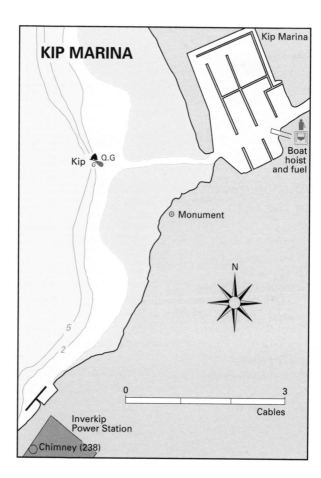

Kip Marina in the process of being surrounded by housing (2006)

TIDES

Constant –0005 Greenock (+0110 Dover)

Height in metres

MHWS	MHWN	MTL	MLWN	MLWS
3·4	2·9	2·0	1·1	0·5

Lights

At night the power station jetty is marked by 2F.G(vert) lights at both ends, and Kip buoy is lit Q.G

Supplies

Calor Gas, diesel, water, telephone. Shops, post office in village ½ mile. Hotel 200 metres.

Facilities

Showers, laundry, chandlery, 50-ton boat-hoist, 16-ton crane, repairs, rigging, mechanical, electronic, slipway. Bar and restaurant at marina.

Communications

Marina office ☎ 01475 521485, VHF Ch 80. Train/bus to Glasgow.

Anchorages on the west side of the Firth

Innellan, 55°54′N 4°57′W, temporary anchorage north or south of the old ferry jetty which lies a mile north of Innellan Beacon.

Dunoon, 56°57′N 4°55′W, temporary anchorage a cable off a stone jetty (which dries) 1½ cables north of the main ferry pier, but you need to be a cable offshore to find a depth of 3 metres.

West Bay, 3 cables southwest of the pier, is an alternative anchorage although more exposed to the south.

Visitors' moorings are provided in West Bay.

In approach, keep clear of The Gantocks, a detached drying reef 3 cables SSE of Dunoon Pier, marked by a red light beacon at its southeast corner and an unlit north cardinal buoy on its northwest side. The passage northwest of The Gantocks is 2 cables wide.

Shops, post office, telephone, hotel, *Calor Gas*, petrol and diesel at garages. Car ferry to Gourock.

Inverkip Power Station, a conspicuous landmark throughout the whole firth (1987)

III. Loch Long to River Clyde

The head of the Firth of Clyde consists of a basin north and east of Cloch Point, south of Loch Long, extending 7 miles from west to east with 3 lochs branching off it. The River Clyde enters from the east, south of Greenock Bank the west end of which is only two cables off Clydeport Container Terminal.

The branch lochs and anchorages in this chapter are described in a clockwise sequence.

Rothesay Sound and the Kyles of Bute are covered in Chapter IV.

CHARTS

Imray chart folio 2900 (1:50,000)
Chart 1994 (1:15,000)

TIDES

Constant 0000 Greenock (+0115 Dover)
Height in metres

MHWS	MHWN	MTL	MLWN	MLWS
3·4	2·9	1·9	1·0	0·4

FAIRWAYS TO PIERS, ETC

Navigating and mooring by small craft near the approach fairway to piers, jetties and quays is restricted by Clydeport plc – and by common sense. Any pleasure vessel of less than 20 metres length within 300 metres of any pier, jetty or quay within the jurisdiction of Clydeport shall keep clear of any vessel approaching or leaving the pier, etc. No vessel of any sort shall be moored so as to encroach on a fairway 100 metres wide forming the ordinary course taken by any vessel approaching or leaving such pier etc.

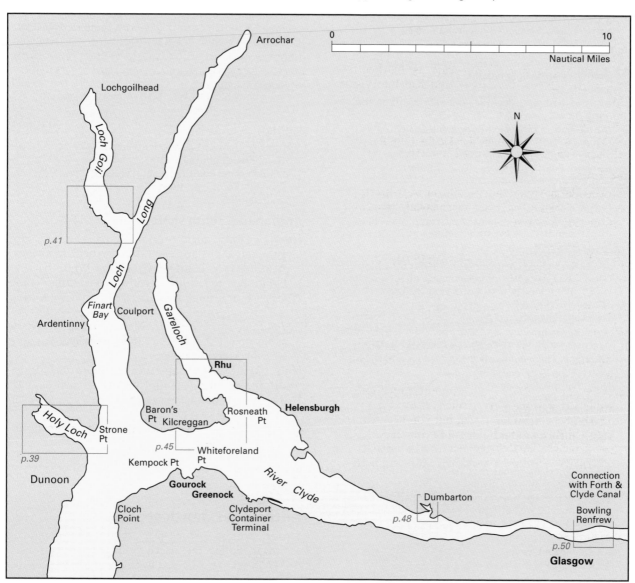

RESTRICTED AND PROHIBITED AREAS

Loch Long and Gareloch are Dockyard Ports, under the control of the Queen's Harbourmaster. Specific areas within these lochs are designated as prohibited areas from which all civilian craft are excluded at all times, and restricted and protected areas, within which no civilian craft may enter or remain during the movement of nuclear submarines or large naval vessels. These are shown on the relevant plans. Guard boats are permanently on patrol.

When restricted/protected areas are closed to non-naval vessels signals are shown from naval establishments and escorting naval vessels in the area and are described where appropriate below. These areas leave space for small craft to continue on a passage without great difficulty, except possibly at Rhu Narrows.

ANCHORAGES

Many Clyde anchorages consist of no more than an indentation in the shore of a loch, or sometimes only a length of shore where there are moderate depths and reasonable holding. Very often the shore dries for up to ¼ mile or, at the head of a loch, more than a mile, with a narrow shelf of moderate depth the edge of which drops suddenly into much deeper water.

It is often not practicable to describe the distance from the shore at which one should anchor; specific hazards are described, but otherwise it is necessary to check the depth while approaching.

By using a large-scale chart, many more occasional anchorages will be found than can be listed.

MARKS

Rosneath Patch ¼ mile north of Whiteforeland Point, on which is a lattice light beacon, is the main hazard in this area.

A lattice mast on Gallow Hill (Rosneath Point) on the north shore is conspicuous.

Ashton buoy a safe-water buoy a mile WNW of Kempock Point, is a turning point in the Firth of Clyde Channel and an important reference point.

Kempock Point and Princes Pier at the west side of Gourock Bay are about 5½ miles ENE of Cloch Point.

Whiteforeland Point, with a conspicuous block of red brick buildings is ¼ mile east of Kempock Point.

Clydeport Container Terminal, with conspicuous blue cranes, stands a mile ESE of Whiteforeland Point.

DEEP-WATER CHANNELS

The Firth of Clyde Channel runs northeast to Ashton buoy, then east to Whiteforeland buoy, about 3 cables NNE of Whiteforeland Point, then ESE to Clydeport Container Terminal.

Loch Long Channel runs due north from Cloch Point.

Ardmore Channel branches ENE from Ashton buoy to pass north of Rosneath Patch and thence to Gareloch.

Kilcreggan Channel follows the north shore, between Loch Long and the Gareloch.

Note that the direction of buoyage changes at Baron's Point at the mouth of Loch Long, so that the starboard-hand light buoy Kil No. 3 is on the northeast side of the channel.

It is essential for yachts to keep out of the way of vessels which can only use the deep-water channels, and a good lookout must be kept for them. Beware also car ferries, whose helmsmen may not be too scrupulous about the Collision Regulations.

Signal flags in the form of numeral pennants of the International Code are flown by ships to indicate which channel they are using, as follows:

1. Firth of Clyde Channel
2. Skelmorlie Channel
3. River Channel
4. Ardmore Channel
5. Loch Long Channel
6. Holy Loch
7. Kilcreggan Channel

Anchorages for large ships are designated north of Ashton buoy and east of Rosneath Patch. Ships leaving a channel for one of these anchorages fly First Substitute pennant of the International Code.

Lights

Many light buoys which do not directly concern yachts may be found on the chart; the principal lights are as follows:

Ashton buoy Iso.5s
Kempock Point beacon 2F.G(vert)10m3M
Whiteforeland buoy LFl.10s
Rosneath Patch beacon Fl(2)10s
Lateral buoys show Fl.R.2s (port hand) and Fl.G.5s (starboard hand)

Holy Loch

55°59′N 4°55′W

CHARTS

1994 (1:15,000), 3746 (1:25,000)

The head of the loch dries out for ½ mile and the shores on either side up to a cable. Submerged rocks extend 1½ cables south of Strone Point, the north point of the entrance to Holy Loch, marked by a south cardinal light buoy ¼ mile south of the point.

TIDES

Constant 0000 Greenock (+0115 Dover)
Height in metres

	MHWS	MHWN	MTL	MLWN	MLWS
	3·4	2·9	1·9	1·0	0·4

Lights

Hunter's Quay ferry slip 2F.R(vert)6m6M
Strone Point light buoy Q(6)+LFl.15s
White Farlane Point light buoy Fl.R.2s
Graham's Point light buoy Fl.G.3s
Sandbank Pier 2F.R(vert)

Anchorages, south shore

Hunter's Quay, north of, but clear of, the ferry slip, although there are several permanent moorings. Also between Hunter's Quay and White Farlane Point, but the shore dries up to a cable; some visitors' moorings are laid here by an hotel for the use of its customers.

Ardnadam, northwest of White Farlane Point; a cable area extends 1¼ cables east and ¼ cable west of Admiralty Pier.

Holy Loch Marina, constructed around the former Admiralty Pier, provides the usual facilities. ☎ 01369 701800. Major expansion is expected over the next few years.

Supplies

At Sandbank include shops, post office, telephone, hotel, water at Holy Loch SC close southeast of Sandbank Pier.

Anchorages, north shore

Strone, west of a stone pier about 2 cables west of Strone Point, the north point of the entrance. Moorings are provided by the Argyll Hotel for the use of its customers ☎ 01369 840227.

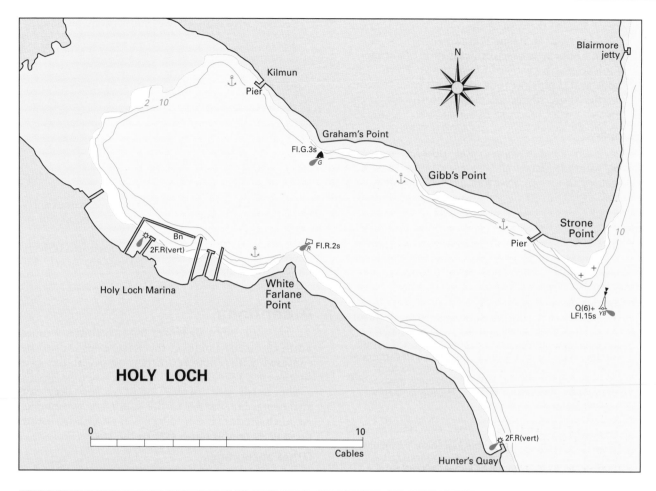

Kilmun

Pier

2 _ 10

Graham's Point

Fl.G.3s
G

Gibb's Point

Strone
Point

Pier

10

Blairmore
jetty

N

Q(6)+
LFl.15s
YB

Bn

2F.R(vert)

Holy Loch Marina

White
Farlane
Point

Fl.R.2s
R

HOLY LOCH

2F.R(vert)

Hunter's Quay

0   10

Cables

Holy Loch Marina (2006)

Gibb's Point, to the west of the point, which is about 6 cables west of Strone Point.

Kilmun, about a cable northwest of a stone pier 3 cables northwest of Graham's Point. An underwater pipeline runs southwest from beacons on the shore about 70 metres northwest of the pier.

Supplies

At Kilmun include shops, post office, telephone, hotel, water at pier.

Visitors' moorings are available with a capacity of 5 tons.

Loch Long

CHART

3746 (1:25,000)

RESTRICTIONS

The whole loch is a Dockyard Port and the restrictions described at the beginning of this chapter apply.

At Coulport on the east shore about 5 miles from the entrance a prohibited area extends 150 metres from the shore, from about 7 cables south to a mile north of Coulport Jetty, and a restricted area extends most of the way across the loch from the jetty leaving a narrow passage along the west shore.

A covered floating dock lies off the jetty and guard boats are constantly on patrol.

Finnart Oil Terminal, also on the east shore 1¼ miles northwest of the north point of the entrance to Loch Goil, is used by very large tankers which have to manoeuvre in a restricted space.

A prohibited area extends 150 metres off Glenmallan Jetty, a mile further northeast with conspicuous refuelling derricks.

DANGERS

Mountains fall steeply to the loch on both sides and there is no road along much of the west shore. Severe squalls can be expected from the mountains.

Overhead power lines across Loch Long south of the entrance to Loch Goil have a clearance of 76 metres.

TIDES

Constant –0005 Greenock (+0110 Dover)
Height in metres

MHWS	MHWN	MTL	MLWN	MLWS
3·4	2·9	2·0	0·9	0·3

Tidal streams throughout are negligible.

MARKS

At the entrance Loch Long RW light buoy marks the centre of Loch Long Channel.

A yellow pile beacon with an X topmark stands a cable SSW of Baron's Point at the east side of the entrance.

Coulport Jetty and Finnart Oil Terminal on the east shore, respectively 4 and 8 miles from the entrance, are conspicuous.

LIGHTS

Loch Long light buoy (centre of the entrance) Oc.6s
Light buoy Kil No.3 off Baron's Point Fl.G.5s
Pile beacon No.3 off Baron's Point Oc(2)Y.10s3M
Blairmore Pier 2F.R(vert)

Ravenrock Point light beacon on the west shore 3 miles from the entrance, Fl.4s12m10M, has a directional light 204° showing NNE up the loch, with narrow F.WRG sectors and very narrow Al.WR and Al.WG sectors at the edges of the white sector

Coulport Jetty 2F.G(vert) at each end (with port closure signals)
Portdornaige light beacon on west shore Fl.6s8m11M
Construction jetty, 8 cables north of Coulport 2F.G(vert)9m5M
Dog Rock, at north side of Loch Goil entrance, Fl.2s7m11M
Finnart Oil Terminal has four sets of lights 2F.G(vert)

Anchorages

Cove Bay, on the east shore ¼ mile north of Baron's Point, the east point of the entrance to Loch Long; many small-craft moorings and a large unlit mooring buoy.

Three moorings are provided by Knockderry House Hotel ☎ 01436 842283 for the use of its customers.

Blairmore, on the west shore, 3 cables north of ferry jetty. Shops, post office, telephone, hotel, EC Thursday.

Ardentinny

At the south point of Finart Bay which lies 4 miles north of Strone Point on the west shore (not to be confused with Finnart, further north on the east shore).

The north side of the point is too deep for anchoring, but depths to the south are reasonable. An uncharted rock is said to lies close inshore below the houses on the south side of the bay.

Other anchorages

Shepherd's Point Finart Bay dries out for 2 cables, dropping abruptly to 20 metres, but depths are reasonable east and northeast of a yellow beacon at the north end of the bay.

Loch Goil

The entrance is on the west side of Loch Long, between Rubha nan Eoin on the south side and Dog Rock, on which stands a white light beacon, on the north side. An unlit mooring buoy lies ½ mile west of Dog Rock and a rock dries 1 metre ¼ cable from the shore inshore of the buoy, 2 cables east of Carraig na Maraig the next point on the north shore.

On the southwest shore, ½ mile northwest of Rubha nan Eoin, a drying spit extends a cable from the shore.

A beacon (metal pole with orange rectangular topmark) stands on Rubha Ardnahein.

'The Perch' (on a submerged reef extending over 2 cables off the mouth of Carrick Burn, 4 cables N of Carrick Castle) and the related rear beacon 700m NW, bearing about 318·5° from The Perch, are both metal columns with orange rectangular topmarks. The Perch is on the shallowest part of the reef, not on its east edge.

Loch Goil is used for submarine trials and is sometimes closed to other vessels. Keep clear of Douglas Pier (a mile from the head of the loch on the west side), and Admiralty buoys and rafts.

Lights

Rubha Ardnahein Fl.R.5s
The Perch Dir F.WRG (317°-W-320°)
Fl.R.3s on same structure
Rear light 312°-vis-322.5°

Swine's Hole

Rubha Ardnahein is a low grassy spit on the southwest side of Loch Goil ¼ mile from Rubha nan Eoin with a thin column with a rectangular orange topmark. A drying spit, Roinn Diomhain, lies ¼ mile southeast of it; the bight between the two spits is a popular anchorage. The bay southeast of Roinn Diomhain is an alternative or overflow anchorage.

Carrick Castle

56°06′.5N 4°54′.5W

Tides

Constant –0005 Greenock (+0110 Dover)
Height in metres

MHWS	MHWN	MTL	MLWN	MLWS
3·3	2·8	1·8	0·9	0·3

Loch Goil; Carrick Castle at bottom left

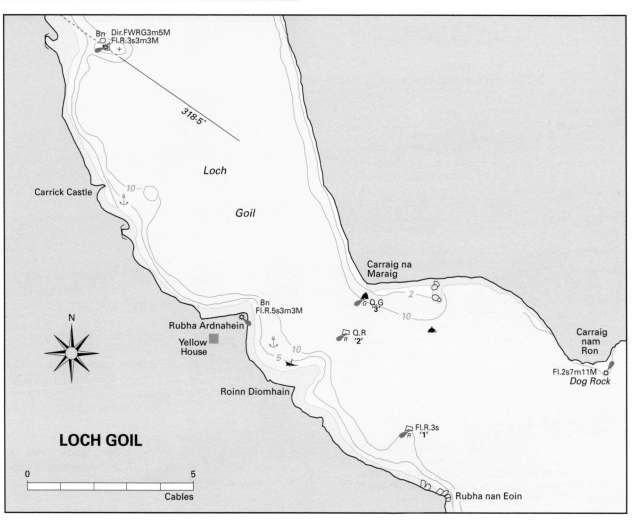

LOCH LONG TO RIVER CLYDE

Lochgoilhead. Shoal water is clearly visible

Carrick Castle, a popular weekend destination

Anchorage

Anchor either north or southeast of the castle, but the bottom is rocky in places and there are some boats on moorings.

Supplies

Shops, post office, telephone, hotel.

Other anchorages

An alternative anchorage is 2 cables NNW of The Perch, off Carrick Burn 4 cables north of the castle. A note on the chart warns: 'Mariners are cautioned against anchoring between Leac Bhuidhe (h mile north of the perch) and Blairlomond (north of Douglas Pier, about 3 miles north of the perch)', however depths are moderate both north and south of the mouth of Cormonachan Burn, 8 cables north of the perch.

Keep clear of Douglas Pier and any Admiralty mooring buoys and rafts.

Lochgoilhead, 56°10′N 4°54′W, any space suitable for anchoring is already occupied by moorings.

Supplies in Lochgoilhead include a small supermarket, restaurant, post office and telephone.

Five visitor moorings, marked '15 tons', with pick-up buoys, are laid among the private moorings in the north east part the loch with landing pontoon on the shore nearby.

Upper Loch Long

CHART 3746 (1:25,000)

The main features, Finnart Oil Terminal and Glenmallan Jetty, are described on preceding pages.

On the northwest shore Cnap Point, ½ mile north of Finnart Oil Terminal, Ardgartan Point 1½ miles from the head of the loch, and the buildings of the former torpedo range ¼ mile northeast of Ardgartan, are conspicuous. An obelisk stands 6 cables north of Cnap Point.

Ardgartan Point has a caravan site on it; the shore dries off for a cable southeast of the point, marked by a perch ESE of the point. The bight north of the point is occupied by moorings (and is very deep).

A small area suitable for anchoring lies south of Ardgartan Point, east of a jetty and two beacons on the shore; also along a narrow strip between Ardgartan and the former torpedo range buildings, but a main road runs along the shore here.

Arrochar

56°12′N 5°45′W

On the east shore anchor in a small bight north of Ardmay Hotel east of Ardgartan, a mile southwest of Arrochar; or between 4 cables southwest and a cable north of the church, or within 1½ cables north of the ruined pier; however the foreshore dries up to

Upper Loch Long, Carraig nan Ron on the left and the tanker terminal on the right (1987)

½ cable and there is only a width of ¼ cable from the LW line with a depth of less than 10 metres.

Supplies

Shops, post office, telephone, hotel, *Calor Gas*, petrol and diesel at garage at the north end of village.

Rail and bus services to Glasgow.

Occasional anchorage between Loch Long and Gareloch.

Kilcreggan,

55°59′N 4°49′W,

East of the pier at the east end of the village; disturbed by passing traffic afloat.

Supplies include licensed grocer, post office, telephone, hotel, petrol.

Gareloch

CHART

2000 (1:10,000)

RESTRICTIONS

The whole loch is a Dockyard Port and a passage 1 cable wide in the approach to Rhu Narrows is a protected channel. Entry to the protected channel is prohibited when a signal consisting of a red over two green lights vertically disposed together with, by day, a red flag with a white diagonal bar is shown at the following places: Faslane Floating Dock; The former Royal Corps of Transport Port Unit, Rhu; Green Island, 2 cables north of Rosneath Point; navy buildings, Greenock; or naval auxiliary craft in the area. Except perhaps at Rhu Narrows there is sufficient space to sail outwith the protected channel.

Gareloch is home to many hundreds of yachts but there is now little to attract a visitor. The eastern shore is largely built up with naval installations, and suburban housing developments filling in the spaces between the Victorian houses. Even the site of McGruer's old boatyard on the west side is now a housing development.

A seaplane operates from Rhu Marina. Attention is drawn to the current Collision Regulations applicable to seaplanes in particular rule 18 (e), and exercise caution when in the vicinity of the seaplane operations.

Gareloch, Rhu Narrows with, beyond, Silvers' yard on the left and the Royal Northern on the right

TIDES

Constant −0005 Greenock (+0110 Dover)

Height in metres

MHWS	MHWN	MTL	MLWN	MLWS
3·4	2·9	1·8	0·9	0·3

Dangers and marks

Perch Rock, an isolated drying rock 1¼ cables east of Green Island which is 1½ cables north of Rosneath Point at the southwest side of the entrance, is marked by a small yellow buoy close to its east side. A red light buoy (No. 24) lies over a cable ESE of the rock.

The bay northwest of Perch Rock dries, and the shore further north dries out for 1 cable.

The shore on the northeast side of the entrance at Cairndhu Point dries out for 2 cables.

The northeast side of the channel is marked by green light buoys and a light beacon.

At Rhu Narrows two red can light buoys mark the west side of the channel.

The conspicuous buildings of the former Royal Corps of Transport Port Unit stand 4 cables NNW of Cairndhu Point. Rhu Marina is 2 cables west of the Port Unit.

Rhu Spit, a further ½ mile west, dries over halfway across the narrows from the northeast shore; a white cylindrical beacon with a green band stands at its southwest end.

North of The Narrows, the moorings of the Royal Northern and Clyde Yacht Club are on the east side, and Stroul Bay and many other yacht moorings on the west side.

Approach

Pass east of No.24 light buoy unless Perch Rock is clearly seen, and keep a good lookout for naval

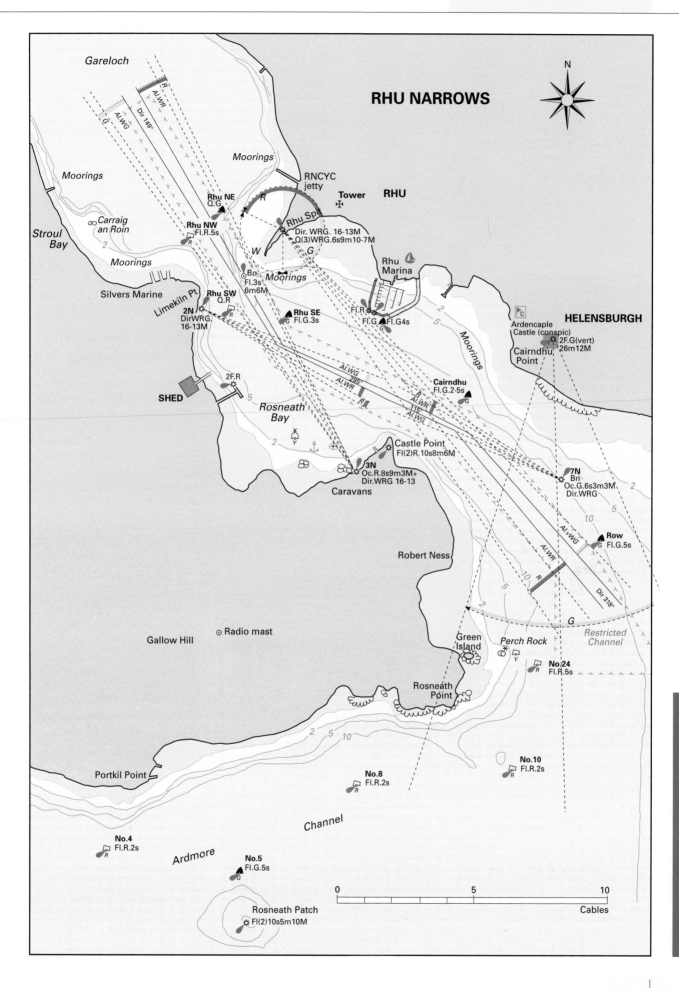

RHU NARROWS

N

Gareloch

Moorings

R
Al.WR
Al.WG
Dir 149°
G

Moorings

RNCYC
jetty

Tower

RHU

Rhu NE
Q.G

R

Moorings

*Carraig
an Roin*

Rhu NW
Fl.R.5s
R

Rhu Spit
Dir. WRG. 16-13M
Q(3)WRG.6s9m10-7M

W

G

**Stroul
Bay**

2

Moorings

Rhu
Marina

Silvers Marine

Bn
Fl.3s
6m6M

Moorings

HELENSBURGH

Limekiln Pt.

Rhu SW
Q.R
R

2N
DirWRG.
16-13M

Moorings

Fl.R

Rhu SE
Fl.G.3s

Fl.G Fl.G4s
G

Ardencaple
Castle (conspic)
2.F.G(vert)
26m12M

**Cairndhu
Point**

2F.R

SHED

Al.WG
295°
Al.WR

Al.WR
115°
Al.WG

*Rosneath
Bay*

R

Cairndhu
Fl.G.2·5s
G

2

Y

Castle Point
Fl(2)R.10s8m6M

7N
Bn
Oc.G.6s3m3M
Dir.WRG

3N
Oc.R.8s9m3M+
Dir.WRG 16-13

Caravans

Robert Ness

10
5

Al.WG

R

Row
G Fl.G.5s
Dir 318°

G

*Restricted
Channel*

Radio mast

Gallow Hill

Green
Island

Perch Rock
Y

No.24
Fl.R.5s
R

Rosneath
Point

No.10
Fl.R.2s
R

Portkil Point

No.8
Fl.R.2s
R

Channel

No.4
Fl.R.2s
R

Ardmore

No.5
Fl.G.5s
G

Rosneath Patch
Fl(2)10s5m10M

0   5   10
Cables

LOCH LONG TO RIVER CLYDE

vessels. Keep to the side of the channel but take care not to wander into shoal water; make sure to pass west of Rhu Spit beacon if going beyond Rhu Narrows.

At Faslane Base, 2½–3 miles north of the narrows on the east shore, a prohibited area from which all craft are excluded extends 150 metres from the piers and floating dock. A restricted area extends from 56°03′N to 56°04′N across the loch from the east shore leaving a passage 1–2 cables wide along the west shore.

Entry to the restricted area at Faslane is prohibited when the following signals are shown on the floating dock: 3F.G(vert) lights supplemented by signal flags International Code Pennant over Pennant 9.

Lights

At night a wealth of leading lights are provided as follows, together with lateral light buoys.

Each of the sectored leading beacons has a narrow central white fixed sector, with alternating white/red and white/green sectors, and red or green sectors as appropriate.

Beacon No.1 VQ(4)Y.5s stands southeast of the entrance leading 080° through Ardmore Channel in combination with

Bn 8N Dir.WRG + Fl.Y3s

No.24 light buoy Fl.R.5s

Row light buoy Fl.G.5s

No.7N Oc.G.6s3m3M and Dir.WRG

Cairndhu light buoy Fl.G.2·5s

Castle Point light beacon Fl(2)R.10s8m6M

Limekiln Point '2N' Dir Lt 295° DirWRG.

Castle Point 3N Oc.R.8s.9m3M and Dir.WRG 149°

Rhu Marina light buoy Fl.G.4s

Rhu Marina entrance SE Fl.G.5s

Rhu Marina entrance NW Fl.R.5s

Rhu Point Q(3)WRG.6s9m10-7M

Dir Lt 318° DirOc.WRG.6s5m14M

Rhu Spit light beacon Fl.3s6m6M

Light buoy south of Rhu Spit Fl.G.3s

Light buoy southwest of Rhu Spit Q.R

Light buoy northwest of Rhu Spit Fl.R.5s

Light buoy north of Rhu Spit Q.G

Mambeg Dir Lt 331° Q(4)WRG.8s

Keep a lookout at night for other traffic and for signal lights particularly at Green Island and the former RCT Port Unit. It is best to keep off the leading lines

Anchorages

Rosneath Bay, anchor not more than ½ cable ESE of a yellow spherical buoy with a cross topmark which is moored north of the front leading beacon on the shore. Drying rocks extend over a cable from the shore.

Rhu Bay, between Cairndhu Point and Rhu Marina, dries up to 1½ cables from the shore and most available space is taken up with moorings.

Rhu Marina This must be one of very few marinas with resident seals, as well as Eider duck nesting on the pontoons at the entrance. It is entered at the south east corner of Rhu Bay. The rock breakwater has been built up to give complete protection from the south, and the entrance is now approached from SSW. A G con. buoy lies off the entrance, which is marked by port- and starboard-hand pyramid beacons.

Rhu Marina approach. The green buoy marks foundations awash for a future breakwater extension. Possibly the only marina with resident seals, on the floating sections of breakwater

Services

Diesel, water, chandlery, *Calor Gas*.

Communications

Rhu Marina ☎ 01436 820238, VHF Ch 37, 80 (office hours).

Supplies

At Rhu; shop, post office, telephone, hotel; more in Helensburgh, 1½ miles.
  Train/bus to Glasgow from Helensburgh.

Other anchorages

Stroul Bay Carraig an Roinn approximately 4½ cables WNW from Limekiln Point at the west side of Rhu Narrows dries 3·0 metres, marked by a stout perch at its east side; an inviting-looking space there is not a suitable place to anchor.

Silvers' Marine on the south side of the bay provides moorings, showers, water, slipping and repairs. ☎ 01436 831222.

Stroul Bay Yacht Haven provides moorings, showers, water, and diesel, ☎ 01436 831430.

Nicholson Hughes Sailmakers are at Silvers' yard ☎ 01436 831356.

Clynder Moorings extend 1½ miles along the west shore. Modern Charters, ☎ 01436 831312, provide moorings and chandlery.

Royal Northern and Clyde Yacht Club moorings occupy the area north of Rhu Spit, and most of the east shore not occupied by the navy is full of individual permanent moorings.

Garelochhead The head of the loch dries for 1½ cables and most of the water with moderate depths is taken up by permanent moorings. Supplies in village.

Helensburgh

56°00′N 4°44′W

A mile east of Gareloch entrance. The shore dries out 1½ cables almost to the head of Helensburgh Pier, and the 2-metre line is 1–2 cables further out. Temporary anchorage clear of the approach to the pier, which is used by excursion steamers. Temporary berth at side of the pier when rise of tide is sufficient. Supplies in town.

Gourock Bay (Cardwell Bay)

55°58′N 4°49′W

The west side of the bay is taken up by ferry quays and small-craft moorings, and the bottom between the quays and the moorings is foul. On the south side of the bay is the detached remains of a naval jetty. The east side of the bay dries off for a cable.
  Land at the slip east of naval jetty.

Services

Moorings available from Ritchie Bros ☎ 01475 632125. Owen Sailmakers ☎ 01475 636196.

River Clyde

CHARTS

1994 covers the channel as far east as Great Harbour, 4°43′W; thereafter 2007 (1:15,000)

TIDES

At Port Glasgow

Constant is +0010 Greenock (+0125 Dover)
Height in metres

MHWS	MHWN	MTL	MLWN	MLWS
3·6	3·0	2·0	1·0	0·4

Glasgow

Constant is +0020 Greenock (+0135 Dover)
Height in metres

MHWS	MHWN	MTL	MLWN	MLWS
4·7	4·1	2·8	1·6	0·8

Tidal streams turn at about local HW and LW. Rates are not strong but out-going streams are increased and in-going streams reduced by heavy rain or melting snow; the out-going stream is enough to raise an unpleasant sea against a fresh westerly wind.

DIRECTIONS

Yachts should give prior notice to the harbourmaster if intending to enter the River Clyde, by phone to 01475 726221 or on VHF Ch 12. Yachts wishing to proceed beyond Bowling must obtain a written permit in advance from the harbourmaster.

The river is entered at Clydeport Container Terminal on the south shore and for the first 3 miles the channel closely follows the shore. The river is navigable for about 16 miles from Greenock but there is at present little to attract a yacht to enter it apart from various laying-up yards. However with the decline in commercial traffic, and extensive riverside development now in progress, Glasgow Harbour may have some attraction in the future.

Custom House Quay, at the centre of a large-scale waterfront redevelopment in Greenock, is ½ mile southeast of the Container Terminal, after which the channel makes a double bend to starboard passing the embankment of the Great Harbour. A mile beyond the east end of Great Harbour the channel begins to leave the south shore and particular care must be taken for the next 4 miles to keep within the buoyed channel. At high water the estuary is over a mile wide here but the buoyed channel is less than a cable.

Clydeport Container Terminal, a conspicuous landmark at the narrow mouth of the river channel. Dumbarton Castle is visible about five miles away

Dumbarton Castle (1999)

Dumbarton Castle on the north side of the river stands on a mound of rock 72 metres high. For the next two miles the south side of the channel is bounded by a stone training wall, the Lang Dyke, a survival from the original 18th-century improvement works, which is submerged except at LWS but marked by stone beacons.

By the east end of the Lang Dyke the channel has been reduced to the character of an inland river although still with a drying foreshore on the south side. Bowling Harbour, a mile further east has been obstructed by several sunken vessels, but should have been cleared by the time this edition is published.

After a further mile the river is crossed by Erskine Bridge (headroom 52 metres) and for a further 3 miles the south bank is not very built-up. The River Cart joins the Clyde on the south side 5½ miles from Erskine Bridge and Rothesay Dock opens on the north side.

PASSAGE NOTES

The Container Terminal has three large blue cranes which are easily seen from Gareloch entrance. If coming from Gareloch steer for the west end of the Container Terminal and pass west of No. 2 red can light buoy.

Keep strictly to the buoyed channel as in some places stone banks lie very close outwith the channel. Keep to the starboard side whenever meeting another vessel.

As large vessels are only able to move near high water and have to keep to the dredged channel which is much narrower than the buoyed channel, the period around high tide should be avoided.

On a passage down river a lightly powered boat of less than about 10 metres will be hard pressed in a fresh westerly wind; in these conditions it may be better to make the passage at low water on the first of the flood when the water will be smoother.

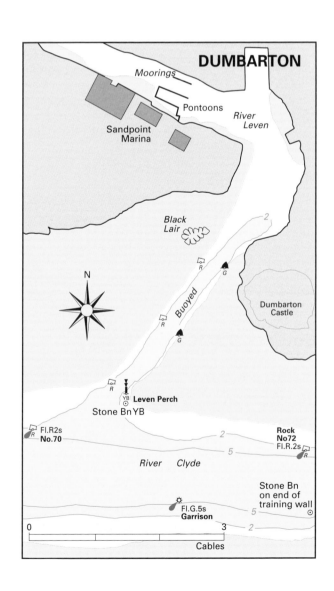

The winding channel of the lower reaches of River Clyde from Dumbarton Castle (1999)

Entrance to River Leven from Dumbarton Castle (1999)

Dumbarton

55°56′N 4°34′W

At the mouth of the River Leven on the north side of the Clyde, 7 miles upriver from the Container Terminal. The Leven is entered ¼ mile southwest of Dumbarton Castle which stands on 72-metre high Dumbarton Rock at the east side of the entrance, between Leven Perch, a cylindrical stone beacon and light buoy No.70 on the west side of the entrance. The channel is marked by miniature lateral buoys of which the first lies ¼ cable northwest of Leven Perch.

The charted depth in the entrance is 2·4 metres, but where the channel bends to the west there is much less and it should be approached on a rising tide. Sandpoint Marina has pontoons in the river, with depths of little more than 1 metre alongside the outer pontoon, but the bottom is soft mud. The yard lays up yachts, carries out repairs, and supplies fuel, water and chandlery; ☎ Dumbarton 01389 762396.

The River Clyde above Dumbarton Castle, with the Lang Dyke on the far side of the channel (1999)

Bowling Basin, the west end of the Forth and Clyde Canal, is entered through a lock from the east end of Bowling Harbour.

The whole canal was re-opened in 2001, although with headroom restricted to 3 metres provision is made for taking down masts.

A Boat Safety Scheme is in operation for boats remaining in the canal, including Bowling Basin. Details should be obtained from British Waterways before entering the canal. ☎ 0141 332 6936.

Maximum dimensions of craft passing through the canal are: length 20m, beam 6m, draught (fresh water) 2m, air draught 3m.

Services

All existing small craft businesses on the Clyde above Dumbarton have been closed down and a new boatyard under the title of River Clyde Boatyard has been established by Clydeport plc in the former Rothesay Dock on the north bank.

Anyone wishing to visit Glasgow by boat can berth at a pontoon (free for private boats for the time being) at Broomielaw Quay on the north bank, east of Kingston Bridge. Security gate and electricity supply. Prior booking necessary (☎ 0141 287 9225) and, to reiterate, prior written consent must be obtained from Clydeport Harbourmaster to navigate upriver from Bowling. New low-level bridges have been built and are under construction across the River Clyde.

Bowling Harbour, Forth and Clyde Canal

The lock keeper can be contacted on VHF Ch 16/74, calling *Bowling Basin* during sea lock operating hours which are 2 hours either side of High Water Greenock +0015.

Open hours are seasonal as follows:

1 April–30 September
0800–2000 hours
1 October–31 March
0800–1600

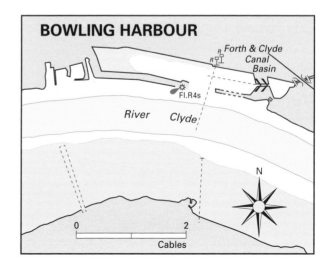

Sandpoint Marina, Dumbarton from the castle

Vessels wishing to use the sea lock should contact the lock keeper in advance on ☎ 01389 877969.

Take care when navigating in Bowling Harbour due to the large number of unmarked wrecks. Keep strictly to leading lines, consisting of two pairs of beacons on the shore, which lead clear of hazards;

On approaching the Lock, follow the lock keeper's instructions, normally mooring on the port side. Two long warps and fenders will be required, and a canvas sheet between fenders and the hull will help to reduce scuffing.

British Waterways operated mast unstepping and stepping facilities are available at Bowling, and Forth and Clyde Canal Licences can be purchased from the lock keeper. Yachts with double spreaders need to make appropriate arrangements.

British Waterways' staff will operate the sea lock and boat safety checks will be carried out at the Lock prior to entering the Canal.

Services
Cycle hire at canal basin.

Top left: Bowling Basin at the entrance to the Forth and Clyde Canal (2006)

Left: Bowling Harbour at low tide, from second leading line (2004)

LOCH LONG TO RIVER CLYDE

IV. Kyles of Bute to Loch Fyne

The sequence of this chapter is from Rothesay Bay through the East Kyle to the Burnt Islands and Loch Riddon, continuing by the West Kyle to the west side of Bute, followed by Loch Fyne and the Crinan Canal.

CHARTS

Imray chart folio 2900 (1:50,000)

2131 (1:75,000). Kyles: 1906 (1:25,000); 2383 (1:25,000) and 2221 (1:36,000) cover the west side of Bute. Chart 1907 (1:25,000) is needed at Toward Point

TIDAL STREAMS

The flood tide enters both Kyles from seaward and the streams meet around the Burnt Islands; the actual point of meeting depends on meteorological conditions, but is normally a few miles east of the islands. The tidal stream in the passages at Rubha Ban and the Burnt Islands may reach 3 knots with the flood usually running eastward.

BUOYAGE

The direction of buoyage in Rothesay Sound and Loch Striven is to northwest and north; in the West Kyle it is to north and in the East Kyle to southeast, changing at Ardmaleish Point, which is marked by a north cardinal buoy on its north side.

LIGHTS

NE of Bogany Point, buoy No.36 is now lit Fl.R.4s.

Rothesay Sound and approaches to East Kyle

55°51′N 5°03′W

CHART

1907 (1:25,000), plan 1867 (1:10,000)

TIDES

Constant −0015 Greenock (+0100 Dover)
Height in metres

MHWS	MHWN	MTL	MLWN	MLWS
3·6	3·1	2·1	1·2	0·6

DANGERS AND MARKS

Toward Point lighthouse on the north side of the entrance to Rothesay Sound from the Firth of Clyde is a white tower 19 metres high, with a lattice tower behind it and two more lattice towers on the hillside further inland.

At Toward Point a drying reef stands 1 cable south of the lighthouse, and No.34 east cardinal buoy lies close southeast of a submerged reef which extends over ¼ mile SSW of the lighthouse.

No.35 green conical light buoy marks Toward Bank with a least depth of 4·3 metres. Unmarked shoals and drying rocks extend two cables out from the north shore between Toward and Ardyne.

The approach from seaward is straightforward but if coming from or going to the upper reaches of the firth, keep south of No.34 east cardinal buoy.

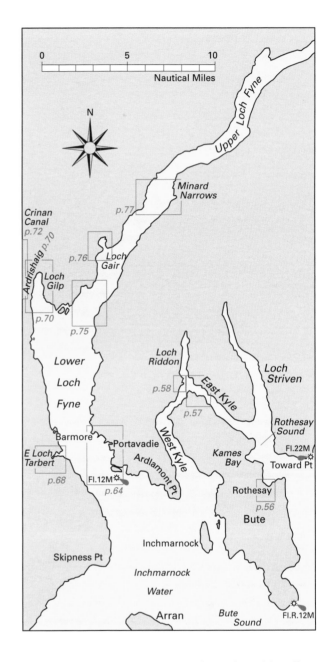

Ardyne green conical light buoy (Fl.G.3s), 3 cables off Ardyne Point, has no navigational significance for yachts.

A stranger might mistake Loch Striven for the East Kyle, but the compass will soon clarify which is which. A boatyard stands on Ardmaleish Point which separates the East Kyle from Kames Bay.

Toward Point with the East Kyle beyond (1987)

Rothesay Harbour, with pontoons for visiting yachts both inside the harbour and south of the west end of the main pier   *Patrick Roach*

Rothesay Bay

55°51′N 5°03′W

The bay is generally clean but a large lit mooring buoy, **Rothesay A,** lies ¼ mile from the head of the bay. Rothesay Harbour is at the south side of the bay.

Port hand beacon NW of Main Pier marks shoal water.

Lights

Buoy no. 36, Bogany Point Fl.R4s
Rothesay A Mooring buoy is lit Fl.Y.2s
SE corner of Main Pier Fl.G.3s
West end of Main Pier 2F.R(vert.)
Albert Pier 2F.R(vert.)
NE of Albert Pier port hand light buoy (Fl.R.5s) marks shoal water
A traffic light system 3 (vert) has been established for the harbour on the roof of the Harbour Office:
    3 R (vert) = harbour closed to all movements,
    3G (vert) = harbour open

Anchorage and moorings

The usual anchorage is off the west side of the bay, where there is a low rectangular building (Kyles of Bute Sailing Club) between the road and the water with a wood behind. Visitors' moorings are provided here. If anchoring check the depth as it is shoal close inshore and the bottom falls away steeply a cable from the shore. Water from a tap below the clubhouse. Bute Berthing Co ☎ 01700 500630.

Pontoons are provided in the Outer Harbour and south of the west end of Main Pier. Yachts able to take the ground can berth alongside in the Inner Harbour.

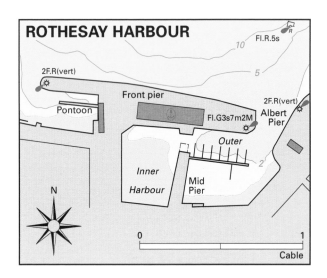

ROTHESAY HARBOUR

Supplies and services

Shops, post office, bank, phone, hotels, chandlers, Calor Gas, swimming baths. EC Wednesday.

Water at pier. Petrol, diesel in town or by tanker. Repairs, see Port Bannatyne. Ferry to mainland.

Communications

Harbourmaster ☎ 01700 503842, VHF Ch 16, 12 (0600–2100).

Kames Bay (Port Bannatyne)

55°52′N 5°04′W

The shores of the bay are drying or shoal up to 2 cables on all sides; in particular rocks dry out a cable NNE of Ardbeg Point at the south side of the bay, and it is shoal 1½ cables north of this point. Many small-craft moorings. A small marina has been established, behind a new stone breakwater, but it is not expected to cater for visiting yachts.

Anchorage

Anchoring is prohibited near a small foul area 2 cables north of the boatyard slip (in any case the depth is about 20 metres). If space can be found anchor between the old pier and the boatyard slip, but the bottom falls away steeply; alternatively well off the northwest side of the bay; the shore dries out up to a cable but there is a shelf with reasonable depths.

Lights

Port Bannatyne breakwater head Fl.R.4s

Supplies and services

Shops, post office, phone, hotels. Water and Calor Gas at boatyard. Boatyards: Ambrisbeg Boatyard ☎ 01700 502719 and Ardmaleish Boat Building Co, ☎ 01700 502007.

Loch Striven

55°57′N 5°05′W

A bleak and rather featureless loch, notorious for squalls, running north for over six miles from the entrance to the East Kyle. Submarine exercises and experimental operations are sometimes carried out.

Anchorages

There are only the most tenuous of anchorages, of which one is at Inverchaolain, northwest of a slight promontory at the mouth of a glen 2 miles north of the NATO fuel jetty on the east side of the loch; the bottom falls away very steeply.

The least insecure anchorage is at the head of the loch on the east side, ¼ mile from the head.

Other berths may be found north of the point 3 cables further south, but much of the bight there dries out.

East Kyle and the Burnt Islands

TIDES

Constant –0015 Greenock (+0100 Dover)
Height in metres

MHWS	MHWN	MTL	MLWN	MLWS
3·2	2·8	2·0	1·2	0·6

DANGERS AND MARKS

The East Kyle is clean outwith a cable from the shore as far as Colintraive Point where there is an extensive drying area in the bight southeast of the point.

Because of the hills close on each side, the Kyles can be very squally. Very strong squalls may be funnelled down Loch Striven and take by surprise a yacht which has thus far survived a passage from west to east.

At Rubha a'Bhodaich (Rhubodach) on the southwest shore a green conical buoy marks the end of a drying bank off the point.

DIRECTIONS

There is a choice of two passages at the Burnt Islands. The passage north of Eilean Mor is narrower but briefer; the tide may be less strong in the southern passage.

In the northern passage the most conspicuous mark is a red lattice beacon but the channel, about 50 metres wide, is defined by two pairs of lateral light buoys.

Pass between the two pairs of buoys, and keep at least ½ cable off the north end of Eilean Fraoich. Tidal streams in both directions tend to set south from Eilean Buidhe.

In the south passage shoals and drying rocks extend deceptively far south and southeast from Eilean Mor.

Pass close north of Wood Farm Rock green conical buoy (No.43).

Pass north of No.44 green conical buoy ¼ cable north of Bear Craig (Channel Point); note that there is a depth of less than 1 metre ¼ cable southeast of the buoy.

At LW springs beware also a rock ½ cable northeast of the buoy with a depth of 1·2 metres.

No.45 red can buoy marks a rock with a least depth of 2·4 metres.

Lights

Rhubodach buoy is lit Q.G

In the north passage all four buoys are lit. In the south channel no buoys are lit.

At night

To be sure of avoiding the reefs at the north end of Eilean Fraoich do not turn south into the West Kyle until Rubha Ban buoy Fl.R.4s shows open of the Buttock of Bute.

Coming from the West Kyle keep Rubha Ban buoy in sight until the two light buoys in the north channel are in line.

Anchorages at Colintraive and the Burnt Islands

55°55′.5N 5°10′W

Southeast of Colintraive Point the shore dries off for 1½ cables. Here and further southeast the bottom falls away sharply.

The best anchorage at Colintraive is west of the point, clear of cables and the ferry mooring and leaving space for the ferry to manoeuvre.

Visitors' moorings are provided by the hotel.

Supplies

Shop (beyond the hotel), post office, phone, hotel, water at the ferry slip.

Anchorages

Balnakailly Bay, south of Eilean Mor and clear of Wood Farm Rock.

Wreck Bay, between Channel Point (Bear Craig) and Buttock of Bute.

In westerly winds, some shelter may be found on the east sides of Eilean Mor or Eilean Buidhe.

An Caladh

55°56′N 5°12′W

A small bay on the west shore ¼ mile WNW of the Burnt Islands sheltered from east by Eilean Dubh which is overgrown with rhododendrons, as is the hillside behind.

A stone beacon in the form of a miniature lighthouse stands on the west side of the south entrance and submerged rocks lie on both sides.

In the middle of the northeast entrance a rock above water is marked by a white stone beacon with a diamond topmark.

A detached drying rock lies north of the beacon, but the beacon in the north entrance in line with the beacon at the south entrance clears it. Any part of a house at the north end of the bay in sight clears the south side of the drying rock.

Anchorage

The west side of the bay dries for about half its width, but twin-keel boats could dry out there. The island shore has some submerged and drying rocks close inshore, and a mooring ring is fixed in the face of the stone cliff. This anchorage is often very crowded.

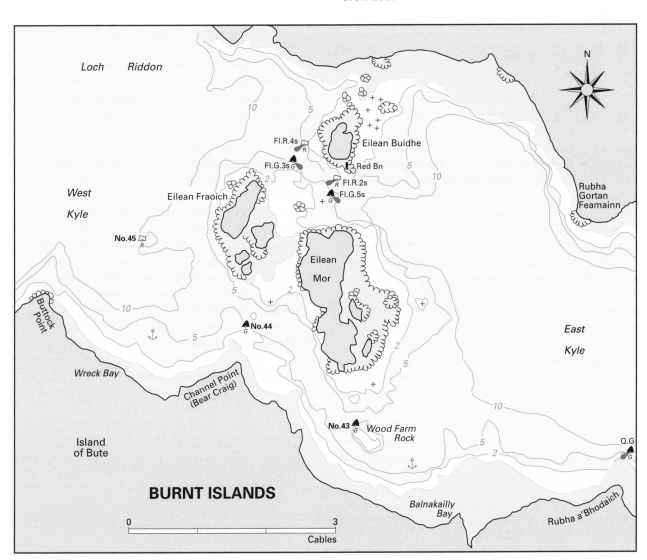

Burnt Islands from northwest

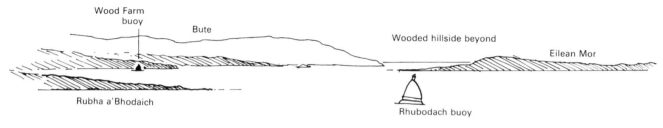

Wood Farm buoy · Bute · Wooded hillside beyond · Eilean Mor · Rubha a'Bhodaich · Rhubodach buoy

Burnt Islands from the east

Burnt Islands from north west, with the stone beacon at the south entrance to An Caladh. This is cruising in mid-February; the photo on page vii was taken in the same area!

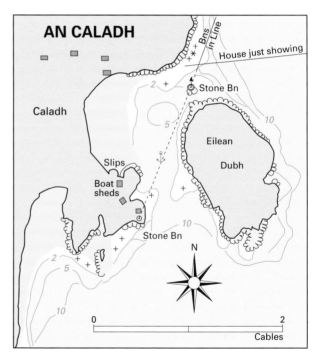

AN CALADH

House just showing · Bns in Line · Stone Bn · Caladh · Eilean Dubh · Slips · Boat sheds · Stone Bn · N · 0 · 2 · Cables

Burnt Islands from south east, showing buoyage in the north channel (2006)

An Caladh from northwest; note the shoal and drying area on the west side (1997)

Eilean Dubh

Beacon

Beacon

An Caladh harbour north entrance. The stone beacon in line with the stone beacon at the south end leads east of the drying rock north of the entrance.

Eilean Dubh

Beacon

An Caladh harbour north entrance. The first house on the right just showing leads south of the drying rock.

An Caladh from west (1987)

Loch Riddon

The head of Loch Riddon dries for 1½ miles and the bottom drops away steeply almost everywhere. Most places suitable for anchoring are already occupied by permanent moorings.

Anchorages

Ormidale, close north of the pier on the west shore, 1¼ miles north of Eilean Dubh at Caladh. The LW line is 2 cables north of the pier and most of the intervening space is taken up with moorings. Fish cages are moored to the south of the pier.

Eilean Dearg, traditionally known as One Tree Island although it has now sprouted three rather half-hearted trees, off the east shore ¼ mile north of Eilean Dubh; there are moderate depths between the island and the shore, but beware a drying patch ½ cable north of the island.

Salthouse, on the east shore ½ mile ENE of Ormidale pier, but the LW line extends across the loch from Salthouse.

Ormidale Pier in Loch Riddon, surrounded by moorings

Head of Loch Riddon, showing banks drying and submerged, and the pool off Salthouse (2000)

Eilean Dearg, Loch Riddon, from west with permanent moorings in the bay south east of the island (2000)

West Kyle

TIDES

Constant −0015 Greenock (+0100 Dover)
Height in metres

MHWS	MHWN	MTL	MLWN	MLWS
3·4	3·1	2·2	1·4	0·9

DANGERS AND MARKS

At Rubha Ban on the northwest shore a mile southwest of the Buttock of Bute a red light buoy marks a drying spit on its northwest side. Half a mile north of Rubha Ban fish cages are marked by yellow light buoys.

From Rubha Ban the villages of Tighnabruaich and Kames stretch for 2½ miles along the northwest and west side of the Kyle, each with a pier and many boats on moorings, as well as some visitors' moorings.

South of Kames shoals and drying rocks lie up to 2 cables off the west shore, and up to 1 cable off the east shore; otherwise the Kyle is clean.

2½ miles south of Kames Pier, Carry Rock light buoy (No.46) marks a rocky spit at Carry Point.

Ardlamont Point red can light buoy (No. 47) marks the east side of drying rocks and shoals extending up to 4 cables south of Ardlamont Point. The extremity of these shoals is WSW of the buoy, so that if coming from or going to Loch Fyne keep at least ¼ mile south of the point.

The West Kyle is often subject to squalls particularly, in westerly winds, off Kames where the wind funnels through a valley west of the village.

LIGHT BUOYS

The buoys at the fish cages north of Rubha Ban are lit Fl.Y.6s at the north end and Fl.Y.4s at the south end
Rubha Ban (No.45) Fl.R.4s
Carry Rock (No.46) Fl.R.4s
Ardlamont Point (No.47) Fl.R.4s
There is no light at Rubha Dubh, but from southward it should show up against the lights at the villages.

Anchorages

Tighnabruaich, 55°54′.5N 5°13′.5W, has less suitable depth for anchoring except off the boatyard ¼ mile west of Rubha Ban. Visitors' moorings are laid in several places off the village. Shops, post office, phone, hotel. Boatyard: Mara Marine, ☎ 01700 811537 or 01436 810971. Slip, 18-ton hoist, moorings, repairs.

Black Farland Bay, on Bute, opposite Tighnabruaich provides good anchorage about the middle of the bay. A rock spit extends ½ cable offshore 3 cables northeast of Rubha Dubh, and a drying and shoal spit extends a cable off Rubha Glas, 7 cables northeast of Rubha Dubh.

Kames, 55°53′.5N 5°14′W, has visitors' moorings off the pier. Alternatively anchor clear of moorings, between Kames and Tighnabruaich piers, but as elsewhere the bottom drops away steeply. Shop, post office, phone, hotel.

Blindman's Bay lies a mile north of Ardlamont Point buoy. Anchor in not less than 5 metres to avoid swinging into shoal water inshore.

Ettrick Bay on Bute, has underwater obstructions charted and reported to extend close inshore.

Inchmarnock and the west side of Bute

Except at Inchmarnock itself all anchorages are exposed to the southwest and are only suitable for occasional use.

DANGERS AND MARKS

Shearwater rock, depth 0·9 metres, lies ½ mile southeast of Inchmarnock and rather west of mid-channel; otherwise the coast of Bute is free of hazards outwith ¼ mile from the shore.

A clearing line for the east side of Shearwater rock is to keep Northpark, a farmhouse near the north end of Inchmarnock, open of the east point of Inchmarnock, but the east point is difficult to identify.

Rubha Ban, with Tighnabruaich beyond (1987)

Tighnabruaich boatyard (1987)

Anchorages

Inchmarnock Anchorage is off Midpark farm at the east side of the island.

St Ninian's Bay, east of Inchmarnock is clean but rocks dry for a cable inside its west point, and the head of the bay dries 3 cables.

Scalpsie Bay, 2 miles ESE of the south end of Inchmarnock, has cables occupying its eastern half, but a reasonable depth for anchoring can be found 2 cables off the farm on the northwest side. Shoals extend ¼ mile south from Ardscalpsie Point at the west of the entrance.

Lower Loch Fyne

CHART
2381 (1:25,000)

TIDES
Tidal streams are not significant in the lower loch.

DANGERS AND MARKS
The fairway of the loch as far as the approaches to Loch Gilp and Otter Spit is completely clean as are the shores outwith a cable. There are few marks of any sort and Tarbert is hidden but Barmore Island, 1½ miles NNW of Tarbert entrance, is conspicuous. Detached drying rocks extend a cable east and 2 cables north of Barmore. Ardrishaig is also conspicuous.

Skate Island (Sgat Mor) light beacon lies off the east shore of the loch 3 miles southeast of Tarbert.

Ardrishaig breakwater light beacon is not very conspicuous.

Otter Spit light beacon in the entrance to Upper Loch Fyne is green, cylindrical.

PASSAGE NOTES
The passage is straightforward, although may be exposed by contrast with shelter in the Kyles or the Crinan Canal. A steep sea can build up off Ardlamont Point, or in the mouth of Loch Gilp in a southerly wind.

LIGHTS
Skate Island (Sgat Mor) light beacon Fl.3s9m12M
Eilean Beithe Fl.WRG.3s.7m5M
Ardrishaig breakwater LFl.WRG.6s9m4M
Otter Spit light beacon Fl.G.3s7m8M

Shelter

Tarbert provides good shelter from all directions but strong westerly winds tend to funnel through the gap from West Loch Tarbert and in these conditions it may be difficult to make the entrance. Ardrishaig gives shelter in the sea lock (unless, unusually, the gates are closed) except in strong east or northeast winds, but in those conditions Tarbert would be easy to approach.

Tides

Constant +0005 Greenock (+0120 Dover)
Height in metres

MHWS	MHWN	MTL	MLWN	MLWS
3·4	2·9	1·9	1·1	0·3

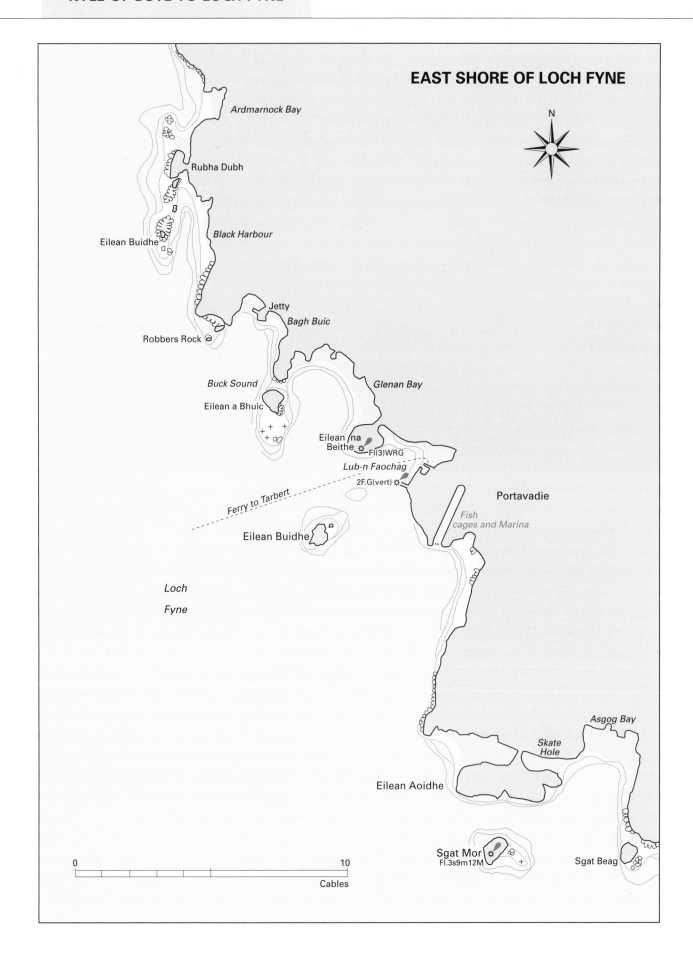

EAST SHORE OF LOCH FYNE

N

Ardmarnock Bay

Rubha Dubh

Black Harbour

Eilean Buidhe

Jetty

Bagh Buic

Robbers Rock

Buck Sound

Glenan Bay

Eilean a Bhuic

Eilean na Beithe

Fl(3)WRG

Lub-n Faochag

2F.G(vert)

Ferry to Tarbert

Portavadie

Fish cages and Marina

Eilean Buidhe

Loch Fyne

Asgog Bay

Skate Hole

Eilean Aoidhe

Sgat Mor
Fl.3s9m12M

Sgat Beag

0   10

Cables

Portavadie (2006)

Glenan Bay, Loch Fyne; Eilean Buidhe at lower right (2006)

Occasional anchorages on north east shore of lower Loch Fyne

In light or offshore winds several bays on the east side of Loch Fyne provide attractive occasional anchorages and there are passages inshore of some of the islets. No supplies or services are available at any of these places.

Ardlamont Bay and Kilbride Bay, 1 and 2 miles respectively northwest of Ardlamont Point, have sandy beaches off which to anchor by day.

Sgat Mor, an island 10 metres high has a white light beacon on it; further north the islands and bays may be difficult to distinguish, but it is essential to do so to identify various drying and submerged rocks.

Asgog Bay, northeast of Sgat Mor (Skate Island) dries up to 1½ cables at the head and the bottom drops quickly from the LW line. Anchor in the northeast or northwest corner, or northeast of the east end of Eilean Aoidhe, in the mouth of an inlet known as Skate Hole.

The passage north of Sgat Mor is straightforward, but a submerged rock lies more than a cable southeast of the northeast point of the island and a drying rock lies ½ cable southeast of the same point.

Portavadie, 1½ miles north of Sgat Mor, was developed as a yard for building oil rigs, but no orders materialised and it was abandoned. A marina is being established, with pontoons in the enclosed dock east of Eilean Buidhe. ☎ 01700 811729. The photo on p.65 is already out of date, and the marina is in the process of being extended.

There is some shelter behind the breakwater northwest of the basin, but the wharf east of the breakwater is not convenient for small boats, and the harbour behind the wharf dries out. There are fish cages in Lub-n Faochag, the bay northwest of Portavadie.

Fuel and water at pontoons. Ferry to Tarbert.

Lights
NW breakwater 2FG(vert)6m4M
Eilean na Beithe Fl.WRG.3s7m5M

Glenan Bay, the next bay northwest of Lub-n Faochag, has the familiar features of a foreshore drying up to a cable, with the bottom dropping sharply from the LW line, but it is possible to anchor off the east and northwest sides.

Eilean Buidhe, west of Portavadie, has drying and submerged rocks, particularly off its northeast side, and Eilean a Bhuic, south of the northwest point of Glenan Bay, has drying and submerged rocks lying up to 1½ cables south of it.

Buck Rock, near the outer limit of these rocks, dries 3·4 metres and therefore rarely covers, but these rocks and the rocks off Eilean Buidhe need to be taken into account when approaching or leaving Portavadie or Glenan Bay.

Buck Sound, the passage between Eilean a Bhuic and the shore is clean.

Bagh Buic (Buck Bay), north of Eilean a Bhuic, is identified by a large modern house on its northeast side, and depths are reasonable for anchoring.

Robber's Rock dries 1·8 metres 1 cable south of the northwest point of the bay; remember also the rocks around Eilean a Bhuic south of the bay.

Black Harbour, about ½ mile northwest of Buck Bay, has some shelter behind a low islet (also named Eilean Buidhe) and drying rocks but depths are moderate at the head of the inlet.

Ardmarnock Bay is separated from Black Harbour by a small peninsula, Rubha Dubh. Rocks above water and drying extend north from the south point of the bay. The north point is clean and there is a boathouse with a slip there. The head of the bay dries, but depths are moderate for anchoring at the south end.

Buck Bay from the east (1987)

Robber's Rock   Eilean a'Bhuie

Buck Sound from northwest

Ardmarnock Bay from north east (1987)

Tarbert

55°52′N 5°24′W

One of the most completely sheltered harbours on the west coast of Scotland, but crowded with moorings, and with a bottom of soft mud. In westerly winds squalls funnel through the gap from West Loch Tarbert.

TIDES

Constant +0005 Greenock (+0120 Dover)
Height in metres

MHWS	MHWN	MTL	MLWN	MLWS
3·4	2·9	1·9	1·1	0·3

MARKS AND APPROACH

The main channel, south of Eilean a'Choich (Cock Island), is a third of a cable wide.

Madadh Maol, a reef extending from the south shore ½ cable east of Cock Island, is marked by a red light column, and reefs off the south side of Cock Island by a green light column.

A drying rock a third of a cable WSW of Cock Island is marked by a green perch with a triangular topmark.

Fishing boats use the main channel, often at a considerable speed, and an alternative passage is north of Cock Island, but a large area of drying and above-water rocks, Sgeir Bhuidhe, lies northwest of the island.

A green conical buoy marks shoal water off Leac Buidhe, the point of the mainland north of Cock Island; a red can buoy marks the northeast point of Sgeir Bhuidhe. A red perch stands near the northwest point of Sgeir Bhuidhe.

Lights

Madadh Maol light column shows Fl.R.2·5s4m

The column south of Cock Island shows Q.G.3m. These two lights in line lead to the entrance clear of the north shore

The perch WSW of Cock Island is lit VQ.G

The perch W of Sgeir Buidhe VQ(9)10s

N end of quay 2F.R(vert)

Mooring and anchorages

Extensive pontoons are provided on the north side of the harbour and visitors should moor to the southeast side.

Some moorings are provided by Tarbert Harbour Authority and the harbourmaster may be able to let you use one of these.

There is unlikely to be space to anchor clear of moorings and clear of the approach to the pier.

Mooring at the quay on the south side is permitted, but it is very much subject to disturbance by fishing boats. In practice all except very large yachts should keep away.

The Deuchlands (Dubh-chaol Linne), the northern arm of Tarbert harbour, is full of permanent moorings; it may appear to have space for anchoring, but drying rocks lie up to a cable from the head.

Outside the harbour, it is possible to anchor on the south side of the entrance, either off the Columba Hotel a cable west of the pier (the foreshore dries out ¼ cable and the bottom drops away sharply),

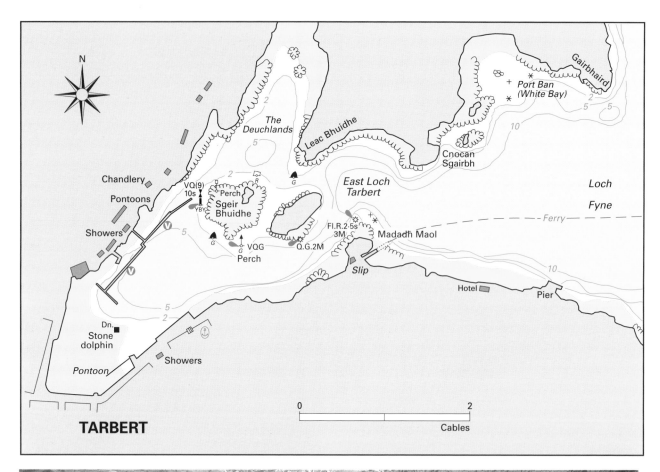

TARBERT

N

Chandlery

Pontoons

Showers

VQ(9)
10s

YBV

Perch
Sgeir
Bhuidhe

VQG
Perch

Q.G.2M

G

The
Deuchlands

Leac Bhuidhe

Cnocan
Sgairbh

Port Ban
(White Bay)

Gairbhaird

East Loch
Tarbert

Loch
Fyne

Ferry

Fl.R.2·5s
3M

Madadh Maol

Slip

Dn.
Stone
dolphin

Hotel

Pier

Pontoon

Showers

0 _____ 2

Cables

Tarbert Harbour entrance (1987)

Tarbert Harbour   *Mike Balmforth*

or a cable east of the pier, off a house with a cupola where there is a wider area with reasonable depth but the bottom is uneven and rocky in places.

Supplies

Shops (EC Wednesday), post office, phone, hotels, *Calor Gas*, petrol, diesel, water at pier and at pontoons.

Services

Boatbuilder: A. MacCallum, ☎ 01880 820209. Sailmaker, chandler and chart agent: W. B. Leitch, near pontoons, ☎ 01880 820287. Showers, coin-operated, at pontoons. Launderette at Leitch's.

Communications

Harbourmaster's office is near the east end of the main quay, ☎ 01880 820344, VHF Ch 16.

Bus to Glasgow. Ferry to Portavadie.

Barmore Island

At the peninsula 1¼ miles north of the entrance to East Loch Tarbert rocks above water and drying lie up to a cable east and 1½ cables northeast of it.

A detached reef, Sgeir Mhada Cinn, stands a cable northeast of Barmore surrounded by rocks.

There are occasional anchorages in the inlets south and northwest of Barmore.

South Bay is clean but its head dries for two cables. Anchor west of a small islet southwest of Barmore.

In North Bay, keep half a cable off Sgeir Mhada Cinn, clear of the hotel's moorings, or if visiting the hotel, pick up one of the moorings.

Loch Gilp

An open, gradually shoaling, loch which dries for nearly a mile at the head, and in which a steep sea builds in southerly winds. Submerged rocks in the entrance are marked by two light buoys.

Big Rock, 7 cables off the west shore 2¾ miles south of Ardrishaig breakwater lies at a depth of 2·1 metres.

TIDES

Constant (Tarbert) +0005 Greenock (+0120 Dover)

Height in metres

MHWS	MHWN	MTL	MLWN	MLWS
3·4	2·9	1·9	1·1	0·3

DANGERS AND MARKS

The buoys should be identified and the red can buoy No.48 left to port, and the green conical No.49 1¾ cables north of it, left to starboard.

The chart shows that at suitable rise of tide and sea conditions alternative courses may be taken.

Keep a reasonable distance off the end of the breakwater as rock footings extend all round the head; also a boat might be concealed behind it.

Duncuan Island has a passage nearly a cable wide between it and the east shore but drying rocks lie off the east shore and shoal patches up to ½ cable north and southeast of the island.

A rock drying 3 metres, ¼ cable SSW of Duncuan, is marked by a green beacon and there is a clear passage over a cable wide between the beacon and submerged rocks further southwest.

LIGHTS

Ardrishaig breakwater light LFl.WRG.6s9m4M at its outer end; white over the fairway, red to the west and green to the east. It is difficult to identify against town lights

Red light buoy　　　　　　　　Breakwater head　　Green conical buoy

Loch Gilp approach

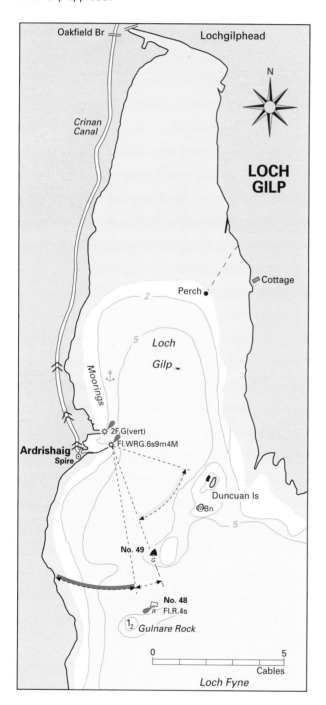

No.48 red can buoy, Fl.R.4s, lies in the middle of the white sector, as is part of Gulnare Rock, 2·4 metres
No.49 buoy Fl.G.5s, lies on the edge of the green sector
Ardrishaig Pier has 2F.G(vert) lights at its SE corner
Entrance to canal sea lock is marked by F.R and F.G lights

Ardrishaig

A pontoon has been established at the north wing wall of the sea lock in Ardrishaig Harbour, and the lock is normally left open (see below).

The pier is used by commercial vessels and is not available for yachts.

The north side of the breakwater dries along most of its length.

The regular anchorage is off the west shore north of the pier. The low water line, ½ mile north of the pier, extends west from a black and yellow sewer outfall beacon 1½ cables off a cottage on the east shore.

Communications

Canal office ☎ 01546 603210. VHF Ch 74.

Supplies

Water taps around canal basin (with hoses). Showers (coin-operated) and toilets at pier and at sea lock, opened by key provided by lock-keeper for boats using the canal.

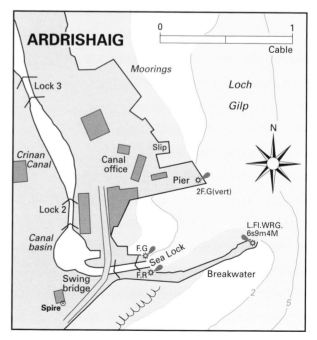

Shops, post office, phone, hotels, bank, *Calor Gas*, petrol diesel (at garage).

Chandlery and boatbuilder, ☎ 01546 603280.

More shops, etc. at Lochgilphead (EC Tuesday at Lochgilphead, Wednesday at Ardrishaig). When passing through the canal, Lochgilphead is only a third of a mile from Oakfield Bridge.

Occasional anchorages

Glac Mhor and Glac Bheag, at the south end of the peninsula between Loch Gilp and Upper Loch Fyne, lie on either side of Eilean Mor.

Glac Mhor, east of Eilean Mor, is protected from the east by Liath Eilean.

Dorus More, the narrow passage between an islet north of Liath Eilean and the mainland is passable but the edges are shoal.

Ardrishaig breakwater provides welcome shelter in southerly winds

Ardrishaig and Crinan Canal entrance (2006)

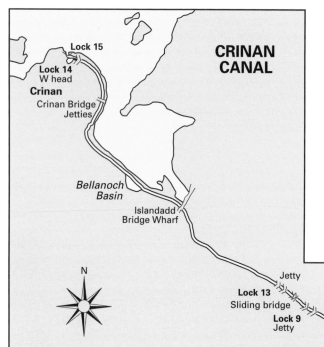

CRINAN CANAL

A local man may be available to help work a yacht through the canal for a fee, and his experience will be found valuable; ask at the canal office (or if going the other way, the duty lock-keeper at Crinan). To avoid delay it is worth arranging help in advance, through the canal office.

Ardrishaig Canal Basin is very small and vessels have to make a right-angle turn between the sea lock and lock No. 2; yachts moored there may be subject to minor damage. To leave a boat for several nights or longer consult the lock-keeper; it may be preferable to lie above lock 2.

The sea lock is normally left open, day and night, and you can usually go straight in unless it is filling or emptying or you are directed to stand off.

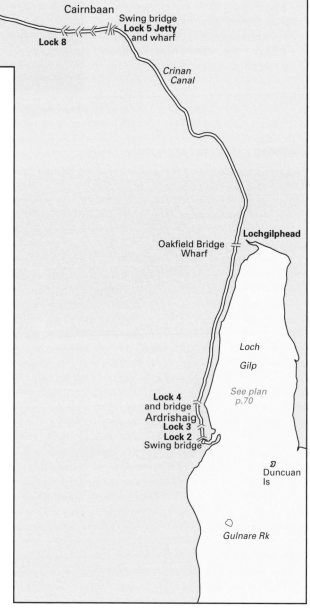

Crinan Canal

The canal through the neck of the Kintyre peninsula avoids the exposed passage round the Mull of Kintyre and, if coming from the upper part of the Firth, saves a distance of about 80 miles.

All locks apart from sea locks are worked by the boat's crew. The operation of gates and sluices takes considerable strength.

The passage through the canal is not without its hazards, and care is needed in positioning and handling fenders and warps, and managing a boat often in company with others which may be less than expertly handled, and possibly with a head or cross wind. Both luck and good management are needed to pass through the canal in less than six hours.

The scenery along the canal is extremely attractive and the passage can make a pleasant change from normal seafaring; it is worth taking it at a leisurely pace.

British Waterways provide a leaflet instructing yachts' crews in the operation of the canal, and this should be followed. It is essential to have an adequate number of stout fenders; four are barely adequate and you may regret not having eight. Two strong warps are needed, each about 20 metres in length, with a large soft eye or a bowline at the landward end.

Under good conditions two experienced people can take an easily managed boat through the canal, but it is preferable to have four. Don't rely on crews of other boats to help out, they may be short-handed too.

Make ready warps and fenders before approaching. There are ladders on both sides.

There is often quite a strong current out of the lock from the runoff from the canal, so it is best to get the bow warp ashore first; however if the lock-keeper is standing by to take your warps he may prefer to take the stern warp, in which case keep some way on to stem the current and avoid being swung across the lock.

In case there is no-one to take ropes, a crew member should be ready to go up the ladder.

If there is a shortage of water (which, although it may seem surprising, is not uncommon) the use of the sea lock may be limited to half tide and above.

Too much water running off the land into the canal may make the gates impossible to open.

The sea lock is operated by a lock-keeper. While the lock is being filled keep both warps tight; the bow warp may have to be led to a winch or windlass to control the boat.

At all 'inland' locks it is usual to take the stern warp ashore first to check way on entering the lock, but during and after heavy rain there may be a strong current out of the lock. Let the water in gradually to begin with and beware of helpful bystanders.

There are seven swing (or sliding) bridges operated by keepers, four of these are at locks.

Hours of operation may vary but are currently as follows:

Seven days a week between May and September: sea locks 0600–2130, inland locks and bridges 0800–1615, both with a lunch break from 1200–1230.

Long-term berths are available at Bellanoch Basin, Ardrishaig, Oakfield Bridge, Cairnbaan and Crinan. These are subject to compliance with British Waterways' Boat Safety Scheme, with which any well-equipped and maintained boat should easily be able to comply.

Services

Oakfield Bridge: (road) fuel station, with small supermarket; swimming pool, supermarket ¼ mile, shops Lochgilphead, ½ mile.

Cairnbaan: hotel, small shop/post office.

Bellanoch Bridge: small shop/post office.

Crinan: boatyard, chandlery, hotel and coffee shop, diesel, water and *Calor Gas*. No food shop.

Facilities for laying up ashore are provided at Cairnbaan; details from the British Waterways office as above.

Mooring

Transit jetties are provided at most locks.

Bellanoch Basin and marina (2006)

Upper Loch Fyne

CHART
2382 (1:25,000)

Upper Loch Fyne is entered about 3 miles east of Ardrishaig by the west side of Otter Spit, which dries for more than half the width of The Narrows from the east shore. The loch winds among hills for over 20 miles northeast from Otter Spit and is generally clean, apart from the spit itself and rocks at Minard Narrows, 6½ miles northeast of the spit.

TIDES
Streams at The Narrows run at 1 knot at springs, turning at HW and LW Greenock, but close to the end of Otter Spit streams, especially on the ebb, run at up to 2 knots.

Constant (Inveraray) +0011 Greenock (+0126 Dover)

Height in metres

MHWS	MHWN	MTL	MLWN	MLWS
3·3	3·0	1·7	0·5	0·2

DANGERS AND MARKS
Otter Spit is marked at its west end by a green cylindrical light beacon 11 metres high.

A submerged rock 7 cables southwest of the light beacon is marked on its northeast side by a red can light buoy, marked 'P'.

Glas Eilean, ½ mile north of Otter Spit beacon, has a red light column at its south end.

The red light buoy 'Q' is of no significance to yachts.

Clach Garbh, 1½ miles north of Otter Spit beacon, is a rock drying 1·5 metres, a cable off the west shore.

PASSAGE
Pass east of buoy 'P' and at least ½ cable west of Otter Spit beacon. If going against the tide keep further off the beacon as the tide runs more strongly close to the spit.

LIGHTS
Otter Spit beacon Fl.G.3s7m8M

Glas Eilean Fl.R.5s12m7M

Both buoys 'P' and 'Q' are lit Fl.R.3s

Shelter
Loch Gair is well sheltered with easy access by day.

Occasional anchorages

Port Ann is an anchorage for light or offshore winds; the head dries off for over a cable. Underwater cables occupy part of the west shore of the bay, southward of a cable beacon.

Otter Ferry, northwest of a stone pier which stands a mile east of Otter Spit beacon. Less than 2 cables northeast of the pier several underwater power cables cross the loch, marked by a beacon on the shore. Pontoon landing stages.

Shops, post office, telephone, bar restaurant, Calor Gas at Largiemore caravan site, 1 mile north. Petrol. Water at craft shop.

Otter Spit from east

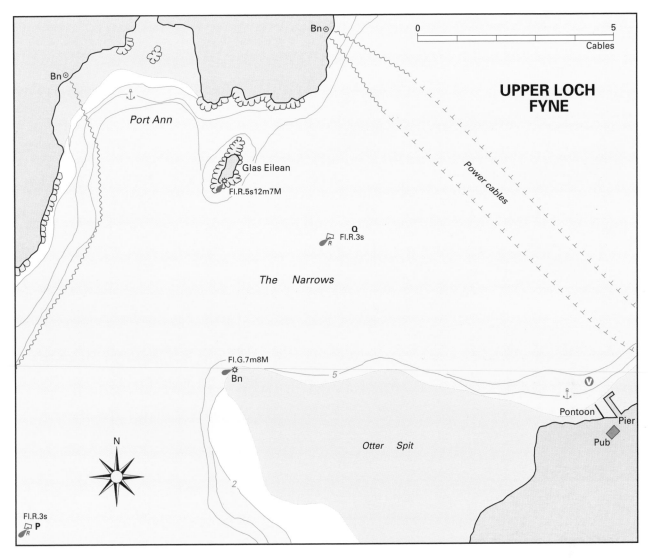

Bn ⊙

0   5
Cables

UPPER LOCH
FYNE

Bn ⊙

Port Ann

Power cables

Glas Eilean

Fl.R.5s12m7M

Q
Fl.R.3s
R

The   Narrows

Fl.G.7m8M
Bn

5

V

N

Otter   Spit

Pontoon
Pier

Pub

2

Fl.R.3s
P
R

Otter Ferry and Oystercatcher Inn (2006)

Loch Gair: note the spit to starboard covers (2006)

Loch Gair

An enclosed pool on the west shore 3 miles north of Otter Spit beacon, easy to enter in daylight and identified by the Pointhouse, a rectangular white tower on the south side of the entrance.

A spit at the inner end of the entrance channel on the north side dries out 1 cable; keep closer to the south side until past the point 2 cables northwest of the Pointhouse.

The foreshore is muddy and the loch is shoal on all sides; at LW the point 2 cables northwest of the Pointhouse is the cleanest place at which to land.

Supplies

Shop, post office, telephone, hotel. Showers at hotel. Hotel has two moorings.

Minard Narrows

6½ miles ENE of Otter Spit several islets, rocks and banks, both drying and submerged, are spread across the loch.

Eilean Aoghainn and Fraoch Eilean constitute the main group with rocks drying and submerged up to 2 cables NNE, marked by 'X' red can light buoy on their east side.

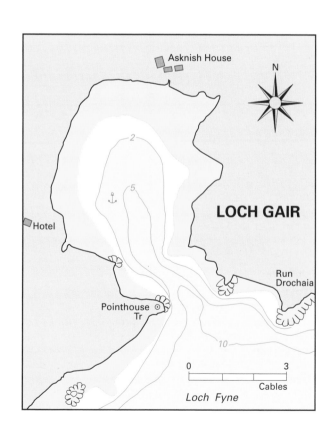

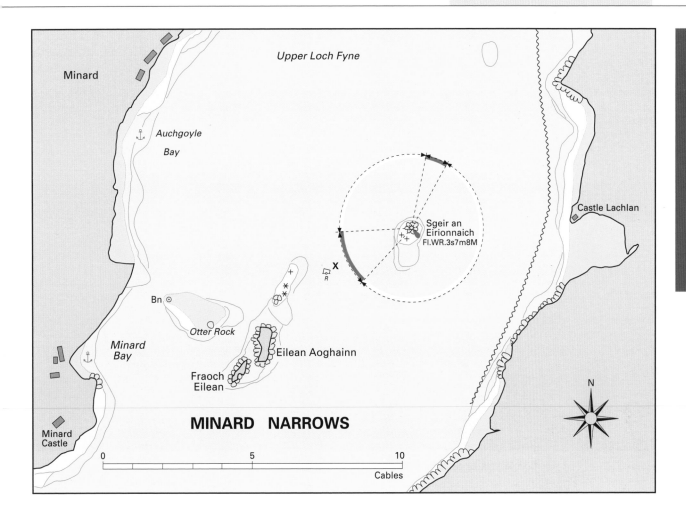

Sgeir an Eirionnaich, 2 cables ENE of the light buoy, has a cylindrical metal light beacon 7 metres high.

Otter Rock (An Oitir), 1 metre high, 1½ cables west of Eilean Aoghainn has a gravel bank drying 1½ cables WNW of it, marked at its WNW end by a black beacon with a spherical topmark.

The main passage is between Sgeir an Eireonnaich and the red light buoy, but others may be taken with careful attention to the chart.

Lights

Sgeir an Eirionnaich Fl.WR.3s7m8M, showing red over the rocks north of Eilean Aoghainn, and also over a shoal to the NNE which is of no concern to yachts.
The red light buoy 'X' shows Fl.R.3s

Anchorages

Minard Bay, the best anchorage in this part of the loch, lies ½ mile west of Fraoch Eilean.

Other occasional anchorages on the west side are at Auchgoyle Bay, 8 cables NNW of Eilean Aoghainn, south of Minard village, and Crarae Bay, 1½ miles north of Eilean Aoghainn and ½ mile southwest of a disused quarry.

Some supplies at Minard. Shop, coffee shop.

Furnace, on the northwest shore, 3½ miles northeast of Eilean Aoghainn, has a very conspicuous active quarry. Shop and Pub.

Other occasional anchorages

Throughout the upper loch occasional anchorages can be found on the chart, but many bays are too deep or shoal. Those most useful are as follows, all on the southeast shore:

Newton, opposite Furnace, either behind the island Innavagaan to the west of Newton village, or off the east end of the village. The shore in front of the main part of the village dries 1 cable.

Strachur, 3 miles ENE of Furnace, off the south end of the bay; the northeast side of the bay dries over a cable. Admiralty mooring buoy. Shop, post office, telephone, hotel. In an area between 1 and 2½ miles NNE of Strachur there are swamped moorings and anchoring is prohibited.

St Catherine's, opposite Inveraray, ¼ mile southwest of the hotel.

Inveraray: see text for clearing line for An Oitir (2006)

Inveraray from the northwest shore at low water. The *Arctic Penguin* museum ship is permanently moored alongside the pier

Inveraray

An 18th-century planned town, one of the west coast's principal tourist attractions. Inveraray Castle, a 19th-century mansion, is open to the public. A drying harbour is formed by the pier at the northeast point of the village.

TIDES

Constant (Inveraray) +0011 Greenock (+0126 Dover)

Height in metres

MHWS	MHWN	MTL	MLWN	MLWS
3·3	3·0	1·7	0·5	0·2

DANGERS AND MARKS

A drying spit, An Oitir, extends 2 cables from the northwest shore southwest of Inveraray. The two-arched bridge north of Inveraray open of the pier 355° leads clear of the spit.

Anchorage

The shore north of Inveraray dries nearly as far as the pier head but depths are suitable for anchoring in Newtown Bay, between An Oitir and Inveraray. The position of the inner end of An Oitir is indicated by the south end of the continuous row of houses (not the detached houses) at Newtown.

Supplies

Shops, post office, telephone, hotels, *Calor Gas*, petrol and diesel at garage south of village. Water at toilet block at the pier.

The *Arctic Penguin* museum ship is moored in a drying berth at the west side of the pier.

Anchorages at the head of Loch Fyne

Cairndow has an extensive raft of fish cages lying in the middle of the loch off Ardkinglas House, marked by cardinal buoys at its south and north points. Anchor ¼ mile from the head of the loch, off the north end of the village; the shore in front of the village dries for a cable. Hotel/restaurant.

Visitors' moorings are provided by Loch Fyne Oyster Bar near the northwest shore. Restaurant and up-market provisions.

V. Kintyre and Kilbrannan Sound

CHARTS

2126, 2131, 2168 (1:75,000), 2221 (1:36,000)

The peninsula of Kintyre extends 40 miles or so south from the mainland, protecting the Firth of Clyde from the open Atlantic, and leaving a gap of 11 miles between its extremity, the Mull of Kintyre, and the Irish coast.

The difference between the times of high water west of Kintyre and in the Firth of Clyde cause strong tidal streams off the Mull; the swell and the prevailing westerly winds ensure that conditions inshore are rarely peaceful.

The simple tactic of passing the point well offshore conflicts with the requirement to keep clear of a Traffic Separation Scheme the east end of which is only 2 miles southwest of the Mull of Kintyre.

Between the Clyde and the west coast of Scotland the passage round the Mull presents a challenge, but there is always the alternative of using the Crinan Canal. However, many local yachtsmen still prefer to go round the Mull; some consider the canal to be more of a challenge!

On passage between the North Channel and the west coast of Scotland the obvious passage is outside the Mull, but if the weather is unfavourable you can take the alternative route by way of Kilbrannan Sound and the canal.

The sequence followed in this chapter is through Kilbrannan Sound from north to south; Campbeltown Loch; round the Mull of Kintyre and northwards along the west side of Kintyre.

SHELTER

Campbeltown Loch provides excellent shelter (although some sea works in with strong easterly winds) and easy access by day or night.

Carradale Harbour in Kilbrannan Sound provides shelter except from strong northerly winds.

See also Chapter VI for Islay and Gigha.

Kilbrannan Sound

55°35′N 5°25′W

In the passage between the east side of Kintyre and the island of Arran any wind tends to be deflected along the line of the sound and increased in velocity. Erins Bank in the middle of the north part of the sound causes overfalls. Tidal streams generally do not exceed ½ knot.

CHART

2126, 2131 (1:75,000), 2221 (1:36,000)

DANGERS AND MARKS

Skipness Point at the north end of the sound has a red can light buoy off its south side, and radio masts and light beacons 1½ miles north of the point.

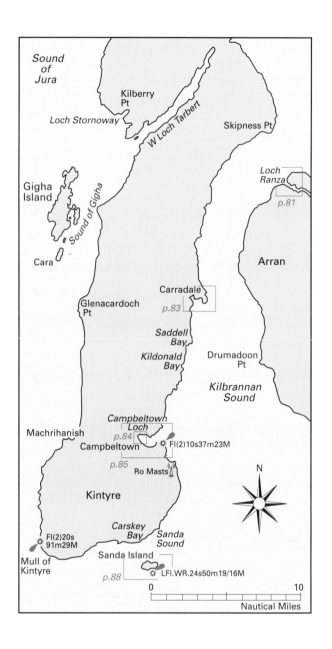

Crubon Rock red can light buoy lies off Carradale Point on the west side of the Sound. Note: this buoy may be withdrawn.

Ross Island, a rock with a jagged outline nearly 4 miles north of Island Davaar is conspicuous from north or south.

Iron Rock Ledges, submerged and drying rocks, extending several cables off the southwest side of Arran between Pladda and Blackwaterfoot are marked by a green conical light buoy nearly a mile offshore, 7 miles west of Pladda.

Otterard Rock with a least depth of 3·2 metres, northeast of the entrance to Campbeltown Loch is marked by an east cardinal light buoy. Unmarked rocks, 1¼ miles north of Island Davaar, lie more than 3 cables offshore.

Island Davaar lighthouse is a conspicuous white tower 20 metres high on Island Davaar at the south side of the entrance to Campbeltown Loch.

LIGHTS

Skipness Calibration Range, ¼ mile NNE of Skipness Point shows Iso.R.8s7m10M 292°-vis-312°, together with an Oc(2)Y.10s24M when the range is in use.
Skipness Point light buoy Fl.R.4s
Port Crannaich breakwater Fl.R.10s5m6M
Crubon Rock light buoy Fl(2)R.12s
Iron Rock Ledges light buoy Fl.G.6s
Otterard Rock east cardinal light buoy Q(3)10s
Island Davaar lighthouse Fl(2)10s37m23M

Loch Ranza

55°43′N 5°18′W

A popular anchorage at the northwest of Arran but subject to violent squalls in offshore winds. Drying and submerged rocks extend about a cable south of Newton Point at the north side of the entrance.

The pier at the south side of the entrance is ruined and unsafe marked by lights 2F.R(vert), and a car ferry operates from a slip at the east side of the pier. At night the ferry usually lies at a mooring in the

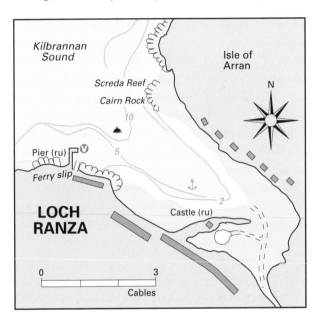

Loch Ranza from northwest at high water (1987)

middle of the loch, but sometimes inside the head of the pier.

The bottom, particularly on the north side is very soft mud, and dragging the anchor is a common experience there. The south shore dries out in places about a cable. A line of permanent moorings lies on the south west side of the middle of the loch, and a line of visitors' moorings on the north east side.

The pool east of the castle has a drying bar and a yacht on a mooring occupies the pool. Yachts able to dry out might have a quiet night aground there if the tide serves, but it should be inspected at low tide first.

TIDES

Constant +0005 Greenock (+0120 Dover)

Height in metres

MHWS	MHWN	MTL	MLWN	MLWS
3·4	2·9	1·9	1·1	0·3

Supplies

Shops (licensed grocer, butcher), post office, telephone.

Carradale Harbour (Port Crannaich)

55°36′N 5°28′W

A small harbour formed by a sheet-piled breakwater a mile north of Carradale Point. Nearly half the width of the harbour dries but there is about 3 metres alongside the breakwater. Fishing boats congregate here particularly at weekends, but yachts are now more welcome.

Light

Fl.R.10s5m6M at the end of the breakwater

Supplies

Shops, post office, telephone, hotels, *Calor Gas*, water.

The head of Loch Ranza from southwest, showing drying banks below water (1988)

Torrisdale Bay and Carradale Bay

55°34′N 5°29′W

Depending on wind direction anchor as depth allows off Torrisdale Castle, a large stone house in the southwest corner of the bay, or in the northeast corner of Carradale Bay. Shoal draft boats may be able to lie in the small river at Waterfoot, in the west corner of the bay, which within living memory was used by 60-foot fishing boats. Keep close to south shore to avoid sand spit on north side of river mouth.

Carradale Harbour (2006)

Waterfoot, Torrisdale Bay (2006)

Waterfoot, Torrisdale Bay river entrance (2006)

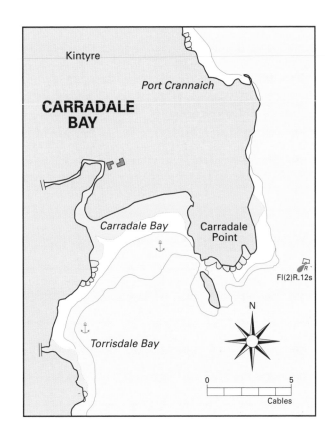

Blackwaterfoot (2006)

Occasional anchorages in southern part of sound

Blackwaterfoot, on Arran ESE of Drumadoon Point, has a tiny boat harbour at the mouth of a river, where sailing coasters used to be towed in by rowing boats. The entrance channel is marked on both sides by posts or withies. The harbour might be used by trailer-sailers. There are shoal rocky patches offshore, but keel boats can anchor off the river mouth in quiet weather.

Saddell Bay, 2¾ miles south of Carradale Point.

Kildonald Bay, 2 miles south of Saddell Bay, with some shelter from south behind Ross Island, but drying rocks lie on the south side of the bay.

Campbeltown Loch

55°25'N 5°35'W

CHART
1864 (1:12,500)

TIDES
Constant +0010 Greenock (+0125 Dover)

Height in metres

MHWS	MHWN	MTL	MLWN	MLWS
2·9	2·6	1·8	1·1	0·6

Off the east side of Island Davaar tidal streams run at up to 2 knots on the flood (northward) and 3 knots on the ebb (southward) with overfalls off the southeast point of the island on the ebb. In strong onshore winds the sea surges round the north end of the island, so give it a good berth, as far as the middle of the channel.

DANGERS AND MARKS
A well sheltered loch on the east side of Kintyre 9 miles north of Sanda Island, identified by a conspicuous lighthouse on the north side of Island Davaar at its entrance.

Otterard Rock with a least depth of 3·2 metres, 1½ miles NNE of Island Davaar lighthouse, is marked by an east cardinal light buoy.

Occasional anchorage in Kildalloig Bay southwest of Island Davaar with some shelter from northwest from the Doirlinn except at high water. An underwater cable, probably well buried, crosses the bay in about 3 metres.

A cable northeast of Macringan's Point on the north side of the entrance Yellow Rocks just dry, but are clear of the channel unless you are tacking or approaching from north very close inshore.

Millmore Bank, marked by a stone beacon and a red light buoy 4 cables west of Island Davaar, intrudes into the south side of the channel.

Millbeg Bank a cable NNW of the red buoy is marked by a green light buoy on the north side of the channel.

West of Millmore Bank the loch opens out; Methe Bank Isolated Danger light buoy 3 cables WSW of Millmore Beacon is of no significance to yachts.

The NATO pier is prominent on the south shore.

Trench Point on the north shore is prominent and a green conical light buoy lies off the end of the point.

A green conical beacon stands near the east end of a drying bank east of Trench Point.

LIGHTS
Otterard Rock light buoy Q(3)10s

Island Davaar lighthouse Fl(2)10s37m23M, obscured from south of 330°

Millmore Bank light buoy Fl.R.10s

Millbeg Bank light buoy Fl.G.2·5s

Methe Bank light buoy Fl.(2)6s

Trench Point light buoy Fl.G.6s

NATO Pier Q.R.7m2M at each end of head

Ldg Lts 240·3° on the south shore are both F.Y.7/28m6M

The naval mooring buoy ½ mile southeast of New Quay is unlit.

Campbeltown Harbour

The harbour, on the southwest shore, consists of two stone quays 7 cables west of Trench Point, Old Quay to the northwest and New Quay to the southeast; the head of Old Quay is used by coasters.

Most of the harbour dries although part of its seaward side has been dredged to 4m.

A terminal for a car ferry to Northern Ireland was constructed at New Pier but is disused at present.

A very large mooring buoy lies 2 cables off the southwest shore ½ mile southeast of New Quay.

Lights at the harbour
New Quay 2F.R(vert)5m4M
Old Quay 2F.G(vert)7m4M

Berths
A pontoon is provided for visiting yachts north west of Old Quay as shown on the plan. The quays are heavily used by fishing boats and yachts moored there may be asked to move.

The head of the loch beyond the harbour is shoal; Campbeltown Sailing Club has moorings east of Dalintober Pier but no visitors' moorings.

Anchorages
Anchorage may be found between Old Quay and the sewer outfall towards Dalintober Pier, but taking care not to be too far inshore, and clear of access to Old Quay and the way out for the lifeboat.

Alternatively about a cable offshore southeast of New Quay. About 4 cables west of NATO Pier the wreck of a submarine is a hazard.

Yachts at anchor must show an anchor light as fishing boats use the harbour at night.

Larger yachts (over 12 metres) should contact the harbourmaster before approaching the harbour.

Supplies and services
Shops, post office, bank, telephone, hotel, *Calor Gas*, petrol, diesel; water at southeast end of green shed on the head of Old Quay. EC Wednesday, harbourmaster ☎ 01586 552552.

Showers at Royal Hotel, White Hart, sailing club and public swimming pool.

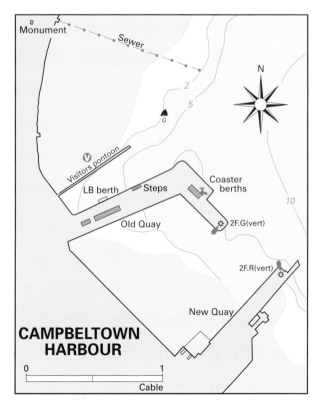

Campbeltown Harbour   *Patrick Roach*

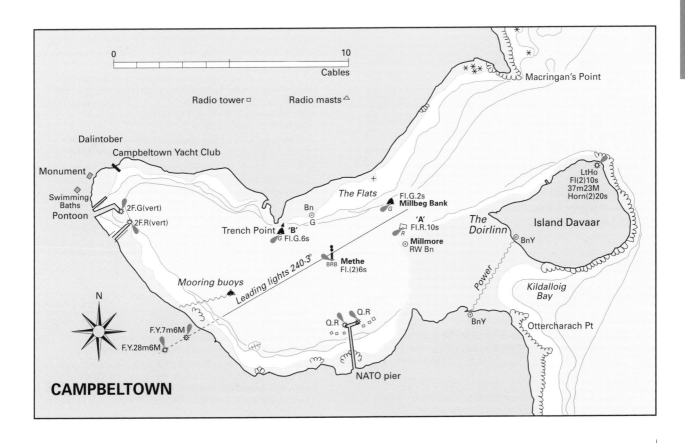

Campbeltown Loch and Davaar Lighthouse

Electronics and marine engineers at the harbour. Marine surveyor. S C McAlister, also responsible for visitors' pontoon, ☎ 01586 552131, mobile 07798 524821. CMC ship chandlers ☎ 01586 551441. Marine electrical engineer Mackinlay and Blair ☎ 01586 552012. Marine electronics engineer L & A Marine ☎ 01586 554479. Campbeltown Sailing Club (Secretary) ☎ 01586 550464.

Slip at harbour suitable for large motor yachts; small boats can dry out beside harbour wall.

Air service to Glasgow twice daily on weekdays; bus to Glasgow three times a day.

Sanda Sound and the Mull of Kintyre

CHARTS

2724 North Channel to the Firth of Lorne (1:200,000) is convenient for passage planning, but at a larger scale (1:75,000) three charts 2126, 2199 and 2798 all overlap at the Mull.

Imray's chart C63 takes you round the Mull to Gigha, and C64 overlaps it, covering from Sanda Island to Islay and Colonsay, together with part of the Ulster coast.

TIDES

In the middle of the North Channel and the Western Approaches spring tides run at over 3 knots and close inshore, over 5 knots.

Tides inshore turn more than an hour earlier than those offshore forming heavy overfalls in unsettled conditions at the boundary between the two streams.

At a point 2 miles SSW of the west end of Sanda the west-going stream begins about –0120 Greenock (HW Dover), and the east-going stream begins about +0440 Greenock (+0600 Dover). The spring rate in both directions is over 3 knots.

On the west side of Kintyre the north-going stream begins rather earlier and ends rather later.

In Sanda Sound the west-going stream begins about –0230 Greenock (–0110 Dover). The east-going stream begins about +0340 Greenock (+0500 Dover). In both directions this stream forms part of an inshore stream turning more than an hour earlier than the streams further offshore with severe turbulence at the boundaries.

Races form on the ebb north of Sheep Island and north of Sanda.

DANGERS AND MARKS

Ru Stafnish on the east side of Kintyre, 5½ miles NNE of Sanda, is identified by three radio masts on a hill ½ mile to the west.

Apart from the general sea conditions the principal dangers are all near Sanda and Sanda Sound.

In Sanda Sound rocks awash and drying extend up to ¼ mile from the mainland from the Arranman Barrels 2¼ miles NNE of Sanda, marked by a red can light buoy, to Macosh Rock northwest of Sanda, also marked by a red can light buoy.

Dun na h-Oighe, a prominent knob on the shore west of Arranman Barrels, is a useful reference point when coming from the north. A radio mast stands near the shore north of Macosh Rock buoy.

Sheep Island, north of Sanda, has drying rocks on all sides, those to the north extending ½ cable. Paterson's Rock dries a mile east of Sanda, marked by a red can light buoy.

Sanda Island lighthouse stands on a rocky promontory (known as 'The Ship') on the south side of Sanda at a height of 50 metres.

Mull of Kintyre lighthouse stands on a steep hillside on the west side of the Mull of Kintyre at a height of 90 metres and is not visible from east of 350°.

The eastern extremity of the Traffic Separation Scheme lies 2¼ miles southwest of Mull of Kintyre lighthouse, limiting the distance off the point at which yachts may round the point unless passing along the northwest-going lane of the scheme.

PASSAGE PLANNING

Sanda, the only anchorage near the Mull, provides less than complete shelter, but is considered an excellent anchorage in settled conditions or if the wind is southerly. The bottom is clean sand and Sanda is used regularly as a staging post for yachts on passage round the Mull.

Distances between anchorages are more significant than is usual on the west coast of Scotland. The shortest distance between anchorages (other than Sanda) on a passage round the Mull is 44 miles.

The distance from a point 1 mile southeast of Arranman Barrels to a point 2 miles southwest of Mull of Kintyre lighthouse is about 11 miles.

From Cove Point southeast of Arranman Barrels to Campbeltown Harbour is 11 miles and to Lamlash Harbour on the east side of Arran 24 miles.

The distance from the point 2 miles southwest of Mull of Kintyre lighthouse to each of the following anchorages is about 24 miles: Ardminish Bay, Gigha; Loch an t-Sailein, Islay; Port Ellen, Islay.

Allowance should be made for sudden, unforecast changes of weather partly because they are more inclined to happen at a turning point such as the Mull and partly because the distance from shelter is greater than usual.

From the Clyde to the west side of Kintyre, if the wind is southwesterly, there is little point in using Sanda Sound. The tidal stream will be either against you or against the wind; no distance would be saved if tacking and motoring would be uncomfortable (to say the least).

Local yachtsmen, however, usually take the inshore passages at Sanda and the Mull, preferring to endure discomfort and save distance. Some people who have been round the Mull many times profess to find nothing to it, and others recount the most picturesque horror stories. It depends partly on luck and partly, no doubt, on the temperament of the storyteller.

The southwest-going tide sets across Paterson's Rock and the buoy is moored south of the rock. For a clearing mark, the east point of Island Davaar open of Ru Stafnish astern leads 1¼ miles east of Paterson's Rock.

Pass at least ½ mile east of Paterson's Rock buoy and a mile south of Sanda, or 2 miles off if the wind is more than Force 3; plan to be south of Sanda about the time that the tide turns to the west.

When the Mull of Kintyre lighthouse comes into sight, the temptation to bear away too soon should be resisted; pass two miles off it, to avoid a south-going eddy inshore.

If the wind is northwesterly Sanda Sound can be used, but if it is any more than light, conditions will probably be unattractive when the west side of the Mull is

Mull of Kintyre lighthouse (1997)

opened up. Standing further offshore will take you into the Traffic Separation Scheme.

Moderate winds between northeast and south present little problem; if making for Gigha or the Sound of Jura in wind directions except between south and west aim to be at the east end of Sanda Sound 2½ hours before HW Greenock.

If making for Islay aim to be clear of the Mull of Kintyre by 4½ hours after HW Greenock, but if late keep well clear of the east-going stream inshore; an adverse tide in the deep water clear of the Mull is much weaker than near the shore.

Passages beyond the Mull are generally straightforward but if there is a heavy swell it will be steeper near the shore.

For the south and east of Islay, the Sound of Islay, and the Sound of Jura see the respective following chapters.

The passage eastward presents fewer problems if only in that easterly winds do not blow from the open sea, but a following westerly wind can build up overwhelming seas.

LIGHTS AROUND THE MULL

At night the waters around the Mull of Kintyre are well provided with powerful lights, but in an area ENE of Sanda Sound three out of the four nearest lights are obscured.

For more than 5 miles northeast of Sanda, Sanda Island lighthouse, Island Davaar and Ailsa Craig lights are all obscured, leaving only Pladda visible, at least 13 miles away, and the two light buoys in Sanda Sound.
Mull of Kintyre Fl(2)20s91m29M
Sanda Island LFl.WR.24s50m19/16M; flash is 8 seconds long. Light is obscured from northeast of 245°, red 245°-267° and white elsewhere.
Arranman Barrels buoy Fl(2)R.12s
Macosh Rock buoy Fl.R.6s
Paterson's Rock Fl(3)R.18s

MORE DISTANT LIGHTS

Altacarry Head Fl(4)20s74m26M; the northeast point of **Rathlin Island**, 12 miles west of Mull of Kintyre
Rue Point Fl(2)5s16m14M; the southeast point of Rathlin Island
Island Davaar Fl(2)10s37m23M obscured from south of 330°; Campbeltown Loch, 9 miles north of Sanda
Ailsa Craig Fl(6)30s18m17M 028°-obscd-145°; 16 miles east of Sanda

Sanda Island

55°17′N 5°35′W

TIDES

Constant –0040 Greenock (+0035 Dover)
Height in metres (estimated)

MHWS	MHWN	MTL	MLWN	MLWS
2·4	2·0	1·4	0·6	0·4

Anchorage

Sanda Island's anchorage is in a bay on the north side of the island.

A reef off the west point of the bay is marked by a green iron beacon with a ball topmark, well inshore of the edge of the reef.

There are drying rocks both in the middle of the bay and at the southeast side. A mooring buoy for the island's service boat lies between the pier and the drying rock in the middle of the bay. This buoy in line with the Boathouse at the south side of the bay, bearing about 164°, leads to a suitable anchorage. Enter from due north along the west side to avoid the drying rocks and anchor northeast of the stone pier. Some swell is likely under most conditions.

Pub meals by arrangement, internet access, most emergency services ☎ 01586 554667 *mobile* 07810 356278.

Other anchorages

Carskey Bay provides temporary anchorage on the mainland shore northwest of Sanda Island and is said to be clear of tide.

The bay lies off low ground at the mouth of a valley ¼ mile west of the conspicuous white hotel at Southend village.

Carskey Rocks dry 2 cables off the west side of the bay and a submerged reef lies off Keil Point at its east side. Some supplies may be found at Southend village.

South Bay, Sanda, east of the lighthouse, provides shelter from northwest winds, but rocks drying up to ¼ mile lie east of its southwest point.

Machrihanish Bay, on the west side of the Mull of Kintyre at the south end of sand dunes 7½ miles north of Mull of Kintyre lighthouse, provides temporary anchorage to wait for more favourable conditions to round the Mull southward, but can be a trap if the wind comes onshore, or particularly if any swell comes into the bay.

Skerrivore rocks extend 4 cables northwest from the southwest point of the bay and submerged rocks lie up to 2 cables off the south shore. Anchor off the mouth of a burn at the southeast side of the bay.

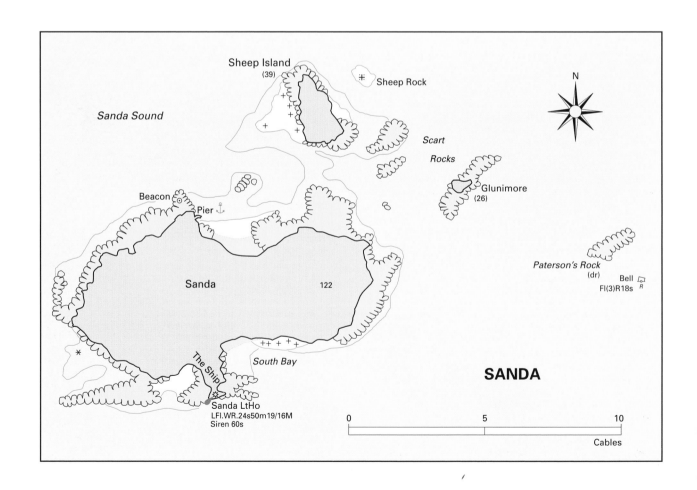

Sanda Island. Note the reef in the middle of the bay is covered, but the mooring off the pier in line with the boathouse leads west of it (2006)

Machrihanish Bay. Note Skerrivore Rocks are covered (2006)

VI. Gigha, West Loch Tarbert and the East Coast of Islay

CHART

2168 (1:75,000),

Caution Chart 2168 is the only one published and is at quite an inadequate scale for exploring inshore. The sketch plans for the east coast of Islay are based on Admiralty surveys of about 1860, together with air photographs and personal visits, but not a detailed recent survey.

TIDES

Between Islay and Kintyre and through the Sound of Jura as far as Fladda the rise and fall of tides is related to a phenomenon known as an amphidrome which is a tidal pivot point where the range is nil. This occurs about halfway between Port Ellen and the Mull of Kintyre, but its exact location moves during the tidal cycle; there is less range of tide on the southeast coast of Islay at the time of spring tides because the amphidrome is nearer to Islay at that time. This (rather simplified) is the reason for the curious observation which used to appear in the Admiralty Tide Tables that 'it is neaps at Port Ellen when it is springs at Machrihanish'.

Sound of Gigha

55°41′N 5°44′W

Gigha is a pleasantly pastoral island with famous subtropical gardens particularly worth visiting especially in May and June.

The main anchorages are on the east side of the island and are uncomfortable in winds from that direction.

CHARTS

2475 (1:25,000), 2168 (1:75,000)

TIDES

The north-going stream begins +0430 Oban (−0100 Dover), and the south-going stream begins −0200 Oban (+0500 Dover).

Constant varies between approximately −0200 Oban (+0500 Dover) at springs, and −0500 Oban (+0300 Dover) at neaps.

Height in metres

MHWS	MHWN	MTL	MLWN	MLWS
1·5	1·3	1·0	0·8	0·6

DIRECTIONS

The sound has the reputation of being difficult to navigate but aids to navigation have been greatly improved, and in moderate weather and reasonable visibility will present little difficulty.

The usual passages and anchorages are on the west side of the sound and shoals and rocks near the mainland side are not described.

To make the information more digestible the approaches from the south and from the north are described separately.

DANGERS AND MARKS AT THE SOUTH END OF THE SOUND

Sgeir an Tru, an unmarked rock drying 1·2 metres, lies ¼ mile off the mainland shore, southeast of Cara.

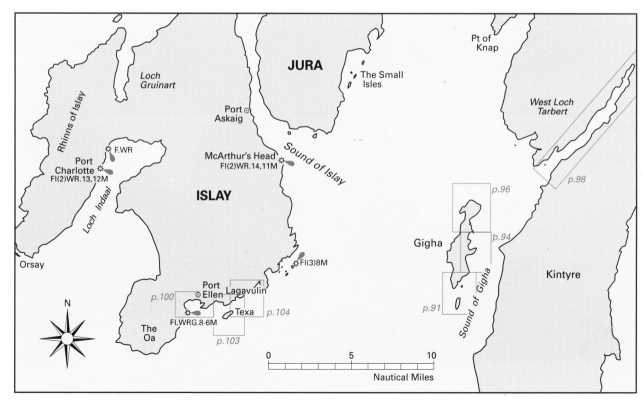

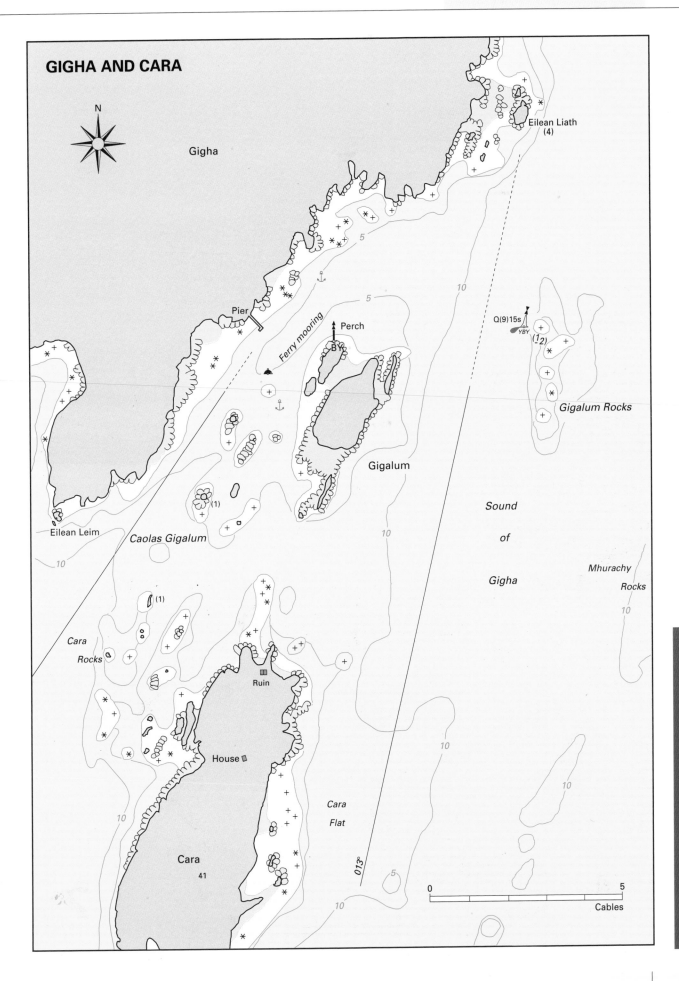

GIGHA AND CARA

Gigha

N

Eilean Liath
(4)

5

10

Pier

Ferry mooring

Perch

B

Q(9)15s
YBY
(12)

Gigalum Rocks

Gigalum

Sound

of

Gigha

Mhurachy

Rocks

10

10

Eilean Leim

10

Caolas Gigalum

(1)

10

(1)

Cara
Rocks

Ruin

013°

House

Cara
Flat

10

Cara

41

5

0   5

Cables

10

Cara and Gigha from south (1985)

The east side of Cara, the most southerly island off Gigha, is clean outwith ½ cable from its east shore, except for a submerged rock 1·8 metres just over a cable northeast of the island.

The east side of Gigalum, north of Cara is clean, and Gigalum Rocks, 4 cables east of Gigalum are marked on their west side by a west cardinal light buoy.

Wee Rocks lie east of Gigalum Rocks, and Sgeir Gigalum lies about a mile northeast of the light buoy.

At Eilean Liath, a group of islets off the east side of Gigha ½ mile NNE of Gigalum, a drying rock lies ¼ cable ENE of Eilean Liath itself.

Approach from south

West side Keep at least a mile off the mainland shore to avoid Sgeir an Tru. Pass at least 2 cables east of Cara and steer to keep Eilean Liath ahead in line with Ardminish Point 1½ miles further north bearing 013°. Pass west of Gigalum Rocks buoy and alter course to pass a cable east of Eilean Liath to avoid the drying rock referred to above.

East side The east side of the sound could be safely negotiated, once Sgeir an Tru is passed, by following the 10-metre contour.

Lights

Gigalum Rocks west cardinal buoy is lit Q(9)15s.
A row of five street lights at Ardminish ferry slip are normally left on at night.

Caolas Gigalum

55°39′N 5°45′W

Caolas Gigalum, the sound separating Cara and Gigalum from Gigha, is full of rocks, most of them above water but less than a metre high. The simplest approach is from the north. Anchor no closer to Gigha than the end of the pier.

Rocks, mostly above water, extend ¼ mile WNW of Cara leaving a passage 3 cables wide southeast of Gigha, but the approach from the southwest is reasonably straightforward. Further north rocks southwest of Gigalum only 0·3 and 0·6 metres high lie within 1½ cables of Gigha, but the most westerly of these is marked by a thin steel perch.

The pier is constructed of concrete piles which are not convenient to lie alongside. There is no regular steamer service, but a boat should not be left unattended at the pier. The berth on the north side, with a depth of about 1·2 metres, is used for fuelling. A berth on the southwest side on the inner side of the pier head has a low-level landing platform and steps and the depth there also appears to be 1·2 metres.

In easterly winds some shelter may be found north of the 3-metre-high rock near the west side of Gigalum, but look out for a submerged rock between the 3-metre rock and the ferry mooring.

Supplies at Ardminish, except for water which is at this pier.

Caolas Gigalum from north, with Eilean Liath in the foreground (2006)

Ardminish

55°40′N 5°44′W

The most popular anchorage on Gigha, with visitors' moorings. Both points of the entrance are very foul; drying rocks extend a cable north of the most northerly rock above water at the south point, marked by an unlit red can buoy; submerged and drying rocks extend a cable southeast from the north point.

Ardminish Bay from southeast   *Patrick Roach*

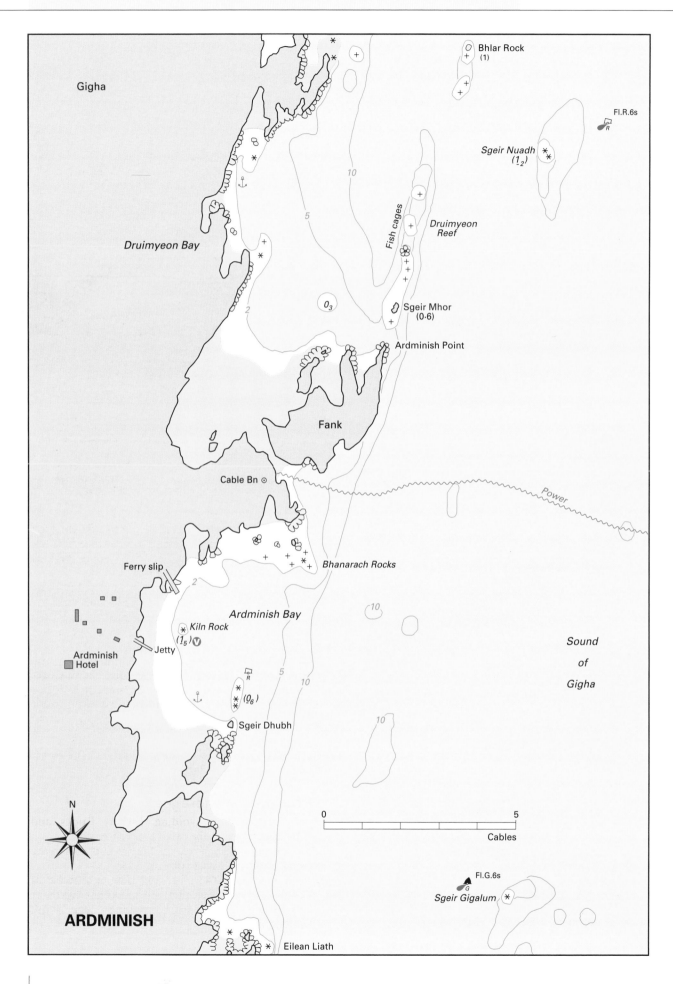

Gigha

Bhlar Rock
(1)

Fl.R.6s
R

Sgeir Nuadh
(1₂)

10

Fish cages

Druimyeon
Reef

Druimyeon Bay

5

2

0₃

Sgeir Mhor
(0·6)

Ardminish Point

Fank

Cable Bn ⊙

Power

Ferry slip

Bhanarach Rocks

2

Ardminish Bay

10

Sound

Kiln Rock
(1₅) Ⓥ

Ardminish
Hotel

Jetty

of

R

Gigha

(0₆)

5

10

Sgeir Dhubh

10

N

0   5
Cables

Fl.G.6s
G
Sgeir Gigalum

ARDMINISH

Eilean Liath

Kiln Rock (Sgeir na h-Atho) dries 1·5 metres close north of the visitors' moorings, a cable ENE of the old ferry jetty at the middle of the west side of the bay.

There is space for anchoring south of the moorings but the southwest side of the bay is shoal, although clean sand apart from obvious rocks.

Keep clear of the approach to the car ferry slip.

Supplies

Shop and post office, telephone, hotel, *Calor Gas* and petrol at shop, water tap on east wall of the Boathouse tea room (stone building by the old jetty); refuse disposal at Boathouse. Water at Caolas Gigalum pier; showers and washing machines at the Boathouse.

Port Mor, at the north end of Gigha (2006)

Eilean Garbh on the west side of Gigha

Druimyeon Bay

55°41′.5N 5°43′W

More peaceful than Ardminish but not very convenient to find a way ashore.

From the north approach by the northwest side of Bhlar Rock.

From the south pass between Ardminish Point and Sgeir Mhor (0·6 metres high) which lies ¼ cable from the point, but keep closer to Ardminish Point to avoid a rock spit extending south from Sgeir Mhor.

A submerged rock with a depth of only 0·3m lies a cable offshore nearly 2 cables northwest of Ardminish Point, and drying rocks lie ½ cable northeast of Rubha Breac.

Fish cages are moored west of Druimyeon Reef.

Good anchorage can be found close to the west shore north of Rubha Breac.

DANGERS AND MARKS AT THE NORTH END OF THE SOUND

An Dubh-sgeir, ½ mile north of Gigha is 3 metres high, with submerged and drying rocks around it.

Gamhna Gigha, 1¼ miles east of the north end of Gigha, is 2 metres high, with a light beacon on it.

Badh Rock, 1½ miles south of Gamhna Gigha, is marked on its west side by a starboard-hand light-buoy.

Bhlar Rock (Sgeir Blath-shuileach), 1 metre high, standing 8 cables WSW of Badh Rock, is the north end of a reef extending nearly a mile from the east side of Druimyeon Bay.

Sgeir Nuadh which dries 1·2 metres, 3 cables southeast of Bhlar Rock, and probably the most dangerous rock in the sound, is marked by a port-hand light-buoy.

Approach from north

Identify Gamhna Gigha and then Badh Rock buoy and pass within a cable west of it. Continue heading south for half a mile before altering course towards Eilean Liath to avoid Sgeir Nuadh.

If, in clear weather, you pass near the northeast point of Gigha and can identify Bhlar Rock on the horizon ahead, you may prefer to pass west of Sgeir Nuadh or straight into the north end of Druimyeon Bay.

To leave Gigha Sound from Ardminish by the north steer to keep Badh Rock buoy on the port bow, bearing not more than 030°, until it is in line with Gamhna Gigha and then pass west of the buoy.

Lights in the north part of Gigha Sound

Sgeir Nuadh light-buoy Fl.R.6s
Badh Rock Fl(2)G.12s
Gamhna Gigha Fl(2)6s7m5M

Occasional anchorages

East Tarbert Bay, avoiding Tarbert Rocks and shellfish floats in the middle of the bay.

Port Mor, at the north end of Gigha, and also in the small inlet northwest of Port Mor.

Eilean Garbh, 55°43′.5N 5°44′.5W, northwest of Gigha. In quiet weather anchor either north or south of the shingle spit connecting Eilean Garbh to Gigha.

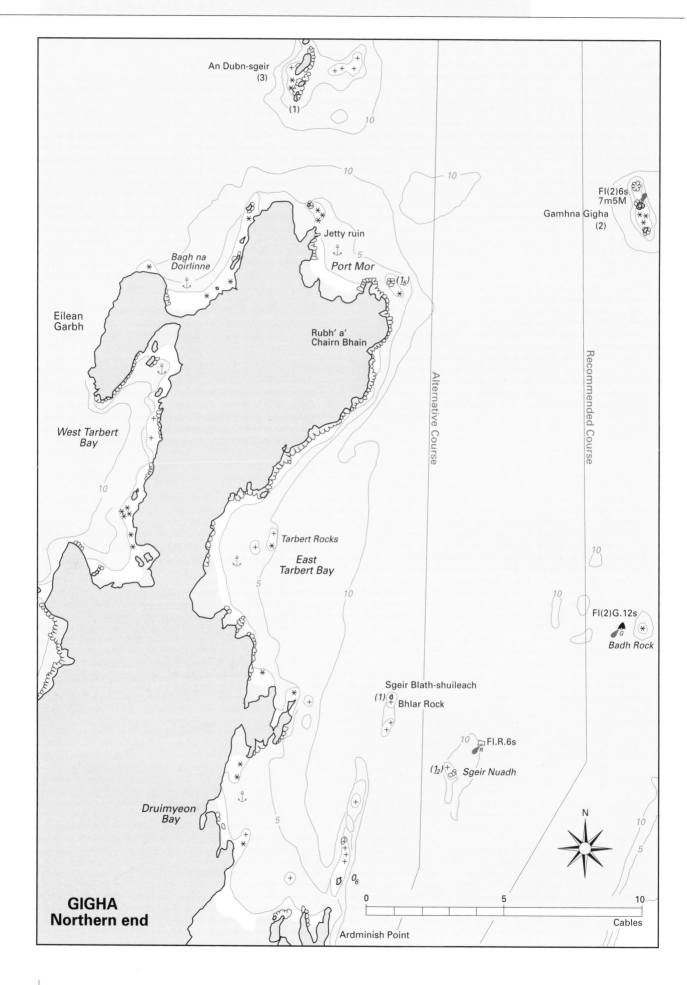

An Dubn-sgeir
(3)

(1)

10

10   10

Fl(2)6s
7m5M
Gamhna Gigha
(2)

Jetty ruin

Bagh na
Doirlinne

5

Port Mor

(1₅)

Eilean
Garbh

Rubh' a'
Chairn Bhain

Recommended Course

Alternative Course

West Tarbert
Bay

10

10

10

Tarbert Rocks

East
Tarbert Bay

10

5

Fl(2)G.12s

G
Badh Rock

Sgeir Blath-shuileach

(1) Bhlar Rock

10   Fl.R.6s
R

(1₂)   Sgeir Nuadh

Druimyeon
Bay

N

5

0₆

10

5

0   5   10

Cables

**GIGHA
Northern end**

Ardminish Point

West Loch Tarbert

55°45′N 5°36′W

A rather narrow, pleasantly wooded loch, with many hazards on either side, but well marked as far as the ferry terminal for Islay is halfway up the loch; a pier at the head is extensively used by fishing boats. Abandoned hulks of fishing boats restrict space for anchoring north east of the pier. Fish cages and shellfish floats are moored off both shores throughout the loch.

CHART

2477 (1:25,000)

TIDES

The in-going stream begins about +0430 Oban (−0100 Dover)

The out-going stream begins about −0200 Oban (+0500 Dover).

Constant is approximately −0200 Oban (+0500 Dover) at springs, −0500 Oban (+0300 Dover) at neaps.

Height in metres

MHWS	MHWN	MTL	MLWN	MLWS
1·5	1·3	1·0	0·8	0·6

DIRECTIONS

The entrance is identified by a conspicuous conical hill, Dun Skeig, 142 metres, on the south side of the entrance.

Approaching from north a light beacon (a steel column) must be identified 2 cables south of Eilean Traighe, a low island on the north side of the entrance.

Pass south of the Eilean Traighe beacon and well north of Corran Point beacon, a mile further northeast 1½ cables off the south shore.

For the next mile keep these two beacons in line astern to clear submerged and drying rocks 4 cables off the south shore. Note that close to Corran Point beacon this line leads over the edge of a drying bank.

Two further beacons at approximately 1½ mile intervals are passed, the first to port and the second to starboard. Kennacraig ferry terminal is ¼ mile further on the southeast shore, with a red light buoy ¼ mile northwest of it marking submerged and drying rocks which extend ½ mile from the northwest shore over a length of a mile.

Beyond Kennacraig the loch narrows and there are unmarked dangers, mostly on the north side. There are no beacons or buoys beyond Kennacraig.

The pier ¼ mile from the head of the loch is owned by Tarbert Fishermen's Association and is heavily used, particularly at weekends. Beyond the pier most of the loch dries.

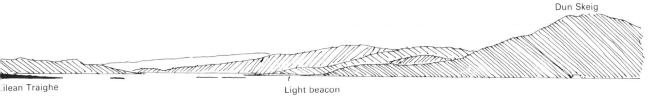

Dun Skeig

Eilean Traighe   Light beacon

West lock tarbert entrance

Head of West Loch Tarbert. Tarbert, Loch Fyne, is visible beyond the head of the loch (1987)

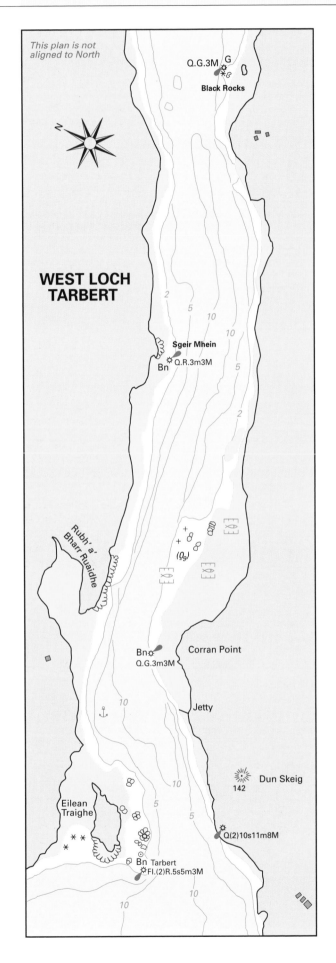

This plan is not aligned to North

N

Q.G.3M G

Black Rocks

WEST LOCH TARBERT

2
5
10
10
5

Sgeir Mhein
Bn Q.R.3m3M

2

Rubh' a' Bharr Ruaidhe

(0₉)

Bn
Q.G.3m3M
Corran Point

Jetty

10

Dun Skeig
142

Q(2)10s11m8M

Eilean Traighe

10
5
5

Bn Tarbert
Fl.(2)R.5s5m3M

10

10

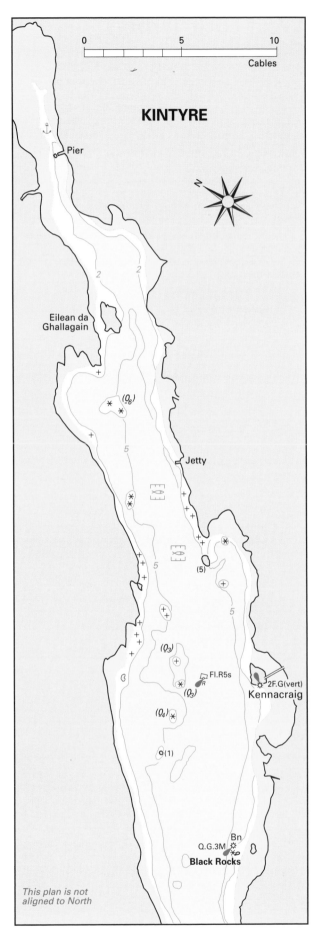

KINTYRE

0   5   10
Cables

Pier

N

Eilean da Ghallagain

(0₆)

2   2

Jetty

5

(0₉)

(5)

5

(0₃)

Fl.R5s

(0₃)

2F.G(vert)
Kennacraig

(0₄)

0(1)

Bn
Q.G.3M

Black Rocks

This plan is not aligned to North

West Loch Tarbert entrance. Eilean Traighe at left

West Loch Tarbert pier

Anchorages and moorings

Northeast of Eilean Traighe, sand and weed. It is disturbed by wash from ferries and fishing boats, as is any part of the loch, but especially southwest of Kennacraig.

Head of the loch, beyond the pier, closer to the southeast shore. Yachts should not be left unattended alongside the pier; you may come back to find six fishing boats rafted up outside you. Water at pier; supplies and services at Tarbert, 1½ miles from the pier (see Chapter IV).

Loch Stornoway provides an occasional anchorage in settled weather with a fine white sandy beach but is dramatically labelled 'dangerous' on the chart.

Drying rocks extend a cable north of Sgeir Choigreach, the outer islet on the south side of the entrance, but Montgomerie Rocks on the north side may extend further south than shown and it is recommended to keep closer to the islets. Clear out if any sea is coming in.

Southeast coast of Islay

The southeast of Islay is rich in history – and distilleries. Dunyveg Castle at the entrance to Lagavulin Bay was the headquarters of the Lords of the Isles after the Norsemen were defeated at the Battle of Largs in 1263, and the finest carved medieval stone cross in Scotland is at Kildalton Chapel, near Port Mor and Glas Uig, north of Ardmore.

The inner passages between Ardmore and Port Ellen have been used by local fishermen and traders for centuries, but have only been brought to the notice of yachtsmen in the last few years by Michael Gilkes.

The Ardmore Isles and the passage inshore of them are designated as a Special Area of Conservation.

There is no published chart of the area at a larger scale than *2168* (1:75,000), but Ordnance Survey *Explorer* map (scale 1:25,000) *No.352* Islay South provides useful detail of this part of the coast.

There are strong tidal streams nearby, in particular at the Oa and the Rhinns of Islay, at the Mull of Kintyre, and in the Sound of Islay.

At Otter Rock the streams run east and west. The west-going stream begins about +0530 Oban (HW Dover) and the east-going stream begins about –0110 Oban (+0610 Dover).

Off Texa Island, tidal streams split, one stream running towards Ardmore, the other towards Rubha nan Leacan at the southeast point of the Oa beginning at about +0530 Oban (HW Dover), and running from those points towards Texa beginning about –0030 Oban (–0600 Dover).

DANGERS AND MARKS

Dangers and marks related to an extended coastal passage are described in sequence from The Oa to Ardmore. Those related to individual anchorages and inshore passages will be described separately.

The Oa, the south point of Islay, which rises to 200 metres, has a tall stone monument at Mull of Oa, its southwest point.

Otter Rock, with a least depth of 3·7 metres, 3 miles south of Texa, is marked by a south cardinal light buoy.

Texa Island is 2 miles east of Port Ellen. Tarr Sgeir, a detached rock 4 metres high, lies 6 cables south of Texa and there are other rocks between Tarr Sgeir and Texa.

Iomallach, 2 metres high, 1¾ miles ENE of the northeast end of Texa and a mile south of Ard Imersay lies at the extremity of an area of rocks south and southwest of Ard Imersay. A detached shoal patch of rock lies southwest of Iomallach and Ruadh Mor, 4 cables southwest of Iomallach has a depth of only 2·1 metres.

Ardmore Point is the most easterly point of Islay. Eilean a'Chuirn, nearly a mile south of Ardmore and 5 miles northeast of Texa, is the most easterly of the Ardmore Islands. Eilean a'Chuirn light beacon is an inconspicuous tower.

The Ardmore Islands run northeast from Ceann nan Sgeirean, 1 mile northeast of Ard Imersay, for 1½ miles, and drying rocks lie up to 3 cables southeast of Ceann nan Sgeirean.

GIGHA, WEST LOCH TARBERT, ISLAY

Port Ellen

55°38′N 6°11′W

The main ferry terminal and harbour on Islay Pontoon berths have been established at the pier. In the photo the finger pontoons have been removed for additional dredging.

CHART

Plan on 2474 (1:15,000)

TIDES

Constant –0530 Oban (+0130 Dover) at springs, and –0050 Oban (+0610 Dover) at neaps.

Height in metres

MHWS	MHWN	MTL	MLWN	MLWS
0·9	0·8	0·6	0·5	0·3

DANGERS AND MARKS

See also the passage notes above, particularly for Otter Rock and Tarr Sgeir.

Carraig Fhada lighthouse, a rectangular white tower, marks the west point of the bay.

The outer limit of submerged and drying reefs extending WSW from the east side of the bay is marked by a green conical light buoy 3 cables 130° from Carraig Fhada.

Rocks above water and submerged extend up to ¼ mile off the west shore SSW of Carraig Fhada.

The Gander, 5 metres high, lies 1½ cables offshore and ½ mile SSW of the lighthouse, and Am Plodan, 0·6 metres high, lies 2½ cables offshore and 4 cables south of the lighthouse.

Otter Gander, with a depth of 2·6 metres, lies ½ mile offshore and 6 cables south of the lighthouse.

LIGHTS

Carraig Fhada (Port Ellen) Fl.WRG.3s19m9-6M
Otter Rock light buoy Q(6)+LFl.15s
Eilean a'Chuirn Fl(3)18s26m8M
Green con light buoy Q.G
Pier head 2F.G(vert)

Port Ellen Pier on the east side of the bay has some shelter from the south behind a line of islets and skerries.

Sgeir nan Ron, which lies a cable west of the pier, is marked by a red beacon with a ball topmark.

A submerged rock lies 2 cables west of this beacon, and north of the beacon there are many submerged and drying rocks.

Approach

From southeast, pass south of Tarr Sgeir 6 cables south of Texa and steer towards Carraig Fhada lighthouse; the lighthouse in line with a group of radio masts on the hill above bearing 310° will lead to the green conical light buoy.

From southwest, if The Gander can be identified, and then Am Plodan, pass a cable east of these rocks. Otherwise keep a mile offshore and approach as from southeast to avoid Otter Gander.

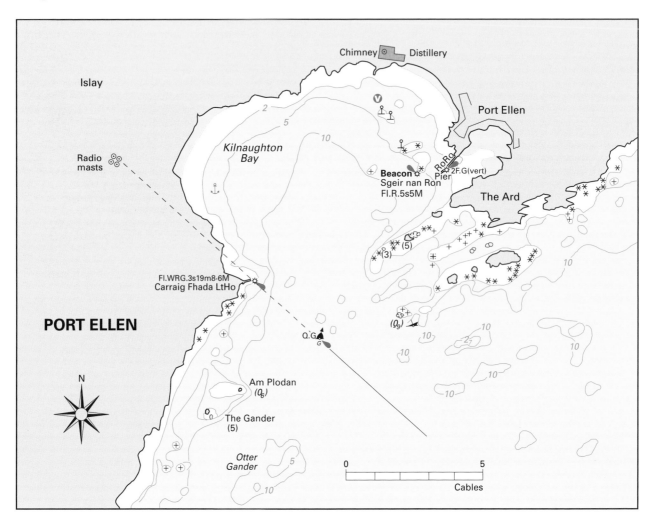

Port Ellen from seaward (2006)

Port Ellen approach from south east

Perch

Approach to Port Ellen

Port Ellen with only the spine jetty of marina in place (2006)

From the green entrance buoy (½M SE of Carraig Fhada lighthouse) steer north until on the line between the lighthouse and the main pierhead. Turn stbd to approx 060°. Approach the pierhead on that bearing, and pass between the south face of the pier and the three green stbd buoys, to the pontoons. Shallow areas lie very close to the south of the buoys, and to the east of the three red buoys which mark the anchors for the ground chains to the east of the pontoons.

Anchorages

In westerly winds some shelter will be found in Kilnaughton Bay 4 cables NNW of the lighthouse.

At the pier anchor close north of the innermost islet south of the pier, clear of the approach to the pier which is used by ferries and by fishing boats.

Visitors' moorings are laid off Port Ellen Distillery at the north side of the bay

Supplies

Shops, post office, telephone, hotels, *Calor Gas*, petrol, diesel at garage, water tap at pier head. Showers are available, and washing machines are being installed, at 39 Frederick Crescent, behind the CalMac office.

Caolas an Eilean

This passage, between Texa and Islay, is 4 cables wide but rocks above and below water lie on the Islay side.

A submerged rock a cable west of Texa, 2 cables south of a line from the north point of Texa to Port Ellen green buoy. At the east end of the passage continue ENE until Lagavulin bears 360°. Anchorage off stone jetty on Texa.

Lagavulin Bay and Loch an t-Sailean

Two distilleries will be seen, Lagavulin, and Ardbeg which is ¼ mile further northeast, both of which have their names conspicuously painted on the wall. Some yachts have encountered underwater obstructions in the entrance, but the following directions have been compiled from information provided by a yacht owner familiar with the bay.

TIDES
At Port Ellen

Constant –0530 Oban (+0130 Dover) at springs, and –0050 Oban (+0610 Dover) at neaps.

Height in metres

MHWS	MHWN	MTL	MLWN	MLWS
0·9	0·8	0·6	0·5	0·3

DANGERS

Rocks above and below water extend over a mile south and southwest from Ard Imersay, which separates Loch an t-Sailein from Loch a'Chnuic.

Iomallach, 2 metres high, is the outermost of these rocks above water. Submerged rocks extend 50 metres southwest from Iomallach, and Ruadh Mor, 4 cables southwest of Iomallach has a depth of 2·1 metres over it.

Approach

55°38′N 6°07′W

Two tripod beacons painted red and green stand in the entrance to Lagavulin Bay, and rocks on either side of the entrance are marked with paint, red to southwest (Gille na Fead) and green to northeast on a detached rock southwest of the castle. The red mark is conspicuous. The more easterly tripod beacon was missing in 2006 (and for several years previously) and replaced by a buoy but, with this information, you should be able to work your way in. From southwest keep at least a cable off the east

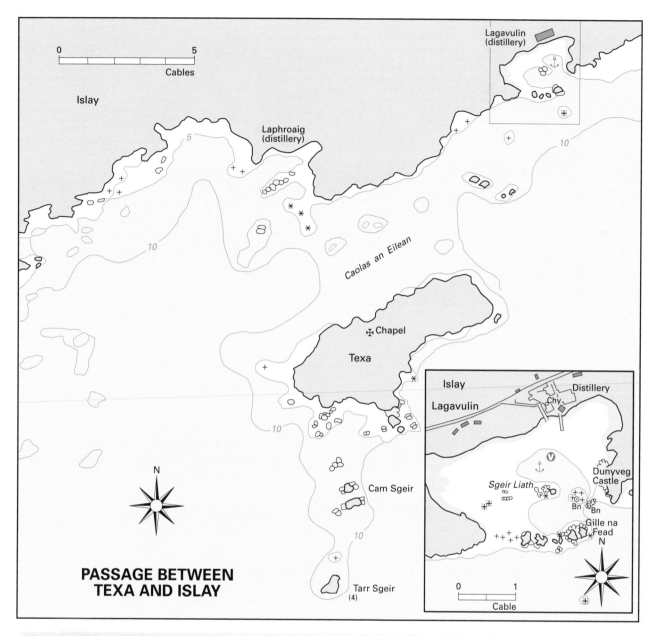

PASSAGE BETWEEN TEXA AND ISLAY

Iomallach, an essential landmark when approaching Lagavulin from northward. Texa on the left and Carraig Fhada lighthouse in the distance

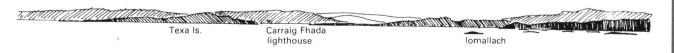

Carraig Fhada lighthouse just open north of Texa Island

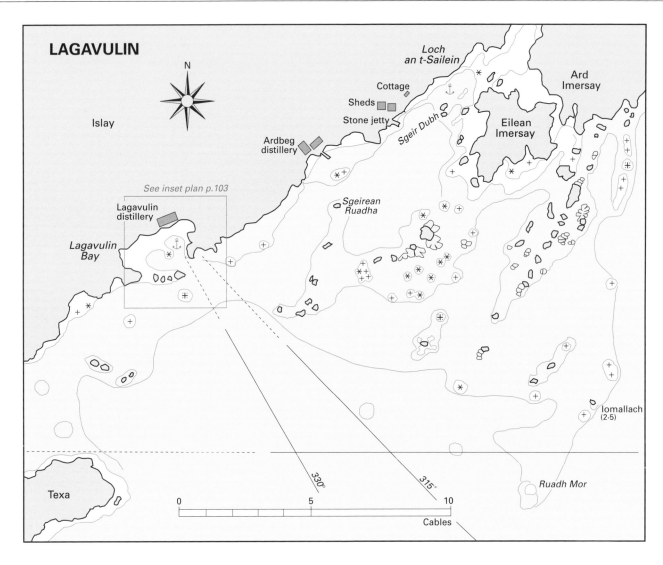

LAGAVULIN

N

Islay

Loch
an t-Sailein

Ard
Imersay

Cottage

Sheds

Stone jetty

Sgeir Dubh

Eilean
Imersay

Ardbeg
distillery

See inset plan p.103

Lagavulin
distillery

Sgeirean
Ruadha

Lagavulin
Bay

Iomallach
(2·5)

Texa

Ruadh Mor

330°   315°

0   5   10
Cables

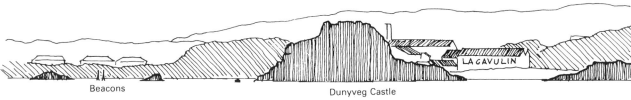

Beacons   Dunyveg Castle

LAGAVULIN

Approach to Lagavulin

Laphroaigh Distillery

Lagavulin Bay from the southeast. Dark patches on either side
of the approach are rocks, for which the text gives clearing marks

end of Texa and steer northeast until Lagavulin
bears 330° to avoid the rock awash south of Gille na
Fead. On this line only the letters LAGA should be
visible on the distillery wall.

From southeast steer with Lagavulin distillery
(taking care not to mistake Ardbeg for it) bearing
315° to pass clear southwest of Ruadh Mor; steer so
that only the letters ULIN are visible in the name on
the wall to the right of the castle.

From east or northeast pass a cable south of
Iomallach and steer west with the north point of
Texa Island in line with Carraig Fhada lighthouse at
Port Ellen. This course takes you over a rock with a

depth of 3·4 metres. Then steer as from southeast
above.

To make for Lagavulin, alter course to port to
keep the Lagavulin distillery chimney in line with the
right-hand beacon. Cross a line joining the two
beacons at an angle of less than 45°, passing 10-12
metres from the west beacon to avoid a large
boulder on the starboard side. Then steer with the
distillery pier 10° on the starboard bow, or direct for
the left-hand visitor's mooring. Do not stray to
starboard of this line. A shoal area of rocks lies on
the west side of the channel northeast of the W
beacon. The northeast part of the bay is very shoal.

Lagavulin Bay entrance

Lagavulin Bay from northwest (1999)

Anchorage and moorings – Lagavulin

Anchor north or northwest of Sgeir Liath in the middle of the bay, in about 2 metres. Mooring rings are fixed at the east and west ends of Sgeir Liath, and the distillery has laid two visitors' moorings marked LAG 1 and LAG 2 at the east side of the bay.

The depth at the head of the pier is 1·2m, and 1·5m on its west side and it may be used by yachts (at owner's risk).

Water is available, and tours of the distillery arranged, at the visitor centre.

Loch an t-Sailein

To make for Loch an t-Sailein turn not less than 90° to starboard as soon as the Lagavulin beacons come into line, to avoid submerged rocks inshore, and steer parallel to, and at least 2 cables off the shore.

Sgeir Ruadh, which stands just above water will be seen ahead, SSW of Ardbeg distillery, with the vestigial remains of an iron beacon, and other rocks which cover at HW about a cable to the south, as well as others about a cable to the north.

Pass *Sgeir Ruadh* on either hand and continue past a stone pier, and a white cottage to port, and Sgeir Dubh to starboard.

Anchor north of *Sgeir Dubh*, avoiding a rocky shelf off the Islay shore.

Ardbeg Distillery provides three visitors' moorings along the north west shore, north of an islet, Sgeir Dubh, off the Distillery Pier. Do not approach south west of Sgeir Dubh, where the apparent passage is foul with rocks. Pick-ups are not provided at the moorings, and yachts' crews should go ashore at the stone jetty south of the distillery. Note that a reef at the head of Loch an t'Sailein is also named Sgeir Dubh. The distillery incorporates a cafe. It is possible to lie alongside the stone pier in the mouth of Loch an t'Sailein (not the pier immediately in front of the distillery) but the stonework is rough. A phone box stands on the main road at the end of the road to the distillery.

The stone jetty at Ardbeg is rough but has deep water alongside

Loch an t-Sailein at Ardbeg showing rocks in the entrance.
Sgeir na Maodail lies at lower right with Sgeirean Rudha above

Passage inshore of Ardmore Islands

55°40′N 6°02′W

The features of this passage are not easy to distinguish and it should only be attempted for the first time in clear quiet weather. The description must be read with the plan.

TIDES

At Port Ellen

Constant –0530 Oban (+0130 Dover) at springs, and –0050 Oban (+0610 Dover) at neaps.

Height in metres

MHWS	MHWN	MTL	MLWN	MLWS
0·9	0·8	0·6	0·5	0·3

DANGERS AND MARKS

Drying rocks extend to 3 cables south of Ceann nan Sgeirean, the southwest end of Ardmore Islands.

Drying rocks 2 cables north of Eilean Bhride are marked by a tripod beacon; a shoal spit lies between 2 and 4 cables WSW of the tripod beacon, with charted depths of 2–3 metres.

A rock awash lies in the middle of the basin 3 cables southwest of Eilean Craobhach.

The passage between Eilean Craobhach and Islay is known as Caolas Port na Lice. Several lines of rocks lie on the southeast side of the passage of which the nearest may cover at a high spring tide. A shoal patch in the middle of the passage appears to be not less than 3 metres deep.

DIRECTIONS

From south or southwest pass east of Iomallach, head NNE to pass northwest of Ardmore Islands and continue as below.

From southeast, the detached islet Garbhsgeir Beg in line with the conical hill Cnoc Rhaonastil (The Cnoc) bearing 316° leads close southwest of drying rocks south of Ceann nan Sgeirean.

When Ceann nan Sgeirean is aft of the beam steer to pass northwest of the tripod beacon.

There is no clear mark to avoid the rock awash in the middle of the bay, but its west side should be cleared by keeping the tripod beacon astern in line with the east point of Eilean Bhride, bearing about 170°.

Steer on this line to within a cable of the skerries at Plod Sgeirean and then turn NNE to head for Caolas Port na Lice.

From northeast keep ½ cable from the southeast side of Ardmore Point to pass inside the line of rocks north of Eilean Craobhach, and outside a line of rocks which are within about 20 metres of Ardmore.

Keep about a cable off Plod Sgeirean, the line of skerries across the mouth of the rocky bay to starboard, until the tripod beacon north of Eilean Bhride is in line with the east point of Eilean Bhride bearing about 170° and steer towards the beacon on that line to avoid the rock awash. Alter course to pass west of Ceann nan Sgeirean. Keep Garbhsgeir Beg in line with the conical hill Cnoc Rhaonastil (The Cnoc) 316° astern or southwest of this line to avoid drying rocks south of Ceann nan Sgeirean.

Anchorages

Eilean Craobhach, 1½ cables off the southwest shore of the island, avoiding the rock awash.

Plod Sgeirean A cairn of stones has been erected on the skerry inshore of the entrance. Enter between the islet which forms the south point of the bay and the first skerry to the northeast, keeping rather nearer to the northeast skerry as submerged rocks lie off the southwest point.

Plod Sgeirean, showing submerged rocks around the skerry to starboard (2006)

Loch a'Chnuich from west. The anchorage is between the islet and the rocks at the right (1987)

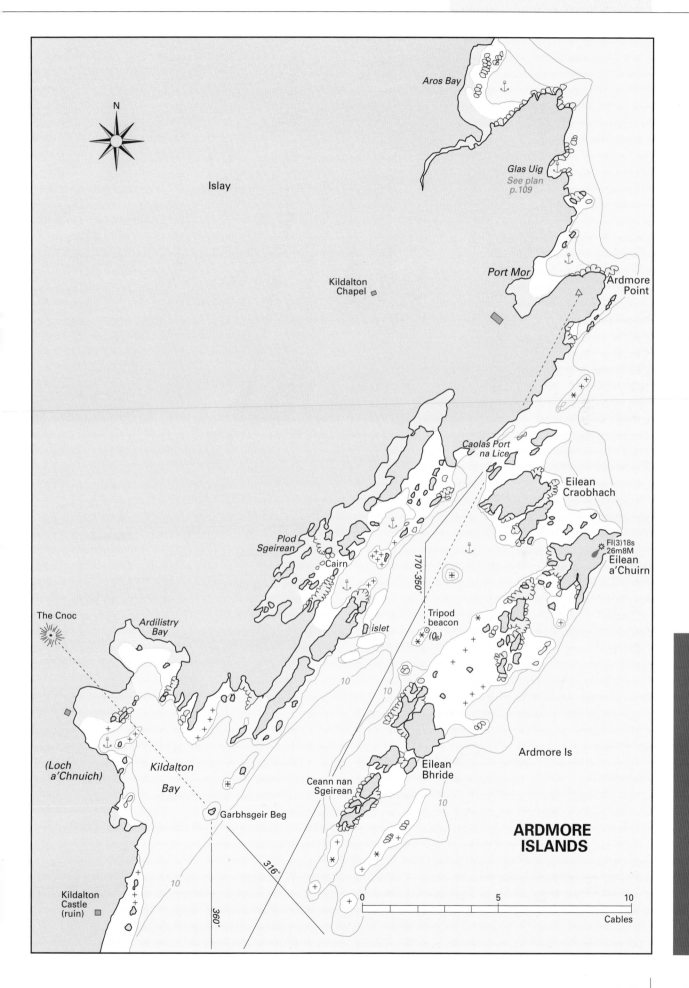

N

Islay

Aros Bay

Glas Uig
See plan
p.109

Port Mor

Ardmore
Point

Kildalton
Chapel

Caolas Port
na Lice

Eilean
Craobhach

Plod
Sgeirean

Cairn

170°-350°

Fl(3)18s
26m8M
Eilean
a'Chuirn

The Cnoc

Ardilistry
Bay

islet

Tripod
beacon (0.6)

(Loch
a'Chnuich)

Kildalton
Bay

Ceann nan
Sgeirean

Eilean
Bhride

Ardmore Is

10

10

10

10

316°

360°

Garbhsgeir Beg

Kildalton
Castle
(ruin)

**ARDMORE
ISLANDS**

0   5   10
Cables

Caolas Port na Lice showing rocks both submerged and above water in the channel (2006)

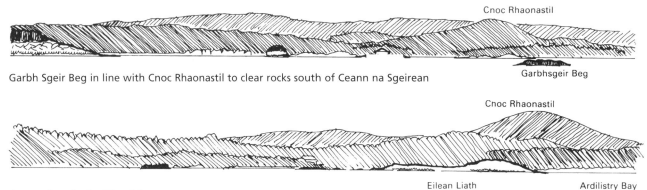

Cnoc Rhaonastil

Garbhsgeir Beg

Garbh Sgeir Beg in line with Cnoc Rhaonastil to clear rocks south of Ceann na Sgeirean

Cnoc Rhaonastil

Eilean Liath   Ardilistry Bay

Approach to Loch a'Chnuich

If anchoring at the south end turn to port when the channel opens out and anchor as far south as depth allows.

To anchor at the north end keep heading towards the shore and turn to starboard when closer to the islet ahead than to the skerry northeast of the entrance, as submerged reefs lie northwest of the skerry.

Kildalton Bay (Loch a'Chnuic) is subject to swell in easterly winds.

Pass either side of Garbhsgeir Beg, but if on its north side not more than a cable away from it to avoid a rock awash WSW of Garbhsgeir Mor, and head towards Ardilistry Bay.

Two detached rocks lie off the southwest shore and then a rocky islet off the promontory which separates Ardilistry Bay from Kildalton Bay (Loch a'Chnuic); when this islet is almost abeam turn to port to pass southeast of it to avoid a reef extending northeast from the second detached rock. Anchor near the southwest shore at the mouth of Kildalton Bay.

Anchorages north of Ardmore Point

See plan page 109

TIDES

At Port Ellen

Constant –0530 Oban (+0130 Dover) at springs, and –0050 Oban (+0610 Dover) at neaps.

Height in metres

MHWS	MHWN	MTL	MLWN	MLWS
0·9	0·8	0·6	0·5	0·3

Port Mor with stone jetty at right and track leading to the road to Kidalton Chapel (2006)

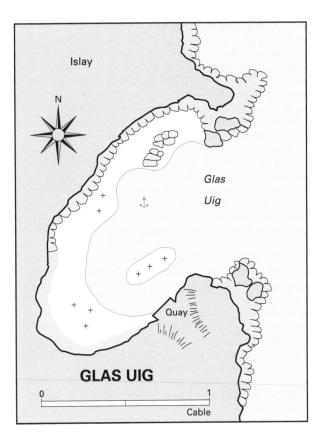

GLAS UIG

0   1

Cable

Glas Uig showing the submerged reef off the jetty on the port side (2006)

Three open bays provide occasional anchorage north of Ardmore Point. These bays are all difficult to identify from seaward, but Ardmore Point has a triangulation point (a short tapering concrete pillar) near its summit and Port Mor has a large white house at its head.

Port Mor is immediately northwest of Ardmore Point. The head of the bay shoals a long way and there is a line of rocks on the northwest side of the bay. The bottom is clean sand.

Glas Uig is very difficult to distinguish and scarcely shows on chart *2168*; it is about 3 cables north of Port Mor. Anchor on the north side of the bay to avoid the submerged reef off the quay very rough on the south side.

Aros Bay is a clean open sandy bay ¼ mile north of Ardmore Point; a pleasant place to spend a fine, windless day. *Thomasina* spent a night there in 1999, the only disturbance being a group of seals in party mood.

Aros Bay with the Paps of Jura beyond (1999)

GIGHA, WEST LOCH TARBERT, ISLAY

Sound of Islay

CHARTS

2168 includes the Sound of Islay and Loch Tarbert at 1:75,000. 2481 covers the Sound of Islay and Loch Tarbert at 1:25,000.

TIDAL STREAMS

Tidal streams in the Sound of Islay run at up to 5 knots with eddies inshore.

The north-going stream begins about +0440 Oban (–0050 Dover), and the south-going stream begins about –0140 Oban (+0515 Dover).

Overfalls form at the north end of the sound on the flood with a northerly wind, and at the south end of the sound on the ebb, where it meets the ebb from the Sound of Jura.

DANGERS AND MARKS

The main dangers are the Black Rocks near the south end of the sound, marked on their southwest side by a G conical light buoy. From either direction this buoy is likely to appear nearer to the Islay shore than might be expected.

Brosdale Island, south of Jura and east of the south end of the sound, has a submerged rock 3 cables south of its southwest side, and Am Fraoch Eilean, 1½ miles west of Brosdale Island, has rocks drying 1½ cables south of it.

At the north end of the sound Sgeir Traigh dries 3·6 metres 4 cables off the shore of Jura 2¾ miles north of Carragh an t-Sruith. Other rocks dry up to ¼ mile offshore for two miles further northeast. These rocks are dangerous, especially if tacking or making for Loch Tarbert, although Sgeir Traigh rarely completely covers. There are few distinguishing marks on Jura, but a prominent rocky streak Sgriob na Caillich (the Witch's Scratch) runs down the hillside to a point about ½ mile northeast of Sgeir Traigh.

Throughout the sound rocks both submerged and drying lie up to a cable from both shores.

Conspicuous marks are, from south to north:

McArthur's Head lighthouse, a 13-metre white tower surrounded by a white-painted wall on a steep hillside on Islay south of the entrance to the sound.

Am Fraoich Eilean, off the Jura shore north of McArthur's Head.

Brosdale Island, 1½ miles further east.

Port Askaig village, 5 miles NNW of McArthur's Head.

Caol Ila distillery, ½ mile north of Port Askaig.

Bunnahabhainn (Bunnahaven) distillery, 2 miles north of Port Askaig.

Rubha a'Mhail (Ruvaal) lighthouse, 45 metres high, at the west point of the north end of the sound, about 3½ miles from Bunnahabhainn.

For dangers beyond the north end of the sound see page 135.

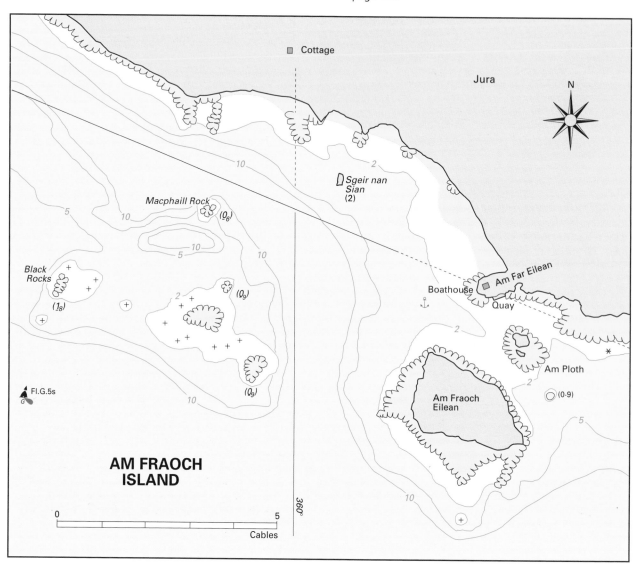

Jura   Brosdale Island   Fraoich Eilean

Boathouse

Sgeir nan Sian

Am Far Eilean under the right fall of Brosdale leads north of Macphaill Rock

LIGHTS

McArthur's Head lighthouse, Fl(2)WR.10s39m14/11M, shows white in Sound of Islay from the northeast coast of Islay to 159°-R-244°-W to the east coast of Islay

Black Rocks light buoy Q.G

Carraig Mor light beacon Fl(2)WR.6s7m8/6M; Islay shore-R-175°-W-347°-R-Islay

Carraig an t-Sruith light beacon Fl.3s8m9M 354°-180°

Rubha a'Mhail lighthouse Fl(3)WR.15s45m24/21M 075°-R-180°-W-075

DIRECTIONS

A passage east and north of the Black Rocks can be used to avoid an adverse tide in the south part of the sound. Approaching from southeast keep at least ¼ mile south of Am Fraoch Eilean; keep the green conical buoy bearing not less than 290°. Identify an isolated cottage on Jura and Sgeir nan Sian, and steer 360° for a rocky bluff between them; as a check on position the boathouse at Am Far Eilean will show up north of Am Fraoch Eilean soon after you turn onto this line. When Brosdale Island passes behind Am Far Eilean alter course to bring the south fall of Brosdale Island over the boathouse bearing 112° astern to pass between Macphaill Rock and drying reefs on the Jura shore.

To make this passage from northwest to southeast, identify Am Far Eilean and Brosdale Island while passing Glas Eilean and reverse the directions given above.

For the passage from the Sound of Islay to Colonsay, and past Colonsay to Mull and to Tiree, see page 143.

TIDES

At Port Askaig

Constant –0030 Oban (+0500 Dover) at springs, and –0110 Oban (+0420 Dover) at neaps.

Height in metres

At Port Askaig

MHWS	MHWN	MTL	MLWN	MLWS
2·1	1·5	1·2	1·0	0·4

At Rubha a'Mhail

3·7	2·8	2·1	1·5	0·6

Note the difference in range in only 6 miles.

Anchorages

Am Far Eilean provides occasional anchorage north of Am Fraoch Eilean and southwest of the boathouse, in 3 metres.

PORT ASKAIG

A temporary berth alongside a well fendered concrete quay. Eddies close inshore make the approach difficult.

Alternatively anchor off the quay in 4 metres, clear of the approach to the quay, but the tide runs strongly here.

Check immediately on berthing that a car ferry is not due to arrive before you intend to leave; it is usually possible to stay overnight (dues charged).

The channel northwest of Am Fraoich Eilean from west. MacPhaill Rock lies left of centre, with Sgeir nan Sian immediately above (2006)

Port Askaig (1984)

Caol Ila Distillery (2006)

Moor towards the south end of the main ferry berth for shelter from the tide. A smaller ferry crosses frequently to Jura from a separate berth at the south end of the quay.

Supplies

Shop, post office, phone, water by hose, hotel, *Calor Gas*, petrol. Ferries to Jura and to mainland. Bus to Bowmore and Port Ellen.

Occasional anchorages

Caol Ila distillery The pier is considered unsafe and is fenced off at the landward end, so that it should only be used in emergency.

Whitefarland Bay, Jura, out of the main tidal stream opposite Caol Ila. Anchor off a boulder on which an anchor is painted in white. The bottom is weedy and holding poor. There is said to be a mooring ring on shore close south of the white mark.

Bunnahaven is a convenient place to wait for a south-going tide; anchor north of the pier.

Port Askaig showing the new approach road (2006)

VII. Sound of Jura

The Gaelic dictionary which I use gives as an alternative name for the Sound of Jura 'an linne rosach' (the channel of disappointment) perhaps because of the strong tides and the awkward seas raised by the wind against tide and the uneven bottom. The seas are at their worst when the wind is southerly, blowing from the open sea against an ebb tide, but eddies on the flood can be just as troublesome.

CHARTS

2168, 2169 (1:75,000) each include part of the sound. Much greater detail is provided by 2396 and 2397 at 1:25,000.

TIDES

Throughout the sound most of the rise and fall occurs within the first three hours of each period. The height of tide is greatly affected by wind and barometric pressure; a southwesterly wind and/or low pressure raising the level by up to a metre, and a northeasterly wind and/or high pressure reducing it by a similar amount.

Throughout the greater part of the sound the north-going stream begins about +0545 Oban (+0015 Dover) and the south-going stream begins about –0015 Oban (–0545 Dover). The rate at the south end of the sound is about 2 knots, and around Skervuile about 3–3½ knots.

Near Ruadh Sgeir at the north end of the sound the north-going stream begins about +0425 Oban (–0105 Dover) and the south-going stream begins about –0155 Oban (+0500 Dover), the rate in each direction being up to 4 knots.

CONSPICUOUS MARKS

The Paps of Jura, a group of three conspicuous hills near the south end of Jura, provide a useful reference point unless they are obscured by cloud.

Na Cuiltean, a rock east of the south end of Jura, with a small white light beacon.

Skervuile, a larger light beacon in the middle of the sound.

The MacCormaig Isles, off the entrance of Loch Sween.

Carraig an Daimh, an isolated rock 11 metres high 1¾ miles north of MacCormaig Isles.

Ruadh Sgeir at the north end of the sound is 13 metres high with a small light beacon.

LIGHTS

McArthur's Head lighthouse on the northeast shore of Islay, Fl(2)WR.10s39m14/11M

Na Cuiltean light beacon Fl.10s9m9M

Eilean nan Gabhar (Goat Island) Fl.5s7m8M; at the south entrance to Craighouse Bay, Jura

Nine-foot Rock buoy Q(3)10s; off the entrance to Lowlandman's Bay

Skervuile light beacon Fl.15s22m9M

Ruadh Sgeir light beacon Fl.6s13m8M

PASSAGE NOTES

There is little to add to the description already given except to emphasise the need to work the tides. If

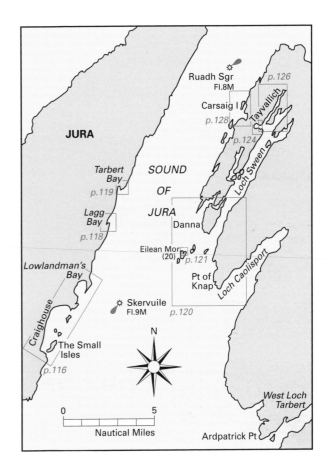

attempting a passage against the tide, some use may be made of eddies in the lee of any projection from the shore, but this will need very careful chartwork, especially on the mainland side. The most useful eddy is off Carsaig Bay.

Submerged reefs extend 4 cables NNE of Ruadh Sgeir at the north end of the sound, and there are strong eddies and overfalls north of that islet on the flood. The flood tide sets NNW across the reefs and must be allowed for if passing east of Ruadh Sgeir.

Anchorages on Jura
Craighouse Bay (Loch na Mile)

55°50′N 5°57′W

An extensive bay sheltered by a row of islands, whose south end is 2½ miles from the southeast point of Jura. In spite of the apparent shelter there is often some swell, usually of a tidal origin, and the holding is poor being sand with patches of weed. There are visitors' moorings NW of the pier.

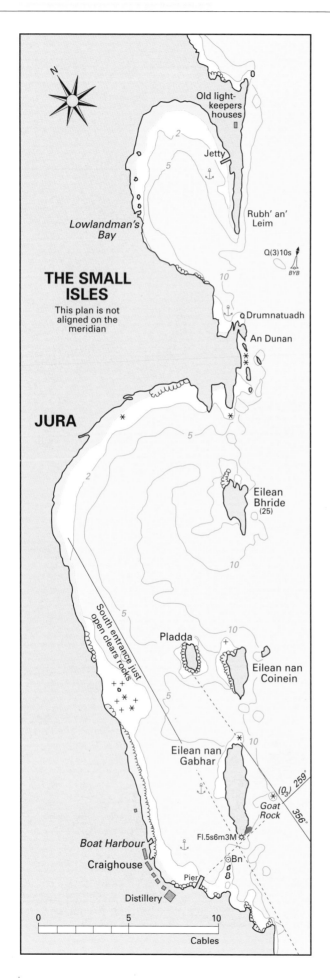

THE SMALL ISLES

This plan is not aligned on the meridian

JURA

Lowlandman's Bay

Old light-keepers houses

Jetty

Rubh' an' Leim

Q(3)10s
BYB

Drumnatuadh

An Dunan

Eilean Bhride (25)

Pladda

Eilean nan Coinein

South entrance just open clears rocks

Eilean nan Gabhar

Goat Rock

(0₂) 259°

356°

Fl.5s6m3M

Boat Harbour

Craighouse

Bn

Pier

Distillery

0   5   10

Cables

TIDES

Tidal streams run strongly across the entrance.
Constant –0130 Oban (+0400 Dover) at springs, and –0430 Oban (+0100 Dover) at neaps.

Height in metres

MHWS	MHWN	MTL	MLWN	MLWS
1·2	0·9	0·7	0·4	0·3

DIRECTIONS

Na Cuiltean light beacon helps to identify the entrance when approaching from the south and the distillery and houses are seen once the entrance is opened.

The main entrance is at the south end of the bay, between the south end of Goat Island (Eilean nan Gabhar) and a drying reef extending north from the south point of the bay.

A small metal light beacon stands at the south end of Goat Island.

An iron beacon with a ball topmark stands about 20 metres south of the end of the reef (not at the end of the reef) on the south side of the entrance.

Goat Rock 1½ cables east of Goat Island dries 0·3 metres. The end of the concrete pier open of the south end of Goat Island, bearing 259° leads south of the rock, and the islet of Pladda, northwest of Eilean nan Coinein, open of the north end of Goat island 356° leads east of the rock.

At night, Na Cuiltean (Fl.10s9m9M) and the light beacon at the south end of Goat Island (Fl.5s6m3M) make the approach fairly straightforward, but look out for being set off course by the tide which may not be so obvious at night.

Because of the poor holding the visitors' moorings are particularly welcome here. Inshore of the moorings the bay is shoal but there are depths of 2 metres east of the concrete pier, which is usually better sheltered from any swell.

There is good depth alongside the pier, but it is of concrete frame construction, so that it is difficult to keep fenders in place, although the range of tide is small.

In easterly winds there is slightly better shelter west of Goat Island, as close to the island as the depth allows.

Anchoring west of Pladda is also possible.

At the north end of the bay the bottom is cleaner.

Luggers, etc. may be able to dry out in the old harbour.

Supplies

Shop, water at pier, diesel, petrol, *Calor Gas*, post office, phone, hotel. Showers at hotel.

Lowlandman's Bay

55°53′N 5°57′W

The former lighthouse-keepers' houses on the rocky ridge which shelters the east side of the bay are conspicuous, and Ninefoot Rock east cardinal light buoy lies east of the entrance.

Much of the bay is shallow and the best anchorage is near the east side, off a stone jetty, southwest of the houses.

Drumnatuadh Bay on the south side of the entrance provides an occasional anchorage in southwesterly winds; the bottom is hard sand.

Further north on Jura several bays provide occasional anchorages but they are all difficult to identify.

Craighouse from southeast   *Patrick Roach*

Lowlandman's Bay, below the Paps of Jura

Drumnatuadh from northwest (1980)

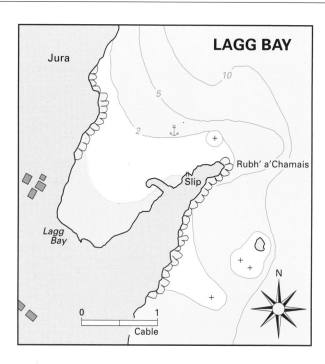

Other anchorages

Lagg Bay, 55°56´.5N 5°51´W, 4 miles north of Skervuile, was the original landing place for the mail ferry crossing to Jura.

A power cable shown on older charts in this bay was disused many years ago.

Take care to avoid a submerged rock ½ cable NNE of the east point of the entrance.

Luggers, etc. may be able to dry out in the old harbour.

Phone box beside the road at west side of the bay.

Tarbert Bay, 55°58´N 5°50´W, 1½ miles north of Lagg Bay, is identified by a dip in the skyline, as it is only ¾ mile from the head of Loch Tarbert on the west side of Jura.

The bay is shallow and almost entirely filled with dense broad-leafed seaweed, but a patch of clear sand north of Liath Eilean has a depth of about 2½ metres (although its extent is said to be diminishing).

Lagg Bay showing submerged rocks. and drying boat harbour on southeast side of bay (2006)

Tarbert Bay, showing submerged rocks

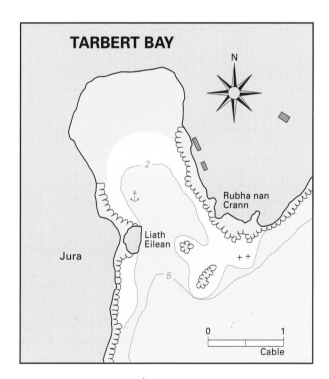

TARBERT BAY

N

Jura

2

Rubha nan
Crann

Liath
Eilean

5

0   1
Cable

To avoid the rocks in the entrance pass within
¼ cable of Liath Eilean heading 360°; from north
and east pass at least 2 cables south of Rubha nan
Crann before turning into the bay.

Lussa Bay, 56°01′N 5°47′W, 3 miles NNE of
Tarbert Bay, is straightforward, but give the east
point of the entrance a berth of half a cable.

Phone box at houses.

Ardlussa Bay, 56°02′N 5°46′W, 1½ miles NNE of
Lussa, provides little shelter except for a shoal-
draught boat.

No provisions are available at any of these
places.

Anchorages on the east side of the Sound of Jura

MacCormaig Isles and approaches to Loch Sween

55°55′N 5°43′W

TIDES
Craighouse

Constant –0130 Oban (+0400 Dover) at springs, and
–0430 Oban (+0100 Dover) at neaps.

Height in metres

MHWS	MHWN	MTL	MLWN	LWS
1·2	0·9	0·7	0·4	0·3

DANGERS AND MARKS

Most of the dangers in the Sound of Jura are
concentrated in this area and affect the approach to
Loch Caolisport and Loch Keills (Loch na Cille) as well as
Loch Sween. On a direct passage through the sound
they are easily avoided by keeping west of Eilean Mor
and Carraig an Daimh.

Clearing marks for avoiding these dangers are all fairly
distant and not easy to identify, but the plan and
illustrations should help. The principal dangers and their
clearing marks are as follows, from south to north:

Bow of Knap and **Ruadh na Brogg**, submerged and
drying rocks ½ mile west and WSW of the Point of Knap
on the north side of the entrance to Loch Caolisport.
Bow of Knap is marked by a W car. light buoy, Fl.(9)15s

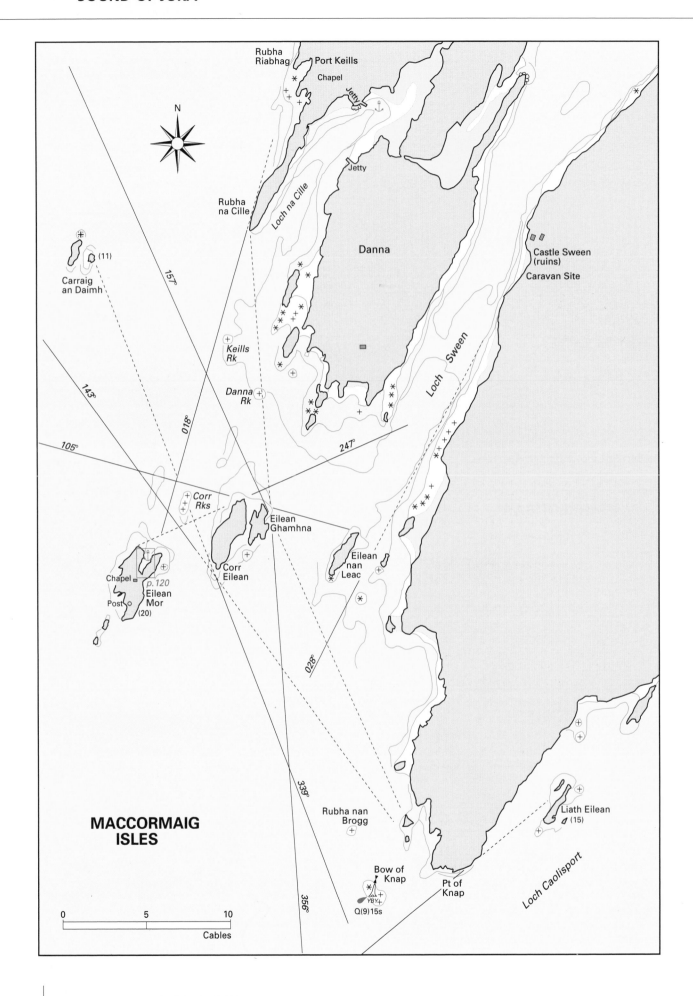

N

Rubha Riabhag   Port Keills

Chapel

Jetty

Jetty

Rubha na Cille

Loch na Cille

Danna

Castle Sween (ruins)

Caravan Site

Carraig an Daimh   (11)

157°

143°

018°

105°

Keills Rk

Danna Rk

Loch Sween

247°

Corr Rks

Eilean Ghamhna

Corr Eilean

Eilean nan Leac

Chapel   p. 120
Post   Eilean Mor   (20)

028°

339°

Rubha nan Brogg

Liath Eilean
(15)

MACCORMAIG
ISLES

356°

Bow of Knap

Pt of Knap

Loch Caolisport

YBY
Q(9)15s

0   5   10

Cables

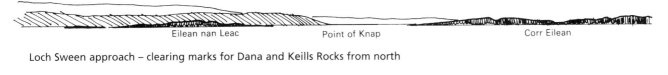

Loch Sween approach – clearing marks for Dana and Keills Rocks from north

Loch Sween approach – clearing marks for Dana and Keills Rocks from south

Rubha na Cille touching Eilean Ghamhna bearing 356° leads 4 cables west of these rocks. Carraig an Daimh touching the southwest point of Corr Eilean bearing 339° leads a cable west of the Bow of Knap.

Corr Rocks, west of the north end of Corr Eilean and NNE of Eilean Mor nearly uncover and weed shows at LW neaps.

Point of Knap just open south of Corr Eilean bearing 143° leads close southwest of Corr Rocks. Rubha Riabhag open west of Rubha na Cille, which looks like a rocky island from this direction, bearing 018° leads a cable west of Corr Rocks. The north end of Eilean nan Leac open north of Eilean Ghamhna bearing 105° leads north of Corr Rocks, but Eilean Puirt Leithe further inshore could be mistaken for Eilean nan Leac, which would take you over the north end of the rocks.

Danna Rock and **Keills Rock** both have a least depth of 1·0 metre.

Rubha Riabhag open of Rubha na Cille bearing 018° (see above) leads close west of Keills Rock. The north end of Eilean Ghamhna touching the Point of Knap bearing 157° leads west of these rocks, but take care not to mistake Keppoch Point, 5 miles further south, for the Point of Knap.

TIDAL STREAMS

Tides run strongly and irregularly among the MacCormaig Isles and it is essential to watch clearing marks continuously.

The north-going stream begins about +0450 Oban (–0040 Dover) and the south-going stream begins about –0110 Oban (+0545 Dover).

Spring rates off the Point of Knap are 1½ knots. Among the islands and off Rubha na Cille, 2 miles north of the MacCormaig Isles, they are around 3 knots, with eddies and overfalls throughout the area.

Loch Caolisport

55°53′N 5°40′W

The name is pronounced, and sometimes written as 'Killisport'. There is no shelter for anchoring except in offshore winds, but any submerged hazards within the loch are close inshore and it is a pleasant place for an occasional visit.

Outside the entrance the Bow of Knap is a dangerous group of drying and submerged rocks 4 cables WSW west of Point of Knap, the north point of the entrance. For marks to clear the west side of these rocks see above. The south side of the Bow of Knap is cleared when Liath Eilean is open south of the Point of Knap.

The best anchorage is near the head of the loch, northeast of Eilean Fada, but there are several inlets, particularly on the northwest side.

Eilean Mor

55°55′N 5°44′W

The most southwesterly of the MacCormaig Isles, identified by the ruined chapel about the middle of the island and a cross on a hill top near the south end.

Like other small islands off the west coast, Eilean Mor had a hermit, who lived in a cave near the south end of the island in the 6th century. The chapel was built in the 12th century, and subsequently became a house and was used at one time for illicitly distilling whisky.

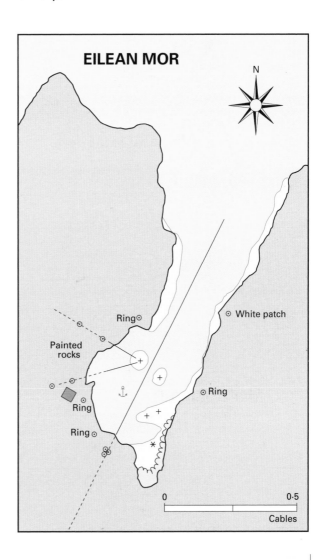

Eilean Mor is a popular anchorage, particularly for day visits. The anchorage is a tiny inlet at the north end of the island with an uneven stony bottom and several individual rocks with depths of less than 2 metres.

The more westerly rock is said to have been blown up by the army, but the other – from personal experience – is still there. Another submerged rock is reported to lie on the leading line (with streaks of white anti-fouling on it), with the drying rock in the SE corner of the inlet bearing 160°.

A visitors' centre is being built on the west side of the inlet, with a rough stone landing place below it.

Approach

For dangers and clearing marks in the approach see page 119. Corr Rocks, 3 cables NNE of the entrance are most dangerous if approaching from the north or from Loch Sween.

The ebb tide divides to run past both sides of the island, and particular care needs to be taken to avoid being set off course; a submerged rock lies ½ cable north of the west point of the entrance.

A cairn of stones on the shore at the head of the loch in line with a cross on the summit of the island leads between two submerged rocks in the basin, the one blown up by the army and its partner, but the cairn may be difficult to identify. There is adequate depth of water inshore of both rocks.

Two pairs of painted marks on the west shore in line intersect on the rock seen off by the army. The east rock has a depth of 0·9 metres.

Mooring

The positions of several mooring rings are outlined in white paint; the inlet is very small and the rings may be needed to prevent a yacht swinging, particularly if several others are there. The bottom consists of stones with weed and some sand and the holding is poor in places.

Loch Sween

55°57′N 5°40′W

A picturesque loch, particularly in its upper parts, with several narrow arms running deep among wooded hills.

TIDES

There are no strong tidal streams. There is effectively a 'stand' of tide for three hours at high water from –0330 to –0030 Oban, and +0230 to +0530 Oban at low water. No official figures are available for the rise of tide in Loch Sween; the nearest are for Craighouse: constant –0130 Oban (+0400 Dover) at springs, –0430 Oban (+0100 Dover) at neaps.

Height in metres

MHWS	MHWN	MTL	MLWN	MLWS
1·2	0·9	0·7	0·4	0·3

DANGERS AND MARKS

Lochfoot Rocks (Sgeir Bun an Locha) on the northwest side of the entrance, normally 1 metre above MHWS, but which could be covered during appropriate meteorological conditions.

Sgeirean a'Mhainn, a long rock 0·3 metre high which occasionally covers, about the middle of the loch, 1½ miles NNE of Castle Sween.

Sgeir nan Ron, a cable from the east shore, and 4 cables east of Sgeirean a'Mhainn dries 1·2 metres.

Castle Sween on the east shore is surrounded by a conspicuous caravan park.

Eilean Mor, MacCormaig Isles, from southwest (1989)

Approach

For dangers and clearing marks outside the loch see page 119. To approach from south by the east side of Eilean nan Leac keep closer to Eilean nan Leac with Castle Sween in sight open of the island bearing 028° to avoid Flat Rock, drying 0·6 metres 2 cables southeast of the island; the passage west of Eilean nan Leac is straightforward.

Approaching from the north part of the Sound of Jura identify the Lochfoot Rocks before turning into the loch. The north end of Corr Eilean in line with the north end of Eilean Mor astern bearing 247° leads southeast of Lochfoot Rocks.

Pass west of the moorings at Castle Sween; there is shoal water inshore both north and south of the moorings.

Identify Sgeirean a'Mhainn and pass it on either side.

At high water this rock is not easy to see (although there may be a pole on it), and it is best to keep well to the west side of the loch, so as to avoid Sgeir nan Ron also.

Beyond this the main fairway of the loch is straightforward. 4½ miles NNE of Castle Sween the loch divides into three parallel branches, with Loch a'Bhealaich (Tayvallich) half a mile to the west.

Anchorage

Taynish Island provides an occasional anchorage for small boats, with limited swinging room north of this island on the northwest shore of the loch.

Tayvallich

56°01′.5N 5°37′.5W

One of the most perfectly sheltered anchorages on the West Coast, but with several rocks both submerged and above water within. Most of the water deep enough for anchoring is occupied by moorings, but the harbour committee tries to keep two areas clear for visiting yachts to anchor, west and southeast of the central reef. The shores are shoal except on the east side.

Tayvallich Bay (2006)

Tayvallich approach

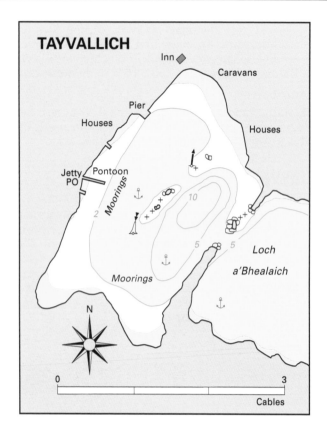

TAYVALLICH

Inn

Caravans

Pier

Houses

Houses

Jetty
PO
Pontoon

Moorings

2

10

5   5

Loch
a'Bhealaich

Moorings

N

0   3

Cables

Tayvallich Bay (2006)

Submerged rocks on the north side of the approach are marked by small perches, the first with a triangular topmark, the second T-shaped. If these perches are not seen, keep towards the south shore as Oib Rocks extend halfway across the approach.

Enter by the more southerly of the two gaps in the outer reef as the other is foul; turn to port and anchor clear of the central reef. This anchorage is deep, and the alternative is to pass round either end of the central reef and anchor to the west of it.

A submerged rock off the south end of the central reef is marked by a small south cardinal buoy which must be passed on its south side. If the buoy cannot be seen, a clearing mark is the south gable of the post office just open; the post office is a buff-coloured building with a red roof by the shore.

In the passage north of the central reef a small south cardinal beacon marks a submerged rock on the north side of the passage. A rock has been discovered at a depth of at least 2 metres in the fairway north of the central reef and in line with the reef. The wooden pier at the northwest side of the bay is used by fishing boats; all vessels are requested not to lie alongside for more than an hour.

An alternative anchorage is outside the bay to the south of the entrance, but the bottom consists of boulders and the holding may not be good in strong winds.

There are no visitors' moorings, and private moorings should not be used without specific prior consent.

Head of Caol Scotnish (1980)

Scotnish Farm

Ruined jetty

Jetty

Scotnish Rock

Caol Scotnish approach

The pontoons in Tayvallich are all private apart from the one attached to the pier adjacent to the shop/coffee shop. This pontoon is owned and managed by the Tayvallich Bay Association and has been extended with two finger berths as can be seen in the photograph. The use of the pontoon is subject to the following rules: Maximum stay one hour, no boats to be left unattended, dinghies to be take to the concrete pier, not left alongside the pontoon. Water is available at the pontoon and there is a collecting box for donations at the head of the pier. Showers and toilets are available at the shop during opening hours. Coffee shop.

Supplies

Grocer at post office towards the south end of the village. Pontoons for loading and unloading at Post Office jetty. Water tap at the pontoon. Phone box beside post office. Refuse disposal skip beside post office. *Calor Gas* at caravan site at north side of the bay. Restaurant (Tayvallich Inn). No fuel.

Caol Scotnish

56°02′N 5°36′W

A narrow inlet two miles long and in places only ¼ cable wide with sheer rocky sides; the upper parts are used for fish farming.

Oib Rocks, a cable south of the entrance, are marked by a perch with a triangular topmark, but a submerged rock lies about 30 metres SSW of the perch; rocks west of the entrance are marked by a perch with a T-shaped topmark. If the Oib Rocks perch is missing keep closer to the south shore until Caol Scotnish is well open.

The main hazards are Scotnish Reef and Scotnish Rocks, 3 cables from the entrance and a cable south of the narrowest part. Scotnish Rocks rarely cover and should be passed close on their west side to avoid the reef; the passage between the rocks and the reef is no more than 20 metres wide.

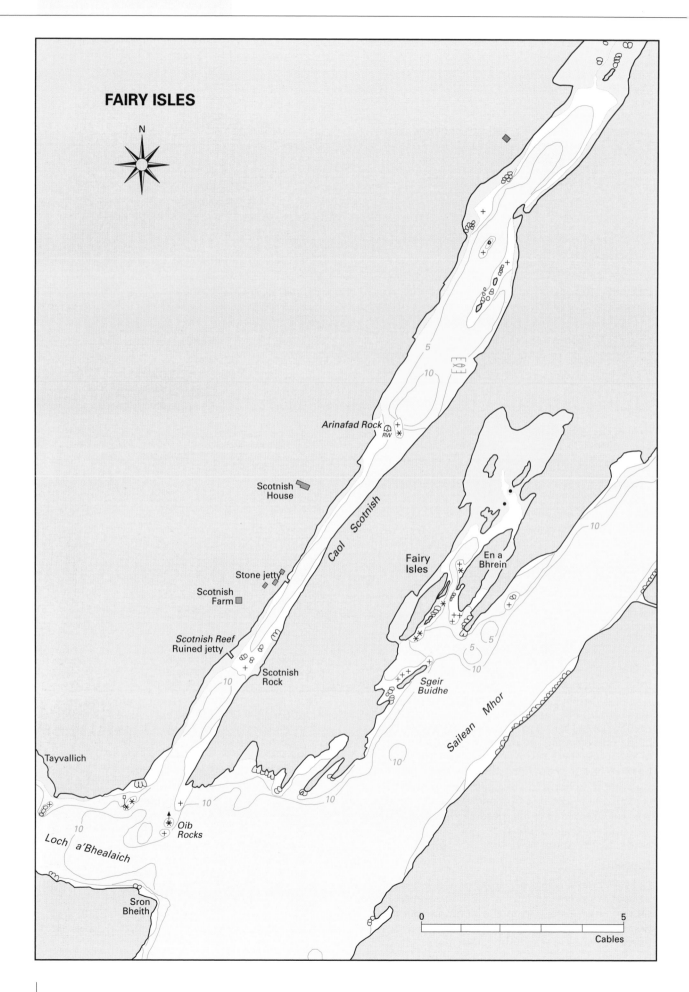

FAIRY ISLES

N

Arinafad Rock
RW

Scotnish
House

Caol   Scotnish

Fairy
Isles

En a
Bhrein

Stone jetty

Scotnish
Farm

Scotnish Reef
Ruined jetty

Scotnish
Rock

Sgeir
Buidhe

Sailean   Mhor

Tayvallich

Oib
Rocks

Loch   a'Bhealaich

Sron
Bheith

0   5

Cables

Half a mile beyond a stone pier on the west side of the narrows, where the kyle opens up, Arinafad Rock which dries just west of mid-channel is usually marked by a small buoy with a topmark of two balls, but it might be confused with other buoys at the fish farm, particularly if its topmark is missing.

In the rest of the inlet most rocks are above water, but there are some drying rocks off the west shore. The head of Caol Scotnish dries 2 cables but the basin before the head is clean. Mud in mid-channel is very soft and if anchoring make sure that the anchor is well dug in.

Fairy Isles

56°02′N 5°35′.5W

An inlet on the west side of Sailein Mhor, the main arm of the head of the loch. The most straightforward anchorage is northwest of Sgeir Buidhe at the south end of the inlet. The north part of the inlet is full of rocks and some years ago the remains of the submerged barrier of an abandoned fish farm was reported to be a hazard.

The north part of the inlet is obstructed by rocks, for which there is no detailed survey, although they appear on the photo to be rather different from the chart, but the air photos give some guidance and a normal keelboat can find her way in. Local yachtsmen state that the artificial obstruction no longer exists. Holding throughout is soft mud.

Achanamara at the eastern arm of the head of Loch Sween, is mostly shoal and occupied by boats on permanent moorings. Port Lunna, the inlet north of Eilean Loain, has been cleared of fish farming installations.

Fairy Isles

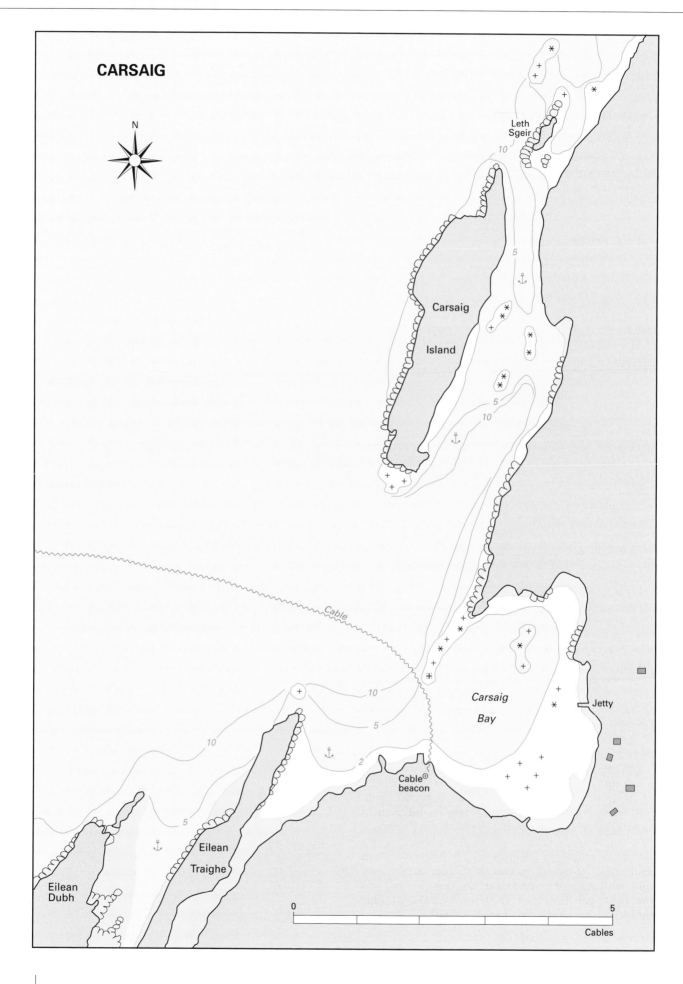

CARSAIG

N

Leth
Sgeir

Carsaig

Island

Carsaig
Bay

Jetty

Cable

Cable⊙
beacon

Eilean
Traighe

Eilean
Dubh

0   5

Cables

Mainland shore of Sound of Jura

Loch Keills (Loch na Cille)

2 miles north of the MacCormaig Isles, Loch Keills is clean with a sandy bottom but the head is shoal and dries for about a mile. Although it is exposed to the south, the strong tidal streams across the entrance tend to keep any swell out of the loch except, of course, at slack water. Anchor just short of a jetty on the northwest side, 1 mile from the west point of the entrance.

Note the clearing marks for Keills Rock on page 121.

The passage inside Eilean nan Coinean, 4 miles ENE of Rubha na Cille, is littered with rocks but can be puzzled out in quiet weather with a large-scale chart; no clearing marks have been identified.

The passage between Eilean Dubh and Eilean Traighe seems to have a least depth of about 0·7 metres.

Carsaig

56°02′N 5°39′W

It is quite easy to mistake the bay north of Eilean nan Coinean for Carsaig Bay, but there are houses at Carsaig and the gap in the skyline there is lower.

Tidal eddies run across the mouth of Carsaig Bay. The entrance to it is partly blocked by a reef which extends more than halfway across the bay from the north point in a SSW direction. Rocks in the bay, both submerged and drying, lie up to 2 cables from the shore, and the parts of the bay which are clear of rocks are full of weed. A power cable crossing to Jura runs out in a northerly direction from a beacon on the south shore.

There is some shelter in either of two inlets southwest of Carsaig Bay, between Eilean Dubh and Eilean Traighe, and between Eilean Traighe and the mainland. Rows of buoys across the mouth of these bays are said to be mooring pickups for fishing boats, not fish-farming equipment; there is space to anchor clear of them, but most of the inlet east of Eilean Traighe dries.

The sound between Carsaig Island and the mainland provides some shelter close to the island, but there are drying rocks to be avoided.

Except in northerly winds, the best shelter is east of the north part of Carsaig Island. Approach from northwest keeping closer to Carsaig Island than to Leth Sgeir which has drying reefs off its southwest end.

A narrow passage 3 metres deep leads to the south anchorage within 20 metres of the promontory on the mainland side northeast of the drying rocks but the tide runs fast here at times and the passage should be investigated first with a dinghy.

Supplies

At Tayvallich (see page 123) ½ mile by road from the jetty in Carsaig Bay.

Other anchorages

Sailean Mor, 2 miles NNE of Carsaig Bay, provides an occasional anchorage but it is exposed to any sea from the north, and the head of the bay dries for 2 cables.

Loch Crinan has a straightforward anchorage off the hotel on the south shore of the loch, uncomfortable in strong west or northwest winds. Yachts can berth at the north face of the pier east of the canal entrance and there is a waiting pontoon at the sea lock. Complete shelter may be found in the canal basin.

VIII. West coasts of Islay and Jura, and Colonsay

Off the Rhinns of Islay, a white lighthouse 46 metres high stands on Orsay island. A detached rock An Coire lies 1½ cables southwest of Orsay, round which very strong tidal streams run.

PASSAGE NOTES TO PASS SOUTHWEST OF ISLAY

If conditions become unfavourable for a passage south of Islay, Port Ellen is a convenient anchorage but tends to be subject to swell. Portnahaven, behind Orsay, provides good shelter but strong tides run across the entrance which can be difficult in deteriorating conditions.

Alternatively, the route by the Sound of Islay is no greater distance for a passage to the west of Mull, with more shelter and more anchorages on the way. Few yachts make a direct passage to the Outer Hebrides by way of Skerryvore, but even this passage is probably no further from the Mull of Kintyre by way of the Sound of Islay. However, the outside passage is discussed below.

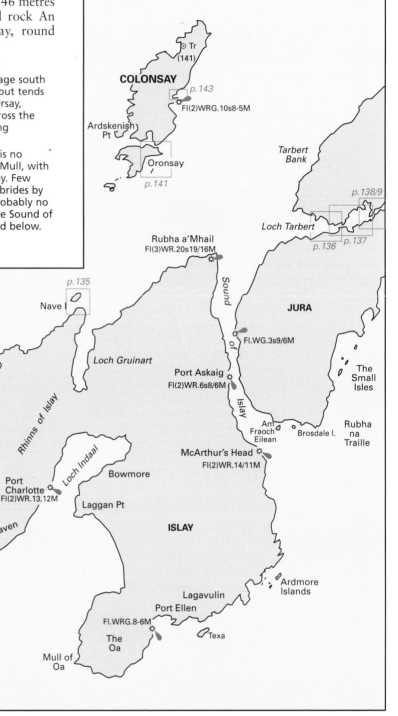

Off the Oa and the Rhinns the northwest-going stream begins about +0530 Oban (HW Dover) and the southeast-going stream begins about –0040 Oban (–0610 Dover). These streams reach a rate of 8 knots at springs off Orsay, Rhinns of Islay, and 5 knots off the Oa.

Overfalls form off the southeast side of the Oa during northwest-going streams and off its southwest side during southeast-going streams.

Because of overfalls, both the Oa and the Rhinns of Islay should be passed at a distance of several miles (overfalls southwest of the Oa are worst with a southeast-going tide). As it is 36 miles from the Mull of Kintyre to the Rhinns of Islay only a motor yacht or fast sailing boat under very favourable conditions could pass these two points in a single tide, and it is normally best to take a foul tide in the open water between Kintyre and Islay, aiming to be at the Oa at slack water.

There are more overfalls in unsettled weather over West Bank, 4 miles northwest of Orsay, as well as over banks six miles further NNW.

Dubh Artach lighthouse, which is distinguished by a broad red horizontal band, stands 28 miles north of Orsay.

Rocks above water and drying extend up to ½ mile southwest and northwest of the lighthouse so that it should be passed on its northeast side.

Skerryvore lighthouse, about 42 miles NNW from Orsay, has no red band.

Port Charlotte (2006)

Bruichladdich pier, extended in 2005 (2006)

Several detached rocks lie up to 3 miles southwest of the lighthouse and there are strong tidal streams over relatively shoal water.

The lighthouse should be passed at least 5 miles to the southwest in a depth of not less than 15 metres.

LIGHTS
Rhinns of Islay (Orsay) Fl.5s46m24M
Rubha an Duin (Port Charlotte) Fl(2)WR.7s15m13/12M
Mull of Kintyre lighthouse Fl(2)20s91m29M
Altacarry Head Fl(4)20s74m26M
Rathlin West Fl.R.5s62m22M
Dubh Artach Fl(2)30s44m20M

Loch Indaal

For passage notes and landmarks in the approach see the beginning of this chapter. Loch Indaal is a broad shallow loch whose interest is mainly in the several small towns and villages around it. Bowmore, the 'capital' of the island, has a distillery which provides guided tours. The Museum of Islay Life at Port Charlotte is worth visiting.

CHART
2168 (1:75,000)

TIDES
Constant –0040 Oban (–0610 Dover)

Height in metres

MHWS	MHWN	MTL	MLWN	MLWS
2·3	1·5	1·5	1·4	0·8

DANGERS AND MARKS
Off Laggan Point, the east point of the entrance, submerged rocks extend WSW for ½ mile, and rocks above water extend up to ¼ mile from the southeast shore. Shellfish floats may be found ½ mile off the northwest shore.

The head of the loch dries for ¼ mile and the shores all round the head are shoal with drying patches.

Port Charlotte and **Bruichladdich** on the west shore are prominent; a white light beacon 13 metres high stands at Rubh'an Duin, ½ mile north of Port Charlotte.

Rubh'an Duin light beacon, Fl(2)WR.7s15m 13/12M, shows white in the approach and in the upper part of the loch, and red over dangers near the east shore.

Anchorage

Occasional anchorage may be found off Port Charlotte.

Newly dredged to 2 metres sand/mud in line with head of stone pier, and 4 metres at head of new T-shaped pier extension completed in December 2005 for monthly oil delivery. The new pier extension has no wave screen, so **no protection** from southerly swells. It provides a safe mooring point in the event of unsettled weather though anything more than a force 3 would be uncomfortable. The pier has new lighting. One fisherman's mooring in line with distillery outfall (defunct) is usable by visitors. One distillery visitors' mooring in 3 metres was planned for Spring 2006. Bruichladdich Mini Market stocks decent food, wine and other supplies.

Supplies

Shops, post office, telephone, hotel, *Calor Gas*, petrol, diesel, water.

Bowmore harbour (2006)

Bowmore

A small drying boat harbour is formed by a curved stone quay, but the 2-metre line is 2 cables offshore.

A rock, and the end of a sewer outfall, 2 cables NNW of the quay are marked by a beacon.

A beacon 2½ cables southwest of the first beacon marks another rock. Anchor north of the north beacon.

Although the harbour has been dredged, there is no depth for the average keelboat, and berths at the pontoons are fully occupied. Yachts, except those able to take the ground, should anchor off.

Supplies

Shops, post office, bank, telephone, hotels, restaurants; petrol and diesel at garage. *Calor Gas* at Bruichladdich. Indoor swimmming pool and laundry at distillery. A whisky and music festival is held at the end of May / early June.

Portnahaven creek. Boatyard and quay are at the right (1987)

Portnahaven

55°41′N 6°31′W

The channel between Orsay and the Rhinns of Islay is well sheltered with a sandy bottom, but strong tides run across the entrance.

TIDES

Constant –0055 Oban (+0605 Dover)

Height in metres

MHWS	MHWN	MTL	MLWN	MLWS
2·6	2·3	1·7	1·3	0·5

DIRECTIONS

The north entrance is obstructed by submerged rocks and should not be attempted.

Keep towards the Islay shore when approaching unless you are certain that the tide is running towards southeast to avoid being carried onto An Coire, southwest of Orsay. Anchor north of the quay on the Islay shore, where the channel opens out.

Small boats can use a creek on the Islay shore northeast of the quay, but the approach is intricate and the creek is often full of local fishing boats. Ian Wallace has provided the following directions:

From southeast head for a white single-storey house on the shore on the northwest side of the entrance until about 20 metres from the shore.

Weed on the reefs at the entrance is usually visible at any state of tide, and a passage a few metres wide through the weed leads diagonally to the opposite shore, towards a house in the terrace ahead which has a rectangular extension on the roof.

Turn to head along the middle of the creek as soon as the reef to port is passed and drop your main anchor almost immediately. There are rings on either shore to which to take lines ashore.

It is possible to berth at the quay at the south side of the creek.

Supplies

Shops, post office, telephone, hotel. Portnahaven Boatyard (Mr Glover ☎ 01496 860222) can repair wood and glassfibre, and can arrange for electrical and mechanical repairs. Slipway and alongside berth.

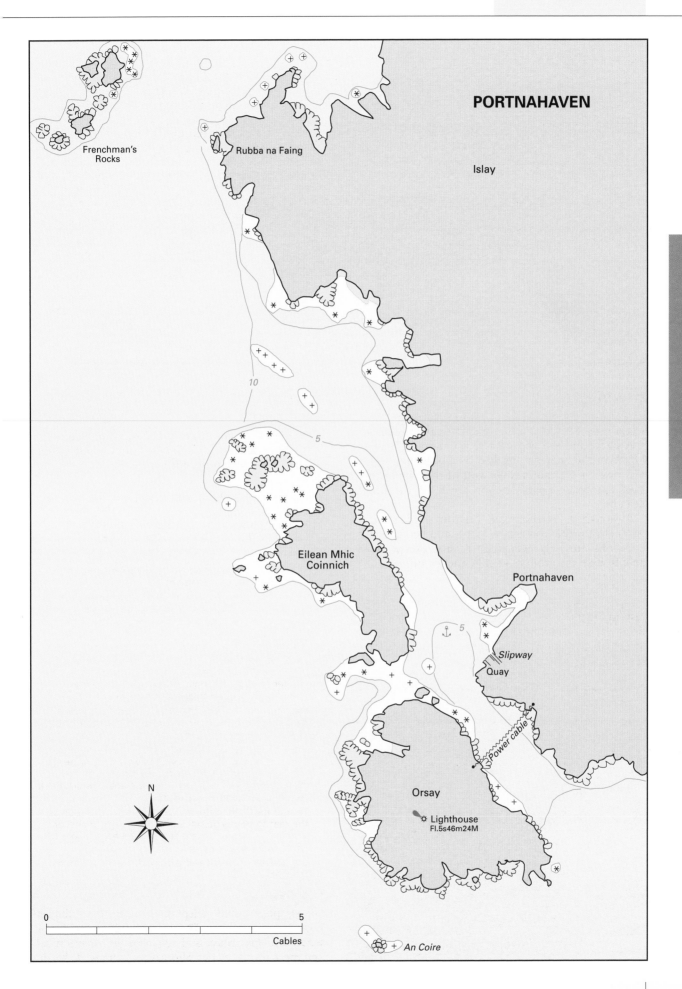

PORTNAHAVEN

Frenchman's
Rocks

Rubba na Faing

Islay

Eilean Mhic
Coinnich

Portnahaven

Slipway
Quay

Power cable

N

Orsay

☼ Lighthouse
Fl.5s46m24M

0   5

Cables

+ *An Coire*

Orsay from southwest (1987)

Nave Island from east (1987)

Northwest coast of Islay

Nave Island lies north of Ardnave Point, at the NNW of Islay. Occasional anchorage southeast of the middle of the island; drying rocks obstruct the south end of the channel.

Approach either from the north of Post Rocks, or round the northeast end of Nave Island, keeping ¼ mile off to avoid a reef at the end of the island and to pass inshore of the Balach Rocks, which lie up to 2 miles northeast of Nave Island.

Loch Gruinart, southeast of Ardnave Point, is inaccessible to any except the most adventurous owners of shoal-draught boats prepared to explore with almost no information. The original Admiralty survey shows the sands at the mouth of the loch as quicksand.

Post Rocks, 1½ miles WNW of Rubha a'Mhail lighthouse at the north entrance to the Sound of Islay, lying up to 7 cables offshore, dry up to 3·3 metres (they rarely cover). A clearing mark for Post Rocks is Beinn an Oir, the highest of the Paps of Jura, in line with Rubha a'Mhail lighthouse bearing 117°.

To the west of the north end of the sound, Post Rocks 1½ miles WNW of Rubha a'Mhail lighthouse.

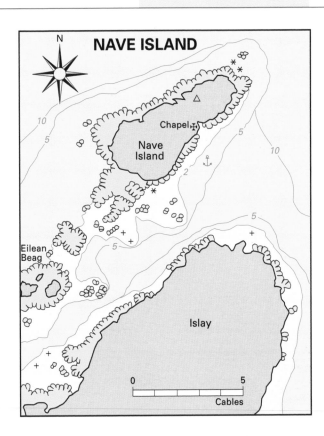

Loch Tarbert, Jura

CHART

2481 (1:25,000)

Possibly the most remote loch in the Inner Hebrides in that it has no road access and is far from any other anchorage. The loch is littered with reefs though navigation is much simplified by the leading lines, originally established by the late H.G.Hasler in 1960.

TIDES

Constant at Scalasaig (Colonsay) –0012 Oban (+0542 Dover).

Height in metres

MHWS	MHWN	MTL	MLWN	MLWS
3·9	2·7	2·2	1·6	0·5

DANGERS AND MARKS

The outer part of the loch has fewer hazards than the inner.

Bo Mor, a submerged rock with a depth of 1·9 metres, lies 4 cables south of Rubh' an t-Sailein, the north point of the entrance.

Eileanan Gleann Righ extend 3 cables from the north shore with drying rocks on their west side but the south and southeast sides are clean.

Off the mouth of Glenbatrick on the south shore opposite Eileanan Gleann Righ a reef Sgeir Agleann extends ½ mile northwards. A submerged rock at its outer end lies 2½cables NNE from the outermost rock above water.

In southerly winds violent squalls spread out from Glenbatrick to cause confusion, just when the navigational hazards need all your concentration.

Anchorages in the outer loch

Glenbatrick Bay provides some shelter on the east side of Sgeir Agleann but the shore dries off 2 cables at the mouth of the river.

Three bays on the north side of the loch provide occasional anchorage:

An Sailein, 4 cables east of Rubh' an t-Sailein; note drying rocks more than a cable west of Eileanan Gleann Righ.

Bagh Gleann Righ Mor, ENE of Eileanan Gleann Righ. There is over 3 metres depth north of the islands but the passage through is blocked by rocks at its west end.

Bagh Gleann Righ Beag, east of Aird Reamhar, which is 6 cables east of Eileanan Gleann Righ.

Leading lines and beacons

The nine remaining lines were surveyed in 2006 and designated for clarity, as on the plans here. Each line is marked by a pair of beacons, concrete obelisks 1.15m high which have been freshly painted (2006) by the Tarbert Estate. All are white, except two pairs in Cumhann Beag which are banded.

Passage to the inner loch

Boghachan Baite, 8 cables ENE of Sgeir Agleann, is a large area of rocks drying up to 2.4 metres, where the cleaner passage is on the south side.

Sgeirean Bhudragain, 3 cables further ESE, is another patch of rocks, up to 3 metres high with extensive drying areas, where the cleaner passage is on the north side.

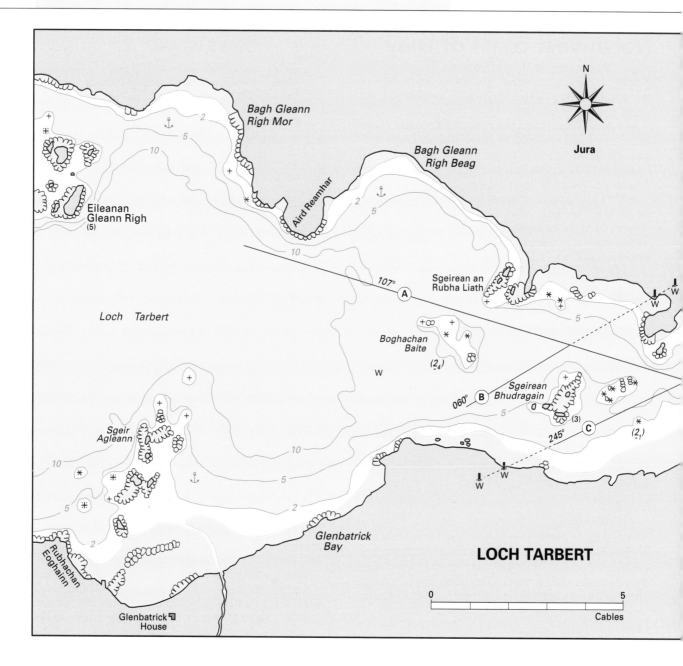

LOCH TARBERT

Loch Tarbert

Bagh Gleann Righ Mor

Bagh Gleann Righ Beag

Jura

Aird Reamhar

Eileanan Gleann Righ
(5)

Sgeirean an Rubha Liath

107°
A

Boghachan Baite
(2.4)

W

060°
B

Sgeirean Bhudragain
(3)

245°
C
(2.1)

Sgeir Agleann

Glenbatrick Bay

Rubhachan Eoghainn

Glenbatrick House

0   5
Cables

Line B, with beacons on the north shore bearing 060°, leads southeast of Boghachan Baite; Line A, bearing 107° towards beacons on the south shore, leads north of Sgeirean Bhudragain (and also north of Boghachan Baite if you prefer to go that way).

Line C, bearing 245° astern from a further pair of beacons on the south shore, leads south of Sgeirean Bhudragain, but this is a trickier passage used mainly by shoal-draught estate boats.

The most popular anchorage is in Cuan Mor Bay northwest of Cumhann Mor, 6 cables ENE of Sgeirean Bhudragain. A drying reef lies on the east side of the bay and two cairns in line on the hillside north of the bay lead close west of it. The head of the bay dries for at least a cable.

From Sgeirean Bhudragain the loch is clean to the narrows of Cumhann (Cuan) Mor, after which the passage to the inner loch is south of an islet 4 metres high. At first the inner loch is very deep, but after half a mile most of it is less than 3 metres deep with patches of less than 2 metres depth. A rock dries 0·6 metres 2 cables off the south shore 8 cables ENE of Cumhann Mor. Sgeirean Druim an Loch, a patch of rocks the highest of which is 0·3 metres above high water, lies towards the head of the loch 1¼ miles northeast of Cumhann Mor.

After passing south of the 4-metre islet east of Cumhann Mor, head northeast to follow that shore until Sgeirean Druim an Loch is identified. The inner loch is shoal on all sides so that it is necessary except for shallow-draught boats, or at neaps, to anchor well offshore; the anchorage off Cruib Bothy, the only man-made feature north of Sgeirean Druim an Loch, is well spoken of, but note that drying rocks lie a cable offshore in the middle of the bay.

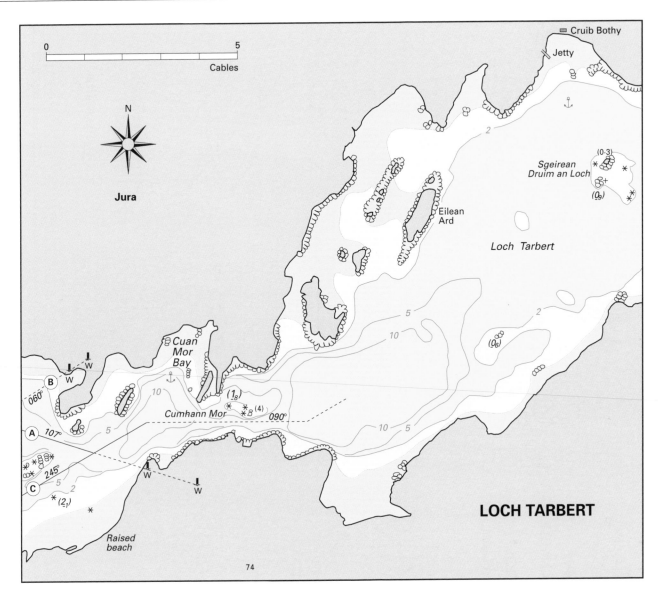

Map labels:

Cruib Bothy

Jetty

0 — 5
Cables

N

Jura

Sgeirean
Druim an Loch
(0.3)
(0₉)

Eilean
Ard

Loch Tarbert

(0₈)

Cuan
Mor
Bay

B
060°
W

A 107°
245°
C
5   2
(2₁)

Cumhann Mor
(1₈)
*B (4)
090°

W
W

5   5
10

10   5

Raised
beach

LOCH TARBERT

74

ISLAY JURA AND COLONSAY

Loch Tarbert entrance. Sgeir Agleann extends from the right; note the detached rock well off its end (1985)

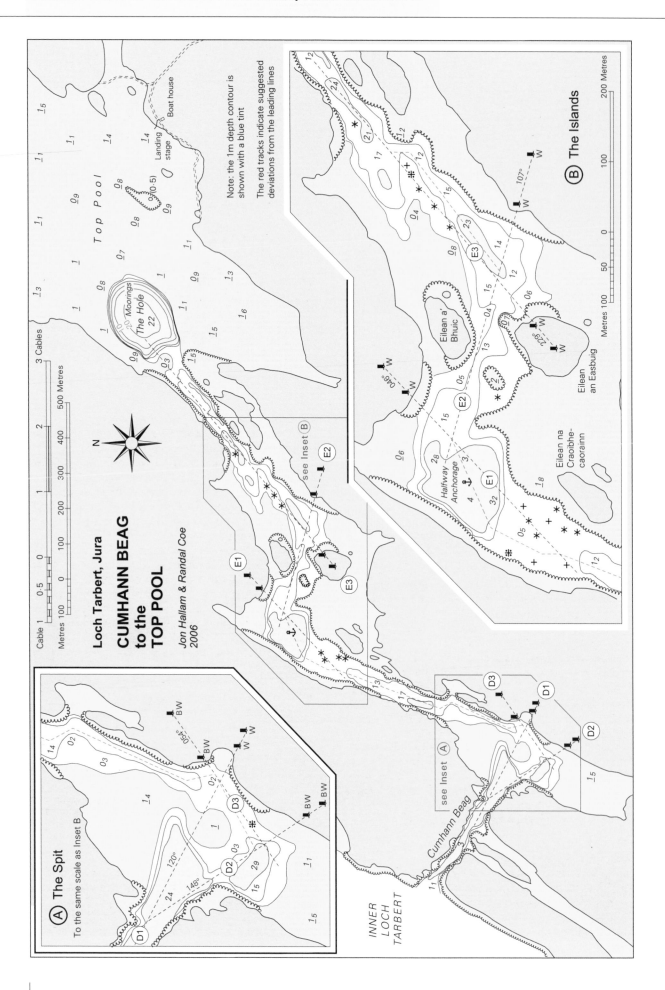

Loch Tarbert, Jura

CUMHANN BEAG to the TOP POOL

Jon Hallam & Randal Coe
2006

Note: the 1m depth contour is shown with a blue tint

The red tracks indicate suggested deviations from the leading lines

(A) The Spit
To the same scale as Inset B

(B) The Islands

Loch Tarbert, Jura, Cumhann Beag from southwest

Cumhann Beag

55°58′N 5°53′W

There is no Admiralty chart coverage. The plan opposite and the narrative below are reproduced courtesy of Jon Hallam and Randal Coe, who in 2006 made the first survey ever of this passage. Minimum depths over the boulders and rocks in these shallow channels may not have been found, and further dangers may exist. Keep a keen eye on the sounder and a lookout on the bow.

Yachtsmen must be warned there are spring rates of 8+ knots through Cumhann Beag. Any passage through these channels must be undertaken close to slack high water. This will usually provide adequate depth for 2m draught and manageable tidal streams. Avoid spring tides. With strong onshore winds, dangerous seas have been reported in the approach.

In this passage there are two groups of leading lines, D1–D3, and E1–E3, which are intended for shallow draught estate boats. Note that the beacons for lines D2 and D3 are banded, black and white. In general it is helpful to follow these leading lines.

The limiting depth for the passage is at the final sill, which dries about 0.3m. Similarly there are other shoals which just dry on lines E1 and E3, probably also over boulder banks, which could be avoided with small deviations off-line. The red tracks on the plan indicate where such deviations are suggested.

Directions

Cumhann Beag lies 3 cables east of Sgeirean Druim an Loch, near the head of inner Loch Tarbert. The canal-like entrance is fairly narrow with craggy cliffs to port. Take centre passage and on the far shore is the first pair of beacons (line D1, approx. 120°). After 2 cables of 'canal' a further two beacons appear to starboard (D2 banded, 148°). These

should be kept in line while passing close by the small headland to starboard. This line avoids an extensive drying spit to port. Past the spit, a third pair of beacons are seen to the NE (D3 banded, 054°). Turn towards these a little before they come in line and then continue until quite close inshore, before turning N up the fairway. Keep close to the E shore for just over 1 cable before making a dog-leg to centre passage.

Steer parallel to the W shore and maintain this heading. As Line E1 (046°) is crossed, approach and follow the W shore over a boulder bank (see plan inset B). Then veer away through the Halfway Anchorage until the next line (E2, 107°) can be seen to starboard. Follow this line until the last pair of beacons (E3, 229° astern) are seen in the gully on Eilean an Easbuig. When in line use these up to the Top Pool but initially veering to avoid the boulder bank off the E end of Eilean a' Bhuic. Approach the sill before The Hole with caution as there may not be enough water at neap tides for a deep keel.

Anchorage is a problem in the Top Pool as there is only The Hole, 22m deep with very steep sides, which does not dry. The NE part of The Hole is taken up with present (and many past) moorings laid for local boats. It is not recommended to anchor anywhere in the Top Pool unless the craft, say a bilge keeler, can safely take the ground. After visiting the pool at HW, a return to Halfway Anchorage is a far safer option, with plenty of swinging room in 4m.

If you are inclined to go ashore, bear in mind that the loch is surrounded by sporting estates and the stalking season starts at the beginning of July. If you would like to go further afield, consult the head stalker, Gordon Muir, ☎ 01496 820207. Your best chance of catching him is in the evening.

Northwest coast of Jura

Several bays provide occasional anchorage in settled weather if there is no swell; chart *2343* is recommended.

Bagh Feith a'Chaorainn (50°07′.3N 05°46′.5W) has been recommended as a great spot while waiting for the tide, and good overnight anchorage in settled weather from the East – but at springs the seaward rocks might let a bit too much sea in. A submerged rock lies ½ cable off the east shore.

Also Bagh Uamh na Giall, which shows on chart 2326, ½ mile further NE. A drying rock lies 1 cable from the shore north of the entrance.

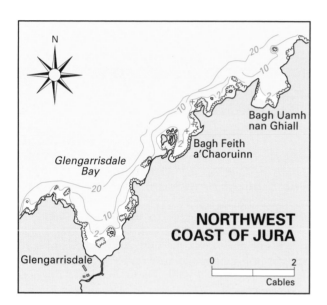

Colonsay and Oronsay

CHARTS

2169 (1:75,000) is the only current chart to show Colonsay and Oronsay, but an old chart 2418 (1:24,430) with depths in fathoms shows the islands in great detail.

TIDES

At Scalasaig

Constant –0012 Oban (+0542 Dover)

Height in metres

MHWS	MHWN	MTL	MLWN	MLWS
3·9	2·7	2·2	1·6	0·5

MARKS

From northeast there is little to distinguish any part of the island, but from the north end of the Sound of Islay Beinn Oronsay (91 metres) shows up as a wedge-shaped hill with a sheer cliff on its south side.

Closer to Colonsay a monument on the skyline between Scalasaig and Loch Staosnaig is the best mark; the lighthouse south of Scalasaig is a low white rectangular building.

Caolas Mor, Oronsay

56°01′N 6°13′W

Occasional anchorage in the sound between Oronsay and the islands southeast of it.

Approaching from the Sound of Islay pass ¼ mile north of Eilean Ghaoideamal and anchor off the boathouse, taking care to avoid the reef Leac nan Geadh which covers.

Coming from northeast steer towards Eilean Ghaoideamal until the boathouse bears 270° and then steer to keep it on that bearing.

Better shelter can be found a cable north of Leac nan Geadh (see above).·

Oronsay anchorage, from southeast. Eilean Ghaoideamal in the bottom left-hand corner   *Patrick Roach*

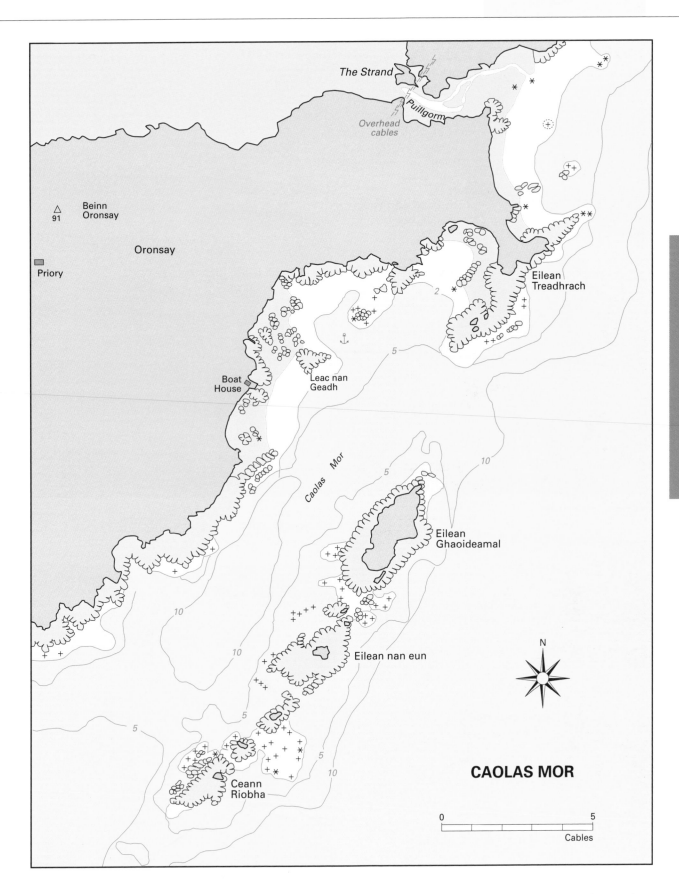

The Strand

Puillgorm

Overhead cables

Beinn
Oronsay
△
91

Oronsay

Priory

Eilean
Treadhrach

2

5

Boat
House

Leac nan
Geadh

Caolas Mor

5

10

10

Eilean
Ghaoideamal

10

10

Eilean nan eun

5

5

10

Ceann
Riobha

CAOLAS MOR

N

0   5
Cables

The bight inside the peninsula Eilean Treadhrach is sometimes preferred, and in southwesterly winds a better berth may be found on the north side of Eilean Treadhrach.

Oronsay Priory is about a mile from the boathouse.

The island is owned by RSPB.

Loch Staosnaig (1987)

Loch Staosnaig

56°03′.5N 6°11′W

The monument on the skyline north of the bay is a good landmark for initial identification. Anchor near the head of the bay towards its south side to avoid power cables which come ashore north of Eilean Staosnaig. Two beacons in line show the approximate line of the cable. As at Scalasaig subject to swell, but with more space.

Scalasaig

56°04′N 6°11′W

CHARTS

Plan on 2474 (1:12,500), 2169 (1:75,000)

TIDES

Constant −0012 Oban (+0542 Dover)

Height in metres

MHWS	MHWN	MTL	MLWN	MLWS
3·9	2·7	2·2	1·6	0·5

DIRECTIONS

Even in westerly winds a swell usually works into Scalasaig and there is very little swinging room. On approaching from southward there is little sign of the village until it bears 270°, and the first mark to be seen is the monument on the skyline. A linkspan for a car ferry has been built on the south side of the pier.

Scalasaig *Patrick Roach*

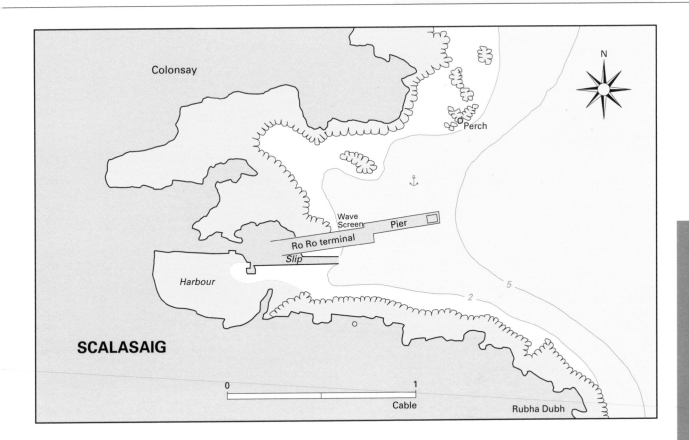

Colonsay

Perch

Wave
Screen   Pier

Ro Ro terminal

Slip

Harbour

SCALASAIG

0   1

Cable

Rubha Dubh

5

2

There is no room for yachts to anchor clear of the ferry terminal on the south side of the pier, and the bottom has been dredged down to bare rock.

Part of the north side of the pier screen near its root has been covered with timber boarding for visiting yachts to lie alongside. Fishing boats often congregate on the north side of the pier overnight.

Supplies

Water at CalMac building, phone box, toilets, rubbish skip at pier. Restaurant 200m south; hotel 400m west; shop and post office 200m north. *Calor Gas,* petrol and diesel in cans.
Piermaster ☎ 01951 200320
Colonsay website www.colonsay.org.uk

Passages past Colonsay to Mull and Tiree

The passage from the Sound of Islay past the east side of Colonsay is straightforward. In good visibility from a point 1 mile northeast of Colonsay steer 330° towards the highest point of the Ross of Mull, Beinn a Chaol-achadh, and the nearest point on the shore there, Rubh' Ardalanish, a distance of about 8 miles. Directions for the passage between the Torran Rocks and Mull are given in the companion volume, *The Yachtsman's Pilot to the Isle of Mull.*

In the passage south of Colonsay, two specific hazards are the Post Rocks 1½ miles west of Rubha a'Mhail lighthouse, and Bogha Chubaidth awash 1½ miles southwest of Oronsay. Rubha a'Mhail lighthouse in line with Beinn an Oir, the highest, and from this direction the central hill of the Paps of Jura, bearing 117° leads well north of Post Rocks, and the lighthouse in line with Beinn Shiantaidh, the more northerly of the Paps bearing 112° leads well south of Bogha Chubaidth.

Once clear west of Oronsay steer 315° to pass northeast of Dubh Artach lighthouse which is distinguished by a broad red band painted round it. Tiree is low-lying but has two hills in its western part, Ben Hynish and Ben Hough, which in clear weather will be the first part of Tiree to be seen.

For the passage south of Tiree see the beginning of this chapter, and for the passage through Gunna Sound see *The Yachtsman's Pilot to the Isle of Mull.*

Appendix

I. CHARTS AND OTHER PUBLICATIONS

Charts published by Imrays are now approved by the Marine and Coastguard Agency for carriage in vessels up to 24 metres. Note that they must be kept up to date by reeference to supplements published on Imrays' website

Charts C63 Firth of Clyde, and C64, North Channel, from Belfast Lough to Crinan are published at around 1:150,000, with inset plans, on waterproof material, in folded format. A Leisure Folio (2900, Firth of Clyde) is published on A2-size sheets, also on waterproof material, in an acetate wallet.

Imray charts are available direct from the publishers, and from most maritime suppliers.

A general chart for the whole west coast of Scotland is Admiralty chart 2635 at a scale of 1:500,000.

The following Admiralty charts relate to the waters covered by this volume. Some of these are essential, and the more you have, the less your pilotage will be fraught with anxiety.

Chart	Title	Scale
2635	West Coast of Scotland	500,000
2724	North Channel to Firth of Lorne	200,000
Areas in Chapter I		
2198	North Channel, South Part	75,000
2199	North Channel, North Part	75,000
2126	Approaches to Firth of Clyde	75,000
1403	Loch Ryan	10,000
1866	Plan of Girvan	6,250
Areas in Chapter II		
2126	Approaches to Firth of Clyde	75,000
2131	Firth of Clyde and Loch Fyne	75,000
2798	Lough Foyle to Sanda	75,000
2220	Firth of Clyde, Pladda to Inchmarnock Southern part	36,000
2221	Firth of Clyde, Pladda to Inchmarnock Northern part	36,000
1866	Plans of Ayr, Troon, Irvine, Ardrossan	6,250–10,000
1864	Campbeltown Loch	12,500
1867	Plans of Millport and Largs Channel	12,500
1907	Little Cumbrae to Cloch Point	25,000
2491	Ardrossan to Largs	25,000
Areas in Chapter III		
2131	Firth of Clyde and Loch Fyne	75,000
1994	Approaches to River Clyde	15,000
3746	Loch Long and Loch Goil	25,000
2000	Gareloch and Approaches	10,000
2007	River Clyde	15,000
Areas in Chapter IV		
1867	Plans of Millport and Largs Channel	12,500
1907	Little Cumbrae to Cloch Point	25,000
2131	Firth of Clyde and Loch Fyne	75,000
1906	Kyles of Bute	25,000
2381er	Lower Loch Fyne	25,000
2221	Firth of Clyde, Pladda to Inchmarnock Northern part	36,000
2383	Inchmarnock Water	25,000
Areas in Chapter V		
2798	Lough Foyle to Sanda	75,000
2126	Approaches to Firth of Clyde	75,000
2131	Firth of Clyde and Loch Fyne	75,000
2168	Approaches to Sound of Jura	75,000
2221	Firth of Clyde, Pladda to Inchmarnock Northern part	36,000
2383	Inchmarnock Water	25,000
1864	Plan of Lamlash Harbour	20,000
2475	Sound of Gigha – Gunna Sound	25,000
2477	West Loch Tarbert and approaches	25,000
Areas in Chapter VI		
2168	Approaches to Sound of Jura	75,000
2474	Plan of Port Ellen	15,000
2475	Sound of Gigha – Gunna Sound	25,000
2477	West Loch Tarbert and approaches	25,000
Areas in Chapter VII		
2168	Approaches to Sound of Jura	75,000
2169	Approaches to Firth of Lorne	75,000
2396	Sound of Jura, South Part	25,000
2397	Sound of Jura, North Part	25,000
Areas in Chapter VIII		
2168	Approaches to Sound of Jura	75,000
2169	Approaches to Firth of Lorne	75,000
2481	Sound of Islay	25,000
2474	Scalasaig and Loch Staosnaig	12,500

Imray, Laurie, Norie & Wilson Ltd are Admiralty chart agents and will supply charts by post:
Wych House, The Broadway,
St Ives, Cambridgeshire PE27 5BT,
☎ 01480 462114, Fax 01480 496109
www@imray.com

Leisure Folio 5610 consists of 11 A2-size sheets, directly reproduced from part of the equivalent full size Admiralty charts, on plain paper, also in an acetate wallet. Leisure Folio 5611, for the area around Oban, extends to Islay and Kintyre. This is a more economical way of buying the most relevant parts of Admiralty charts. Small Craft editions of full-size Admiralty charts are published folded, on lighter paper than the 'professional' equivalent, but otherwise identical, and also more economically priced.

The Admiralty, in combination with RYA, are publishing on CDs Electronic Chart Plotters and Chart Packs, which provide an economic and space-efficient combination for those who are happy to use a computer on board. Chart Pack 11 contains 18 facsimile Admiralty charts within the Clyde area, and Chart Pack 12 contains 20 charts from Kintyre to the head of Loch Linnhe.

Admiralty charts are available from Admiralty Chart Agents, which are established in most major ports and yachting centres in the UK. Imrays are Admiralty Chart Agents and can supply Admiralty charts, publications and products by post.

The following agents are established within the area of this Pilot:
Kelvin Hughes, 5 St Lukes Place, Glasgow G5 0TS,
☎ 0141 429 6462
W.B.Leitch and Son, Tarbert, ☎ 01880 820287
Some other outlets, mostly larger marinas and yacht centres, may supply Admiralty charts and publications, especially 'Leisure Products', although sometimes at a premium.

Throughout the West Coast of Scotland there are a few areas where an older chart, usually at a larger scale than

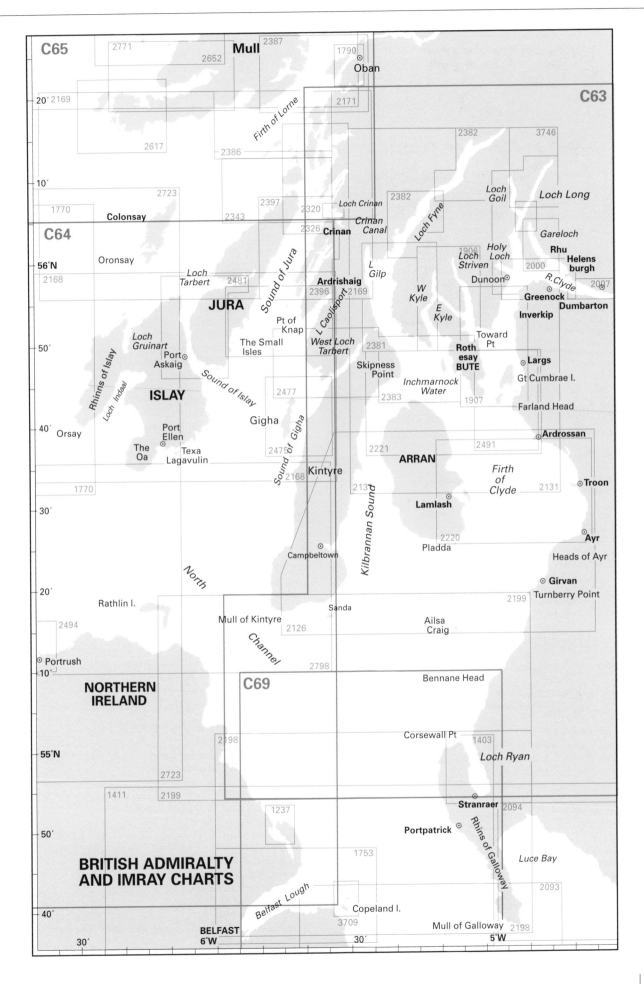

C65

2771
Mull
2387
2652
1790 ⊙
Oban

C63

20′ 2169

Firth of Lorne

2171

2617

2382

3746

2386

10′

Loch
Goil

Loch Long

2723

1770

2397

2320

Loch Crinan

2382

Colonsay

2343

Crinan
Canal

Loch Fyne

Gareloch

C64

2326

Crinan

Rhu

Helens
burgh

1906

Holy
Loch

2000

R.Clyde

56°N

Oronsay

Loch
Tarbert

2481

Ardrishaig

Loch
Striven

Dunoon ⊙

Greenock

2007

2168

2396

2169

L
Gilp

W
Kyle

Inverkip

Dumbarton

JURA

L Caolisport

E
Kyle

Toward
Pt

50′

Pt of
Knap

West Loch
Tarbert

2381

Roth
esay

Largs

Loch
Gruinart

The Small
Isles

BUTE

Gt Cumbrae I.

Port
Askaig

Skipness
Point

Inchmarnock
Water

ISLAY

2477

2383

1907

Farland Head

Sound of Islay

Gigha

40′ Orsay

Port
Ellen

Texa

2475

ARRAN

2491

Ardrossan

Firth
of
Clyde

2221

The
Oa

Lagavulin

Sound of Gigha

2168

Kintyre

2131

Troon

1770

2133

30′

Kilbrannan Sound

Lamlash

Ayr

2220

Pladda

Heads of Ayr

Campbeltown

North

2199

Girvan

Turnberry Point

20′

Rathlin I.

Sanda

Ailsa
Craig

2494

Mull of Kintyre

2126

Channel

2798

⊙ Portrush

10′

Bennane Head

NORTHERN
IRELAND

C69

Corsewall Pt

1403

55°N

Loch Ryan

2723

1411

2199

Stranraer

2094

1237

50′

Portpatrick ⊙

Rhins of Galloway

BRITISH ADMIRALTY
AND IMRAY CHARTS

1753

Luce Bay

2093

Belfast Lough

40′

Copeland I.

Mull of Galloway

2198

BELFAST
6°W

3709

30′

30′

5°W

APPENDIX

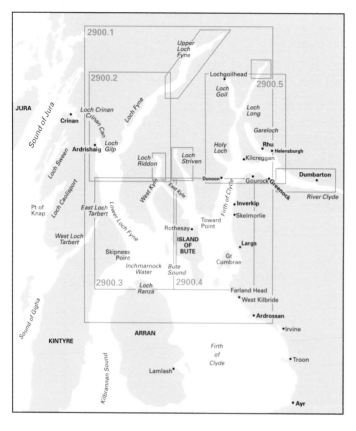

Imray 2900 The Upper Clyde

2900.1 Upper Firth of Clyde and Loch Fyne
1:130 000

2900.2 Loch Fyne - Ardrishaig to Inverary
1:50 000
Continuation of Upper Loch Fyne
Plan Ardrishaig Marina

2900.3 Lower Loch Fyne and Inchmarnock Water
1:50 000
Continuation of Loch Riddon,
Plans Tarbert, Loch Ranza, Burnt Islands

2900.4 Firth of Clyde
1:50 000
Plans Largs Marina, Kip Marina, Rothesay,
Millport, Loch Striven

2900.5 Loch Long and Gareloch
1:50 000
Continuation of River Clyde
Plans Loch Long, Bowling, Dumbarton,
Rhu Narrows

current ones, provides much more detail than the
published chart and, with due caution, can be used to
supplement the current chart. The only instance of this in
the area covered by this Pilot is the islands of Colonsay
and Oronsay, for which chart 2418 was published in 1855
at a scale of 1:24,430, whereas the current chart at a scale
of 1:75,000 can only show far less detail. Photocopies may
be obtained from the National Library of Scotland Map
Room, 33 Salisbury Place, Edinburgh EH9 1SL. ☎ 0131
623 3970. An enlargeable image of this chart may be
inspected on the web at:
http://www.nls.uk/maps/early/scotland.cfm?id=1265
    All current Imray charts, and all Admiralty charts of the
area within the Clyde are to WGS84 / ETRS89 datum. Not
all Admiralty charts of areas west of Kintyre have yet been
converted, although the Leisure Folio (5011) has been
converted to WGS84.

Some waters are not covered by Admiralty charts at a
sufficiently large scale for inshore navigation, and it is
useful to have Ordnance Survey Explorer maps at
1:25,000. This applies especially to Colonsay and Oronsay
(map 354), South East Islay and the Ardmore Islands (map
352), and the rest of Islay (map 353). OS maps, both at
1:25,000 and 1:50,000, are worth having to supplement
chart detail. A free index sheet of all OS maps is available.
    The Cruising Almanac, valid for two years, is published
by the Cruising Association in conjunction with Imrays.
    *The Clyde Cruising Club Sailing Directions and
Anchorages* are also available from the CCC and from
chandlers.
    The Admiralty *West Coast of Scotland Pilot* (NP 66),
republished every three years, contains additional useful
information.
    The Admiralty tidal stream atlas for the *North Coast of
Ireland and West Coast of Scotland* (NP 218) is very
useful.
    Tide tables are essential, preferably for Greenock and
Oban and giving heights of each high and low water; often
supplied by local chandlers, boatyards and marinas, as
well as chandlers in Glasgow.
    Alternatively, of course, there are the full Admiralty
Tide Tables Vol. 1 (NP 201) or *Reed's Almanac*.

Pilotage books

*Clyde Cruising Club Sailing Directions: Kintyre to
    Ardnamurchan*, 2007
Clyde Cruising Club Sailing Directions: Firth of Clyde,
    2005
West Coast of Scotland Pilot (NP66), Hydrographer of
    the Navy, 2004
Adjacent Areas
East and North Coasts of Ireland Sailing Directions,
    Irish Cruising Club, 1999
Isle of Mull, Martin Lawrence, Imray, 2004

General books

The Scottish Islands, Hamish Haswell-Smith, Canongate
    2004
An Island Odyssey, Hamish Haswell-Smith, Canongate
    1999
Isles of the West, Ian Mitchell, Canongate 1999

Contact phone numbers and websites

Imrays – Charts, sailing directions ☎ 01480 462114
    www.imray.com (including amendments)
Clyde Cruising Club – Racing and cruising events; Sailing
    Directions ☎ 0141221 2774 www.clyde.org
Citylink bus travel enquiries ☎ 0990 505050
    www.citylink.co.uk
Rail travel enquiries ☎ 0345 484950
    www.railtrack.co.uk
CalMac (Macbraynes) ferry enquiries ☎ 01475 650100
    www.calmac.co.uk/timetables
Sail Scotland
    ☎ 01309 676757 www.sailscotland.co.uk
Clyde Coastguard ☎ 01475 729988
Belfast Coastguard ☎ 02891 463933
Clyde Yacht Clubs Association ☎ 0141 887 8296
Clydeport – Estuary Control ☎ 01475 726221
RYA Scotland ☎ 0131 317 7388
    www.ryascotland.org.uk
Association of Scottish Yacht Charterers
    ☎ 01852 313219
    www.asyc.co.uk
West Highland Anchorages and Moorings Association
    ☎ 01631 566220
    www.whamassoc.org.uk

II. GLOSSARY OF GAELIC WORDS COMMON IN PLACE NAMES

Many varieties of spelling are found, so it is as well to search for possible alternatives; variations of the same word are listed together but usually at least have the same initial letter. Many words beginning with a consonant take an 'h' after the initial letter in certain cases; notably in adjectives the genitive and the feminine gender and genitive cases of nouns, so that most of the words below could have an 'h' as the second letter.

There is no possibility of guiding the reader on pronunciation except to say that consonants followed by an 'h' are not often pronounced, and that 'mh' and 'bh' at the beginning of a word are pronounced as (and of course in anglicised versions often spelt with) a 'v' *Mhor* is pronounced – approximately – *vore*; *claidheamh* is something like *clayeh*, and *bogha* is *bo'a*.

Some names, particularly those of islands ending in 'a' or 'ay', are of Norse origin. Anyone at all familiar with French and Latin will see correspondences there, for example Caisteil – also Eaglais and Teampuill.

Many words are compounds made up of several often quite common parts, frequently linked by *na/nam/nan*. The following are the most usual forms of words which commonly occur in Gaelic place names. They often set out to describe the physical features and so give some clues to identification. Some of them occur almost everywhere; most lochs have a Sgeir More and an Eilean Dubh, or vice versa.

Gaelic	*English*
a, am, an, an t-	the
abhainn (avon)	river
acairseid	harbour (acair = anchor)
achadh (ach, auch)	field
allt	stream, burn
ard, aird	promontory
aros	house
ba	cattle
bairneach	limpet
bagh ('bay')	bay
ban	white, pale; female (ban-righ = queen), as noun: woman
bealach	narrow passage
beg, beag, beaga	small
ben, beinn	mountain
beul (bel)	mouth of (belnahua = mouth of the cave)
bodach	old man
bogha (bo')	a detached rock, usually one which uncovers
breac	speckled (as noun: trout)
buachaille	shepherd
buidhe (bhuidhe, buie)	yellow (also: pleasing)
bun	mouth of a river
cailleach	old woman
caisteil	castle
camas	bay
caol (a' chaolais)	narrow passage (kyle)
caorach	sheep
ceall, cille (kil...)	monastic cell, church
ceann (kin...)	head
clachan	usually a group of houses (clach = stone)
claidheamh	sword (hence 'claymore' = great sword)

cnoc (knock)	rounded hill
coire (corrie)	cauldron, hollow among hills, whirlpool
craobh	tree
creag	cliff, rock (crag)
darroch	oak tree
dearg ('jerrig')	red
deas	south
dobhran	otter
donn	brown (dun)
druim	ridge
dubh (dhu)	black, dark, (disastrous)
dun, duin	fortified place, usually prehistoric
each	horse
ear	east
eilean (or eileach)	island
fada	long
fir, fear	man
fraoch, fraoich	heather
garbh	rough
geal	white
gille	boy
glas	grey (sometimes green)
gobhar (gour)	goat (gabhar = she-goat)
gorm	blue
gamhna	stirk, year-old calf
iar	west (easily confused with Ear)
iolair	eagle
keills, kells	church
kin... (ceann)	head of
liath	grey
mara	sea
meadhonach	middle-sized
meall	lump, knob
mor (more, mhor, vore)	large, great (often only relatively)
muc, muck	pig (often a sea-pig = porpoise or a whale)
na, na h-, nam, nan	of (the)
naomh (nave, neave)	holy, saint
...nish (ness)	point of land
poll, puill	pool
righ ('ree')	king
ron, roin	seal
ruadh, rudha	red, reddish
rubha (rhu)	point of land, promontory
sailean	creek
sgeir, sgeirean (skerry)	rock, above water or covering
sron	nose (as a headland)
sruth	stream, current
tigh	house
tober	well
traigh	beach
tuath (or tuadh)	north
uamh	cave

III. SUBMARINE EXERCISE AREAS

SUBFACTS are available through Faslane Operations Room (FOSNNI), ☎ 01436 674321 Ext.3206/6778.
SUBFACTS may also be obtained using the Faslane Fisherman's Hotline ☎ 01436 677201

Transmissions of:
0121   Belfast CG
0088   Cullercoats (GCC)
0070   Clyde
0072   Clyde CG
0075   Oban CG
0065   Portpatrick (GPK)
0079   Stornoway CG

1.   Tiumpan X5816
2.   Minch North X5817
3.   Stoer X5818
4.   Shiant X5815
5.   Minch South X5814
6.   Ewe X5813
7.   Trodday X5715
8.   Rona West X5716
9.   Rona North X5717
10.   Lochmaddy X5713
11.   Dunvegan X5714
12.   Portree X5720
13.   Rona South X5718
14.   Raasay X5719
15.   Neist X5711
16.   Bracadale X5709
16A   Crowlin X5705
17.   Ushenish X5712
18.   Hebrides North X5710
19.   Canna X5708
20.   Rhum X5707
21.   Sleat X5706
22.   Barra X5633
23.   Hebrides Central X5632
24.   Hawes X5635
25.   Eigg X5636
26.   Hebrides South X5631
27.   Ford X5630
28.   Tiree X5634
29.   Staffa X5627
30.   Mackenzie X5626
31.   Mull X5628
32.   Linnhe X5624
33.   Jura Sound X5623
34.   Fyne X5603
35.   Minard X5602
36.   Tarbert X5517
37.   Skipness X5516
38.   West Kyle X5518
39.   Striven X5520
40.   East Kyle X5519

41.   Goil X5604
42.   Long X5606
43.   Cove X5605
44.   Gareloch X5620
45.   Rosneath X5506
46.   Cumbrae X5507
47.   Garroch X5508
48.   Laggan X5509
49.   Blackstone X5542
50.   Place X5541
51.   Colonsay X5543
52.   Boyle X5540
53.   Orsay X5539
54.   Islay X5538
55.   Otter X5535
56.   Gigha X5534
57.   Earadale X5533
58.   Lochranza X5515
59.   Davaar X5514
60.   Brodick X5510
61.   Irvine X5511
62.   Lamlash X5513
63.   Ayr X5512
64.   Skerries X5537
65.   Rathlin X5536
66.   Kintyre X5531
67.   Sanda X5530
68.   Stafnish X5523
69.   Pladda X5522
70.   Turnberry X5521
71.   Torr X5528
72.   Mermaid X5529
73.   Ailsa X5524
74.   Maiden X5529
75.   Corsewall X5526
76.   Ballantrae X5525
77.   Magee X5407
78.   Londonderry X5401
79.   Beaufort X5408
80.   Ardglass X5402
81.   Peel X5403

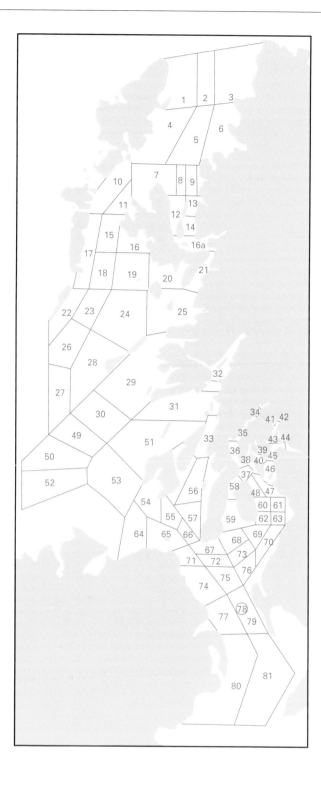

Index